Johnson on
Johnson

I have indeed concealed nothing from you, nor do I expect ever to repent of having thus opened my heart.

Johnson to Hester Thrale, October 1777

Write to me often, and write like a man.

Johnson to Boswell, August 1784

Johnson on Johnson

A selection of the personal and
autobiographical writings of
Samuel Johnson (1709–1784)

*Selected, with an introduction
and commentary, by*
JOHN WAIN

E. P. Dutton & Co., Inc.
New York
1976

ISBN: 0-525-13725-4
Library of Congress Catalog Card Number: 75-42757

Introduction

James Boswell's *Life of Johnson* is generally regarded as the best biography in the English, or perhaps in any, language; the show-case example of the biographer's art. Yet Boswell himself, on his very first page, modestly presents his book as a *pis-aller*. If Johnson had only written his own life, 'the world would probably have had the most perfect example of biography that was ever exhibited'. But, says Boswell sadly, it was not to be. Although Johnson, 'at different times, in a desultory manner, committed to writing many particulars of the progress of his mind and fortunes, he never had persevering diligence enough to form them into a regular composition'. Besides, he adds even more sadly, Johnson burnt most of these personal records just before his death.

That an autobiography by Johnson would have been excellent is beyond doubt. But we should still have needed Boswell. Johnson's writing is terse, weighty, magisterial. Boswell's is gossipy, inquisitive, rambling. They had different approaches to biography just as they had different approaches to the keeping of diaries. Boswell kept the kind of voluminous journal which offers a copious—indeed, a compulsive—record of moods, emotions, reflections, a complete fever-chart of his tempestuous inner life. Johnson would never have done this, not only because his temperament was different from Boswell's but because his generation was different. Boswell was a contemporary of Rousseau; his life overlapped with Byron's. To him, the quirks of the individual psychology were of absorbing interest. If a man had feelings and appetites and terrors which set him apart from other men, it was his delightful duty to analyse them as fully as possible. Johnson is the tail-end of the previous epoch, an epoch stretching back from him at least three thousand years. He takes his starting-point from 'general nature'. To him, the most important features of a man's character are those which he shares with the greatest number of other people. Johnson did not even believe in 'genius' in the sense of an inborn gift for some special activity. To him, a gifted man was gifted generally, his mind was strong and active over the whole range of its activities, and the accidental circumstances of life gave him a nudge towards this or that profession. 'The true Genius,' he wrote in his *Life of Cowley*, 'is a mind of large general powers, accidentally determined to some particular direction.' He always insisted that this generalization applied to him personally. On their Hebridean tour he remarked to Boswell, 'I could as easily apply to law as to tragic poetry.' *Boswell*. 'Yet, Sir, you did apply to tragic poetry, not to law.' *Johnson*. 'Because, Sir, I had not money to study law.'

So little store did Johnson set by the notion that every human mind is cast in a unique mould, and that the uniqueness is its supremely valuable quality. He believed that every man shared the common fate of humanity, a life in which there was everywhere 'much to be endured, and little to be enjoyed', and that one's duty was to use the common gifts of fortitude and compassion that the Creator had given to all men. The kind of diary that Boswell kept, that Boswell considered it part of his character to keep, would have seemed to Johnson unduly self-regarding. The individual mind was simply not worth so many hours of fascinated scrutiny.

Johnson's diaries and 'annals', then, are useful to the biographer in search of hard facts, but offer few self-revelations. I would expect this to be true even of the material which, to Boswell's sorrow, Johnson destroyed a few days before his death. These papers included two quarto books in which Johnson had written, according to Boswell, 'a full, fair, and most particular account of his own life'. Perhaps this account was a continuous process, for Johnson took one of the volumes with him on his journey to the Hebrides with Boswell. The other was left behind at Boswell's house in Edinburgh. In the few days before they set out, Boswell ferreted out these two volumes, read a good deal in them, and even managed to copy out some of the material. He confided to Johnson, at some unspecified time later, that he had had to fight down an impulse to steal the books, even though it would have meant the end of his friendship with Johnson. 'It had come into my mind to carry off those two volumes, and never see him more. Upon my enquiring how this would have affected him, "Sir, (said he,) I believe I should have gone mad."' It is tempting to conclude from this that the quarto volumes contained material of devastating intimacy. Personally I doubt it. Johnson looked often enough into the dark places of his mind, but he did not write essays about what he found there.

Failing intimate diaries, a biographer looks next for letters. Here, the Johnsonian haul is much richer. Johnson's letters have always been regarded as an important part of what he has left us; read with the same eagerness as his formally published work, and probably more so than most of it. Hester Thrale, under her new married name of Piozzi, published over three hundred of them in *Letters to and from Samuel Johnson*, 1788. Boswell, in the *Life* (1791), published every letter of Johnson's he could get hold of, to him or anyone else, to the number of 344. George Birkbeck Hill, Johnson's devoted Victorian editor, gathered all the letters not found in Boswell and published them in 1892. Hill knew of 1,043 Johnson letters; the most recent edition, by R. W. Chapman (Oxford 1952) numbers 1,515. It would be natural to assume that such a bulky documentation must contain all the essential clues to Johnson's nature. Surely we can look into the inner world of a man from whom we have over 1,500 personal messages?

Yes and no. But more yes than no, provided we know what we are looking for. Johnson, who did not indulge in self-analysis when writing for his own eye, was unlikely to be more explicit to other people. The bulk of his letters are practical: an arrangement to meet, a request for the loan of a book, the answer to some specific question. They give the flavour of a life; and if the analysis of motive is rare, the expression of warm and strong feeling is much commoner.

Most of all, it is the incidental touches—asides, almost—which, like 'please to tell Kitty', suddenly reveal the man, to readers alert enough not to miss their chances. Johnson, like most of us, addresses different correspondents in differing tones and styles. When conveying to the Earl of Bute his thanks for the Pension, or rebuking Chesterfield for first neglecting and then 'encumbering him with help', he is grave, stately, ironic where irony is called for; when writing to men of about his own generation such as Baretti or Reynolds, he is companionable and informative; in letters to younger men he is equally companionable but with a vein of fatherly reflectiveness and advice-giving. To women, he is in general softer and warmer, but still there are variations from one recipient to another. The celebrated bluestocking Mrs Montagu he addresses in a vein of stately compliment ('To be ignorant of your eminence is not easy but to him who lives out of the public voice'); his wife is 'Dearest Tetty', her grown-up daughter 'Dear Miss' and 'you little Gipsy'; Hill Boothby, a woman of his own age whom he dearly loved, is addressed in terms of heartfelt admiration and fondness, but without anything in the nature of domestic familiarity: she is 'my dearest dear', 'my sweet angel', but not a woman to be patted on the cheek. Hester Thrale, 'my Mistress', is addressed in a blend of the domestic and the respectful, with a recurrent vein of gigantesque gallantry. If she is in trouble or suffering, he drops all playfulness and writes to her in grave, sober terms of consolation and advice, rather like a softer and more intimate version of his letters to Boswell at crises of the latter's life. In his private as well as his public utterances, he is ready with counsel and instruction. To a lady who has asked him for a favour on behalf of her son—both of them total strangers to him—he patiently spells out the reasons why such an action would not square with his conscience. ('You ask me to solicit a great man, to whom I never spoke, for a young person whom I had never seen, upon a supposition which I had no means of supposing to be true.')

Johnson's letters are of supreme value in helping us to an understanding of his character; even more so, in my opinion, than his recorded conversations, where he is often talking for victory and delighting in the contest. It was Boswell, above all, who presented Johnson to later generations as a great talker, and in their minds the talker sometimes superseded the thinker and writer; so let us quote Boswell's own opinion on the matter.'

> Exulting in his intellectual strength and dexterity, he could, when he pleased, be the greatest sophist that ever contended in the lists of declamation; and, from a spirit of contradiction, and a delight in shewing his powers, he would often maintain the wrong side with equal warmth and ingenuity; so that, when there was an audience, his real opinions could seldom be gathered from his talk; though when he was in company with a single friend, he would discuss a subject with genuine fairness.

When writing a letter, Johnson was 'in company with a single friend'; and that he understood very well the nature of epistolary communication is shown by his wise and luminous letter to Mrs Thrale, about letter-writing:

Dear Madam
   You talk of writing and writing as if you had all the writing to yourself. If our Correspondence were printed I am sure Posterity, for Posterity is always the authours favourite, would say that I am a good writer too. Anch' io sonô Pittore. To sit down so often with nothing to say, to say something so often, almost without consciousness of saying, and without any remembrance of having said, is a power of which I will not violate my modesty by boasting, but I do not believe that every body has it.
   Some when they write to their friends are all affection, some are wise and sententious, some strain their powers for efforts of gayety, some write news, and some write secrets, but to make a letter without affection, without wisdom, without gayety, without news, and without a secret is, doubtless, the great epistolick art.
   In a Man's Letters you know, Madam, his soul lies naked, his letters are only the mirrour of his breast, whatever passes within him is shown undisguised in its natural process. Nothing is inverted, nothing distorted, you see systems in their elements, you discover actions in their motives.
   Of this great truth sounded by the knowing to the ignorant, and so echoed by the ignorant to the knowing, what evidence have you now before you. Is not my soul laid open in these

veracious pages? do not you see me reduced to my first principles? This is the pleasure of corresponding with a friend, where doubt and distrust have no place, and everything is said as it is thought. The original Idea is laid down in its simple purity, and all the supervenient conceptions, are spread over it stratum super stratum, as they happen to be formed. These are the letters by which souls are united, and by which Minds naturally in unison move each other as they are moved themselves. I know, dearest Lady, that in the perusal of this such is the consanguinity of our intellects, you will be touched as I am touched. I have indeed concealed nothing from you, nor do I expect ever to repent of having thus opened my heart.

I am, Madam, Your most humble servant,

Lichfield Oct. 27. 1777 Sam: Johnson

Of the same order of importance as the letters, though not precisely the same kind, are the *Prayers and Meditations*. We can make the better use of this somewhat heterogeneous collection if we have some idea of its history. Johnson, all his life, composed prayers for his own use at solemn times or important junctures. His custom was to review his life at Easter, and try to assess what spiritual progress he had made in the preceding twelve months (he usually had depressingly little to report), and he also composed prayers on beginning a new enterprise or embarking on the study of a new subject. The anniversary of his wife's death, which took place in 1752, usually found him at prayer; and he besought help for his infirmities and afflictions both mental and physical.

These prayers it was his intention one day to publish. Though composed for his own use, they were general enough not to begin and end with his own individual case. True to his premise of general nature, Johnson wrote his prayers in dignified, widely applicable terms. Though he sweated in terror of the Divine Judgment, he did not rush into his Maker's presence screaming or babbling. There is a stately eighteenth-century courtesy in his devotions which will not allow him to address God in less measured tones than he addresses his fellow-men. Hence his prayers, even at their most personal and urgent, are suitable for general use, and he so intended them. But in his last months, enfeebled by disease and with many other calls

on his failing energies, he found himself unable to complete the
task of setting his prayers in order and preparing them for the
printer. Accordingly, he enjoined this duty on his young friend
George Strahan, Vicar of Islington and son of that William
Strahan, printer, who was one of Johnson's oldest friends and
business associates.

The young vicar took his responsibility very seriously, no
doubt realizing full well that it was his privilege to transmit to
the world one of the masterpieces of English devotional literature. (Who, since the days of the Tudor Prayer Book, has written
prayers that are anything like as moving as Johnson's? I can
think of only one candidate for mention, Robert Louis
Stevenson.) Strahan edited Johnson's material carefully:
even, one might say, heavily. As Johnson handed it to him,
it consisted of fourteen paper-bound books, some with loose
leaves inserted. Many of the prayers were dated by Johnson,
and in some cases Johnson also noted the occasion of the
prayer's composition. Strahan gave numbers to the prayers,
not consecutively but in an order that may represent some
attempt, not carried through, to group them according to
theme; he supplied titles where he thought these would be
helpful ('On leaving Mr Thrale's family' is one); and occasion-
ally he made deletions. Most of these deletions occur at points
where Johnson is accusing himself too rigorously as a sinner
and a backslider. One of the most notorious of Strahan's inter-
ferences with Johnson's text is to be found in Johnson's
supremely moving last prayer, December 1784. Johnson,
feeling at last that he was reconciled to God and might hope
for salvation, prayed, 'Forgive and accept my late conversion.'
By conversion he meant not the change from non-belief to
belief, but a change of heart, a progression from an unblessed
to a blessed state of life. Strahan, fearing that readers would
imagine that Johnson had passed many years as a sceptic
and that this might set a bad example, altered it to 'enforce
and accept my imperfect repentance'. He meant well.

Apart from a few such interventions, Strahan evidently felt
it to be his obligation to publish everything in the bundle of
fourteen notebooks. Accordingly he called them not just
Prayers but *Prayers and Meditations*. The title is to some extent

a misnomer. The jottings we find interspersed among the prayers are not so much meditations as diary entries. How Johnson invited home a shabbily dressed man he had seen regularly in church, and 'found him a kind of Methodist, full of texts, but ill-instructed'; how on the way home from church one morning he was accosted in the street by Edwards, an old College acquaintance: 'I did not at first recollect the name, but gradually as we walked along recovered it, and told him a conversation that had passed at an alehouse between us.' Sometimes the jottings are of everyday trivia. 'In the afternoon it snowed. At night I wrote to Taylor about the pot, and to Hamilton about the *Foedera*.' At other times they are more closely related to Johnson's religious life. At times of ritual solemnity he tries to fast, as long as it does not make him too drowsy to keep his mind on his devotions; we learn the details, how he ate buttered cake and drank coffee one afternoon, and another afternoon had potatoes and apples, but found himself 'feeble and unsustained'. His physical state is often mentioned. He cannot go to church because of his cough; he hopes the warm weather will mend it. One night 'I took wine, and did not sleep well.' Now and then we hear of his work. 'I have written a little of the Lives of the poets, I think with all my usual vigour.' But it is the prayers that stay in the mind. 'Almighty and most merciful Father, who hast granted me to prolong my life to another year, look down upon me with pity. Let not my manifold sins and negligences avert from me thy fatherly regard. Enlighten my mind that I may know my duty; that I may perform it, strengthen my resolution.' 'O Lord, forgive me the time lost in idleness; pardon the sins which I have committed, and grant that I may redeem the time misspent, and be reconciled to thee by true repentance, that I may live and die in peace. . . .' 'O Lord, calm my thoughts, direct my desires, and fortify my purposes. If it shall please thee to give quiet to my latter days, and so support me with thy grace that I may die in thy favour for the sake of Jesus Christ our Lord.' 'Strengthen me, O Lord, in good purposes, and reasonable meditations. Look with pity upon all my disorders of mind, and infirmities of body.'

Strahan acted quickly, rushing out the *Prayers and Meditations* in August 1785, only five months after Johnson's death. This made it the first of Johnson's works to appear posthumously, well ahead of even the earliest biographies. So that from the beginning Johnson was placed firmly before the attention of the public as a pious man, a fervent believer not only in the revelations of Christianity but in the duty of orthodox worship. His example became, and has remained, an important example to all Christians and especially to all Anglican worshippers. Small wonder that there is a statue of him, *Dictionary* in hand, outside the Cathedral in his native Lichfield. It is at the south end, looking down Dam Street towards the Dame School where he learnt to read.

We come last, but might with equal appropriateness have come first, to the personal references in Johnson's published work: those moments when he makes an unmistakeable appearance onstage. Even that innocuous description will hardly pass unchallenged, for Johnson's references to himself are seldom as 'unmistakeable' as some writers' would be. In the case of a writer whose material is for the most part entirely imaginary— a novelist, to use the classic instance—there is a definite cut-off point at which he ceases to invent and begins to speak of people who actually existed and events that actually took place. This is not to say that the deepest self-revelation will necessarily be found in the overtly autobiographical writing; when telling a 'true' story the writer is often adept at dressing it up, allowing the reader to gather only what he is meant to gather and no more, and he may reveal far more about himself in those unguarded hours when the imaginative lava is flowing. The problem of interpretation remains; but at least there is no problem of classification. We can say unequivocally that Kipling's *Something of Myself* is autobiographical, and *Kim* is not. In Johnson's case, on the other hand, the main problem is one of definition.

Though he had a vivid imagination, Johnson was not a purely imaginative writer. Throughout his work, he is in general not inventing so much as advising and instructing. When he invents, as he frequently does, the invention is at the service of the applicable moral lesson. Johnson is concerned above all to pass on the lessons of his experience, to produce writing that shall minister directly to piety and morality. When he writes a fable, as in *The Hermit of Teneriffe* or *Rasselas*, he makes an implicit bargain with the reader, who is to understand that the invention is at the service of the impulse to clarify moral issues. Imagination is there, but in harness. 'Never trust the artist, trust the tale,' said D. H. Lawrence, and in our reading of purely imaginative work this is a good principle. But in Johnson the 'tale' is there because it dramatizes the opinions of the artist. There is no separation. We feel Johnson's presence and are meant to feel it. Though he lived at a time which saw the rise of the realistic novel, with all its power to affect people's thinking and living, Johnson showed no sign of its influence. In his nearest approach to a novel, *Rasselas*, the *personae* all speak in the same idiom and it is the idiom of Johnson. This is not the result merely of a failure to write like Fielding or Richardson; it is a Johnsonian decision. He has no wish to get himself out of the way, to merge with the lives of his characters as Shakespeare or Chekhov merge. He comes before us as the story-teller, and the story he tells us is one that will help us to live our lives. 'The end of writing is that men may the better enjoy life, or the better endure it.'

As a critic of literature, there were moments when Johnson applied this demand too narrowly. The tunnel vision which brought some qualities in literature into such clear focus, made other qualities invisible. But the principle remains a steady and fruitful one throughout Johnson's own practice as a writer. Since he is writing to provide general principles of conduct, and then to energize those principles by vivid language or interesting narrative, he works as close to generalization as possible. Everything he writes, and for that matter almost everything he says in his recorded talk, presses towards the general statement. So that the more personal his writing is, the more it enforces impersonal truth. His poetry, very strongly flavoured with his individual temperament, conforms exactly to the Augustan demand for 'general nature'. His terse, masterly biographies are moral tales. His *Ramblers* and *Idlers* are lay sermons. And so strongly is this principle ingrained in his nature that he always seems to be most universal when he is most personal. In the final paragraphs of the Preface to the *Dictionary*, when he appears before us to take his curtain call at the close of that stupendous nine-year performance, he does so as Sam Johnson, lonely, toil-worn, so habituated to lonely suffering that the verdict of the world hardly reaches his ears. 'Success and miscarriage are empty sounds.' But also as Sam Johnson, scholar, writer, man of letters, proud of his vocation and certain that it is of all sublunary endeavours the most important. 'The chief glory of every people arises from its authors.' The individual, standing in the full shaft of light, is identical with the moving spirit of the whole vast impersonal enterprise. This is the unique Johnsonian flavour; unique, because though so many neo-classical writers have it, none has it so strongly as he; it is the flavour we find when the Idler says goodbye to his readers, or Imlac discourses on madness, or when Johnson rebukes Chesterfield or remembers Gilbert Walmsley. In all these passages he reveals himself, yet always so as to stand in the perspective of some large general truth which touches life at many points.

Which is, perhaps, why those of us who have grown used to Johnson find that we cannot do without him. If we do not hear his voice, there is no other that falls on our ear in quite the same way. As one of his friends remarked after his death (and was quoted, at exactly the right point, by the indispensable Boswell) : 'He has made a chasm, which not only nothing can fill up, but which nothing has a tendency to fill up. Johnson is dead.—Let us go to the next best:—there is nobody; no man can be said to put you in mind of Johnson.'

JOHN WAIN

1975

Sources

Johnson's *Annals* and *Prayers and Meditations* were both included by George Birkbeck Hill in his indispensable *Johnsonian Miscellanies* (2 vols, 1897). Hill annotated with a lavishness that goes beyond the needs of this volume; where I have, here and there, kept one of his footnotes, I have indicated it by [G.B.H.].

Otherwise, footnotes have been kept to a minimum, the essential information (it is hoped) being incorporated in the commentary and Who's Who. In Johnson's diary of his French journey (VI, 10) the footnotes are Boswell's, except for those signed M., which are by Edmund Malone.

Mrs Piozzi's *Anecdotes of Samuel Johnson, LL.D.* are also in Hill's *Miscellanies*, and there is a useful pocket edition with an introduction by S. C. Roberts (Cambridge University Press, 1932).

All Johnson's letters reproduced in this volume are taken from the standard edition, *The Letters of Samuel Johnson*, edited by R. W. Chapman, 3 vols, 1952 (omitting Chapman's footnotes), and reproduced by permission of the Oxford University Press, Oxford. In the Contents, I have given each letter the number assigned to it by Chapman; if only to encourage the reader to consult his three volumes with their wealth of explanation and commentary and their seven magnificent indexes. Dr Chapman worked on Johnson's letters from 1919 to 1952; what he did not know about them, I for one am content to go on not knowing.

Contents

Contents

IV CHARACTERS

V JOHNSON AND WOMEN

Contents

Chapter I

Childhood and Youth

Johnson was born on 7 September 1709; or on 18 September, if we reckon by the Gregorian Calendar adopted by England in 1752, and which he himself began to use on 1 January 1753. His birthplace was his father's bookselling shop in Breadmarket Street, now the Johnson Museum; his parents, Michael and Sarah (qq.v.).

We begin with his own account of his earliest years, written probably in his fifties. The manuscript, which has not survived, was printed in 1805 by one Richard Wright under the title, *An Account of the Life of Dr. Samuel Johnson, from his birth to his eleventh year, written by himself.* Wright headed the first page ANNALS, and perhaps this was Johnson's own name for the fragment.

1. ANNALS [1]
1709–10

Sept. 7, 1709, I was born at Lichfield. My mother had a very difficult and dangerous labour, and was assisted by George Hector, a man-midwife of great reputation. I was born almost dead, and could not cry for some time. When he had me in his arms, he said, 'Here is a brave boy.'

In a few weeks an inflammation was discovered on my buttock, which was at first, I think, taken for a burn; but soon appeared to be a natural disorder. It swelled, broke, and healed.

My Father, being that year Sheriff of Lichfield, and to ride the circuit of the County next day, which was a ceremony then performed with great pomp; he was asked by my mother, 'Whom he would invite to the Riding?' and answered, 'All the town now.' He feasted the citizens with uncommon magnificence, and was the last but one that maintained the splendour of the Riding.

I was, by my father's persuasion, put to one Marclew, commonly called Bellison, the servant, or wife of a servant of my father, to be nursed in George Lane, where I used to call when I was a bigger boy, and eat fruit in the garden, which was full of trees. Here it was discovered that my eyes were bad; and an issue was cut in my left arm; of which I took no great notice, as I think my mother has told me, having my little hand in a custard.

It is observable, that, having been told of this operation, I always imagined that I remembered it, but I laid the scene in the wrong house. Such confusions of memory I suspect to be common.

My mother visited me every day, and used to go different ways, that her assiduity might not expose her to ridicule; and often left her fan or glove behind her, that she might have a pretence to come back unexpected; but she never discovered any token of neglect. Dr. Swinfen told me, that the scrofulous sores which afflicted me proceeded from the bad humours of the nurse, whose son had the same distemper, and was likewise short-sighted, but both in a less degree. My mother thought my diseases derived from her family.

In ten weeks I was taken home, a poor, diseased infant, almost blind.

I remember my aunt Nath. Ford told me, when I was about . . . years old, that she would not have picked such a poor creature up in the street.

In . . . 67, when I was at Lichfield, I went to look for my nurse's house; and, inquiring somewhat obscurely, was told 'this is the house in which you were nursed.' I saw my nurse's son, to whose milk I succeeded, reading a large Bible, which my nurse had bought, as I was then told, some time before her death.

Dr. Swinfen used to say, that he never knew any child reared with so much difficulty.

[2]
1710–11

In the second year I knew [? know] not what happened to me. I believe it was then that my mother carried me to Trysul, to consult Dr. Atwood, an oculist of Worcester. My father and

Mrs. Harriots, I think, never had much kindness for each other. She was my mother's relation; and he had none so high to whom he could send any of his family. He saw her seldom himself, and willingly disgusted her, by sending his horses from home on Sunday; which she considered, and with reason, as a breach of duty. My father had much vanity, which his adversity hindered from being fully exerted. I remember, that, mentioning her legacy in the humility of distress, he called her *our good Cousin Harriots*. My mother had no value for his relations; those indeed whom we knew of were much lower than hers. This contempt began, I know not on which side, very early: but, as my father was little at home, it had not much effect.

My father and mother had not much happiness from each other. They seldom conversed; for my father could not bear to talk of his affairs; and my mother, being unacquainted with books, cared not to talk of any thing else. Had my mother been more literate, they had been better companions. She might have sometimes introduced her unwelcome topic with more success, if she could have diversified her conversation. Of business she had no distinct conception; and therefore her discourse was composed only of complaint, fear, and suspicion. Neither of them ever tried to calculate the profits of trade, or the expenses of living. My mother concluded that we were poor, because we lost by some of our trades; but the truth was, that my father, having in the early part of his life contracted debts, never had trade sufficient to enable him to pay them, and maintain his family; he got something, but not enough.

It was not till about 1768, that I thought to calculate the returns of my father's trade, and by that estimate his probable profits. This, I believe, my parents never did.

[3]

1711–12

This year, in Lent —12, I was taken to London, to be touched for the evil by Queen Anne. My mother was at Nicholson's, the famous bookseller, in Little Britain. I always retained some memory of this journey, though I was then but thirty months old. I remembered a little dark room behind the kitchen, where the jack-weight fell through a hole in the floor, into which I once slipped my leg.

I remember a boy crying at the palace when I went to be touched. Being asked 'on which side of the shop was the counter?' I answered, 'on the left from the entrance,' many years after, and spoke, not by guess, but by memory. We went in the stage-coach, and returned in the waggon, as my mother said, because my cough was violent. The hope of saving a few shillings was no slight motive; for she, not having been accustomed to money, was afraid of such expenses as now seem very small. She sewed two guineas in her petticoat, lest she should be robbed.

We were troublesome to the passengers; but to suffer such inconveniences in the stage-coach was common in these days to persons in much higher rank. She bought me a small silver cup and spoon, marked SAM. I. lest if they had been marked S. I. which was her name, they should, upon her death, have been taken from me. She bought me a speckled linen frock, which I knew afterwards by the name of my London frock. The cup was one of the last pieces of plate which dear Tetty sold in our distress. I have now the spoon. She bought at the same time two teaspoons, and till my manhood she had no more.

My father considered tea as very expensive, and discouraged my mother from keeping company with the neighbours, and from paying visits or receiving them. She lived to say, many years after, that, if the time were to pass again, she would not comply with such unsocial injunctions.

I suppose that in this year I was first informed of a future state. I remember, that being in bed with my mother one morning, I was told by her of the two places to which the inhabitants of this world were received after death; one a fine place filled with happiness, called Heaven; the other a *sad* place, called Hell. That this account much affected my imagination, I do not remember. When I was risen, my mother bade me repeat what she had told me to Thomas Jackson. When I told this afterwards to my mother, she seemed to wonder that she should begin such talk so late as that the first time could be remembered.

[*Here there is a chasm of thirty-eight pages in the manuscript.*]
—— examination. We always considered it as a day of ease; for we made no preparation, and indeed were asked commonly

such questions as we had been asked often before, and could regularly answer. But I believe it was of use at first.

On Thursday night a small portion of Æsop was learned by heart, and on Friday morning the lessons in Æsop were repeated; I believe, not those in Helvicus. On Friday afternoon we learned *Quæ Genus*; I suppose that other boys might say their repetition, but of this I have now no distinct remembrance. To learn *Quæ Genus* was to me always pleasing; and *As in Præsenti* was, I know not why, always disgusting.

When we learned our Accidence we had no parts, but, I think, two lessons. The boys that came to school untaught read the Accidence twice through before they learned it by heart.

When we learned *Propria quæ Maribus*, our parts were in the Accidence; when we learned *As in Præsenti*, our parts were in the Accidence and *Propria quæ Maribus*; when we learned *Syntaxis*, in the former three. *Propria quæ Maribus* I could repeat without any effort of recollection. I used to repeat it to my mother and Tom Johnson; and remember, that I once went as far as the middle of the paragraph, 'Mascula dicuntur mono-syllaba,' in a dream.

On Saturday, as on Thursday, we were examined. We were sometimes, on one of those days, asked our Catechism, but with no regularity or constancy.

The progress of examination was this. When we learned *Propria quæ Maribus*, we were examined in the Accidence; particularly we formed Verbs, that is, went through the same person in all the Moods and Tenses. This was very difficult to me; and I was once very anxious about the next day, when this exercise was to be performed, in which I had failed till I was discouraged. My mother encouraged me, and I proceeded better. When I told her of my good escape, 'We often,' said she, dear mother! 'come off best, when we are most afraid.' She told me, that, once when she asked me about forming verbs, I said, 'I did not form them in an ugly shape.' 'You could not,' said she, 'speak plain; and I was proud that I had a boy who was forming verbs.' These little memorials sooth my mind. Of the parts of Corderius or Æsop, which we learned to repeat, I have not the least recollection, except of a passage in one of the Morals, where it is said of some man, that, when he

5

hated another, he made him rich; this I repeated emphatically in my mother's hearing, who could never conceive that riches could bring any evil. She remarked it, as I expected.

I had the curiosity, two or three years ago, to look over Garretson's Exercises, Willymot's Particles, and Walker's Exercises; and found very few sentences that I should have recollected if I had found them in any other books. That which is read without pleasure is not often recollected nor infixed by conversation, and therefore in a great measure drops from the memory. Thus it happens that those who are taken early from school, commonly lose all that they had learned.

When we learned *As in Præsenti*, we parsed *Propria quæ Maribus* by Hool's Terminations; and, when we learned *Syntaxis*, we parsed *As in Præsenti*; and afterwards *Quæ Genus*, by the same book; sometimes, as I remember, proceeding in order of the rules, and sometimes, particularly in *As in Præsenti*, taking words as they occurred in the Index.

The whole week before we broke up, and the part of the week in which we broke up, were spent wholly, I know not why, in examination; and were therefore easy to both us and the master. The two nights before the vacation were free from exercise.

This was the course of the school, which I remember with pleasure; for I was indulged and caressed by my master, and, I think, really excelled the rest.

I was with Hawkins but two years, and perhaps four months. The time, till I had computed it, appeared much longer by the multitude of novelties which it supplied, and of incidents, then in my thoughts important, it produced. Perhaps it is not possible that any other period can make the same impression on the memory.

[4]
1719

In the Spring of 1719, our class consisting of eleven, the number was always fixed in my memory, but one of the names I have forgotten, was removed to the upper school, and put under Holbrook, a peevish and ill-tempered man. We were removed sooner than had been the custom; for the head-master, intent upon his boarders, left the town-boys long in the lower school.

Our removal was caused by a reproof from the Town-clerk; and Hawkins complained that he had lost half his profit. At this removal I cried. The rest were indifferent. My exercise in Garretson was somewhere about the Gerunds. Our places in Æsop and Helvicus I have totally forgotten.

At Whitsuntide Mrs. Longworth brought me a 'Hermes Garretsoni,' of which I do not remember that I ever could make much use. It was afterwards lost, or stolen at school. My exercise was then in the end of the Syntax. Hermes furnished me with the word *inliciturus*, which I did not understand, but used it.

This task was very troublesome to me; I made all the twenty-five exercises, others made but sixteen. I never shewed all mine; five lay long after in a drawer in the shop. I made an exercise in a little time, and shewed it my mother; but the task being long upon me, she said, 'Though you could make an exercise in so short a time, I thought you would find it difficult to make them all as soon as you should.'

This Whitsuntide, I and my brother were sent to pass some time at Birmingham; I believe, a fortnight. Why such boys were sent to trouble other houses, I cannot tell. My mother had some opinion that much improvement was to be had by changing the mode of life. My uncle Harrison was a widower; and his house was kept by Sally Ford, a young woman of such sweetness of temper, that I used to say she had no fault. We lived most at uncle Ford's, being much caressed by my aunt, a good-natured, coarse woman, easy of converse, but willing to find something to censure in the absent. My uncle Harrison did not much like us, nor did we like him. He was a very mean and vulgar man, drunk every night, but drunk with little drink, very peevish, very proud, very ostentatious, but, luckily, not rich. At my aunt Ford's I eat so much of a boiled leg of mutton, that she used to talk of it. My mother, who had lived in a narrow sphere, and was then affected by little things, told me seriously that it would hardly ever be forgotten. Her mind, I think, was afterwards much enlarged, or greater evils wore out the care of less.

I staid after the vacation was over some days; and remember, when I wrote home, that I desired the horses to come on Thursday of the first school week; and then, and not till then, they should be welcome to go. I was much pleased with a rattle to my whip, and wrote of it to my mother.

When my father came to fetch us home, he told the ostler, that he had twelve miles home, and two boys under his care. This offended me. He had then a watch, which he returned when he was to pay for it.

In making, I think, the first exercise under Holbrook, I perceived the power of continuity of attention, of application not suffered to wander or to pause. I was writing at the kitchen windows, as I thought, alone, and turning my head saw Sally dancing. I went on without notice, and had finished almost without perceiving that any time had elapsed. This close attention I have seldom in my whole life obtained.

In the upper-school, I first began to point my exercise, which we made noon's business. Of the method I have not so distinct a remembrance as of the foregoing system. On Thursday morning we had a lesson, as on other mornings. On Thursday afternoon, and on Saturday morning, we commonly made examples to the Syntax.

We were soon raised from Æsop to Phædrus, and then said our repetition on Friday afternoon to Hunter. I remember the fable of the wolf and lamb, *to my draught—that I may drink*. At what time we began Phædrus, I know not. It was the only book which we learned to the end. In the latter part thirty lines were expected for a lesson. What reconciles masters to long lessons is the pleasure of tasking.

Helvicus was very difficult: the dialogue *Vestitus*, Hawkins directed us to omit, as being one of the hardest in the book. As I remember, there was another upon food, and another upon fruits, which we began, and were ordered not to pursue. In the dialogue of Fruits, we perceived that Holbrook did not know the meaning of *Uvæ Crispæ*. That lesson gave us great trouble. I observed that we learned Helvicus a long time with very little progress. We learned it in the afternoon on Monday and Wednesday.

Gladiolus Scriptorius.—A little lapse, we quitted it. I got an English Erasmus.

In Phædrus we tried to use the interpretation, but never

attempted the notes. Nor do I remember that the interpretation helped us.

In Phædrus we were sent up twice to the upper master to be punished. The second time we complained that we could not get the passage. Being told that we should ask, we informed him that we had asked, and that the assistant would not tell us.

The bald account is supplemented by a precious page or two from Hester Thrale's *Anecdotes*:

2. The remembrance of what had passed in his own childhood, made Mr. Johnson very solicitous to preserve the felicity of children; and when he had persuaded Dr. Sumner to remit the tasks usually given to fill up boys' time during the holidays, he rejoiced exceedingly in the success of his negotiation, and told me that he had never ceased representing to all the eminent schoolmasters in England, the absurd tyranny of poisoning the hour of permitted pleasure, by keeping future misery before the children's eyes, and tempting them by bribery or falsehood to evade it. 'Bob Sumner (said he), however, I have at length prevailed upon: I know not indeed whether his tenderness was persuaded, or his reason convinced, but the effect will always be the same.' Poor Dr. Sumner died, however, before the next vacation.

3. Mr. Johnson caught me another time reprimanding the daughter of my housekeeper for having sat down unpermitted in her mother's presence. 'Why, she gets her living, does she not (said he), without her mother's help? Let the wench alone,' continued he. And when we were again out of the women's sight who were concerned in the dispute: 'Poor people's children, dear Lady (said he), never respect them: I did not respect my own mother, though I loved her: and one day, when in anger she called me a puppy, I asked her if she knew what they called a puppy's mother.' We were talking of a young fellow who used to come often to the house; he was about fifteen years old, or less, if I remember right, and had a manner at once sullen and sheepish. 'That lad (says Mr.

Johnson) looks like the son of a schoolmaster; which (added he) is one of the very worst conditions of childhood: such a boy has no father, or worse than none; he never can reflect on his parent but the reflection brings to his mind some idea of pain inflicted, or of sorrow suffered.'

I will relate one thing more that Dr. Johnson said about babyhood before I quit the subject; it was this: 'That little people should be encouraged always to tell whatever they hear particularly striking, to some brother, sister, servant, immediately before the impression is erased by the intervention of newer occurrences. He perfectly remembered the first time he ever heard of Heaven and Hell (he said), because when his mother had made out such a description of both places as she thought likely to seize the attention of her infant auditor, who was then in bed with her, she got up, and dressing him before the usual time, sent him directly to call a favourite workman in the house, to whom she knew he would communicate the conversation while it was yet impressed upon his mind. The event was what she wished, and it was to that method chiefly that he owed his uncommon felicity of remembering distant occurrences, and long past conversations.'

Johnson's boyhood years were diversified by one great event—a protracted visit he paid from the autumn of 1725 to the summer of 1726 to his older cousin Cornelius Ford at Pedmore near Stourbridge. Ford, a scholar, wit, and man of the world who had recently taken Holy Orders and was enduring boredom in a country rectory, welcomed his awkward but intelligent cousin, and gave him the run of his library, discussed with him what he read, and told him many first-hand anecdotes of famous writers, thus laying the foundation of that vast, ramifying knowledge of the literary scene which ultimately bore fruit in the *Lives of the Poets*. He is enshrined there himself; in the *Life of Fenton* we find a casual anecdote of some long-faded geniality on an evening out, when Fenton was 'in the company of Broome his associate, and Ford a clergyman, at that time too well known, whose abilities, instead of furnishing convivial merriment to the voluptuous and dissolute, might have enabled him to excel among the virtuous and the wise'.

About his more formal teachers, we have Johnson's memories as recorded by Boswell.

4. He was first taught to read English by Dame Oliver, a widow, who kept a school for young children in Lichfield. He told me she could read the black letter, and asked him to borrow for her, from his father, a bible in that character. When he was going to Oxford, she came to take leave of him, brought him, in the simplicity of her kindness, a present of gingerbread, and said he was the best scholar she ever had. He delighted in mentioning this early compliment: adding, with smile, that 'this was as high a proof of his merit as he could conceive'. His next instructor in English was a master, whom, when he spoke of him to me, he familiarly called Tom Brown, who, said he, 'published a spelling-book, and dedicated it to the UNIVERSE; but, I fear, no copy of it can now be had.'

He began to learn Latin with Mr. Hawkins, usher, or under-master of Lichfield school, 'a man (said he) very skilful in his little way'. With him he continued two years, and then rose to be under the care of Mr. Hunter, the headmaster, who, according to his account, 'was very severe, and wrong-headedly severe. He used (said he) to beat us unmercifully; and he did not distinguish between ignorance and negligence; for he would beat a boy equally for not knowing a thing, as for neglecting to know it. He would ask a boy a question, and if he did not answer it, he would beat him, without considering whether he had an opportunity of knowing how to answer it. For instance, he would call up a boy and ask him Latin for a candlestick, which the boy could not expect to be asked. Now, Sir, if a boy could answer every question, there would be no need of a master to teach him.' . . . Indeed Johnson was very sensible how much he owed to Mr. Hunter. Mr. Langton one day asked him how he had acquired so accurate a knowledge of Latin, in which, I believe, he was exceeded by no man of his time; he said, 'My master whipt me very well. Without that, Sir, I should have done nothing.' He told Mr. Langton, that while Hunter was flogging his boys unmercifully, he used to say,

'And this I do to save you from the gallows.' Johnson, upon all occasions, expressed his approbation of enforcing instruction by means of the rod. 'I would rather (said he) have the rod to be the general terrour to all, to make them learn, than tell a child, if you do thus, or thus, you will be more esteemed than your brothers or sisters. The rod produces an effect which terminates in itself. A child is afraid of being whipped, and gets his task, and there's an end on't; whereas, by exciting emulation and comparisons of superiority, you lay the foundation of lasting mischief; you make brothers and sisters hate each other.'

When Johnson saw some young ladies in Lincolnshire who were remarkably well behaved, owing to their mother's strict discipline and severe correction, he exclaimed, in one of Shakespeare's lines a little varied,

'*Rod*, I will honour thee for this thy duty.'

That superiority over his fellows, which he maintained with so much dignity in his march through life, was not assumed from vanity and ostentation, but was the natural and constant effect of those extraordinary powers of mind, of which he could not but be conscious by comparison; the intellectual difference, which in other cases of comparison of characters, is often a matter of undecided contest, being as clear in his case as the superiority of stature in some men above others. Johnson did not strut or stand on tip-toe; he only did not stoop. From his earliest years, his superiority was perceived and acknowledged. He was from the beginning, "Ἄναξ 'ανδρῶν, a king of men. His schoolfellow, Mr. Hector, has obligingly furnished me with many particulars of his boyish days; and assured me that he never knew him corrected at school, but for talking and diverting other boys from their business. He seemed to learn by intuition; for though indolence and procrastination were inherent in his constitution, whenever he made an exertion he did more than anyone else. In short, he is a memorable instance of what has been often observed, that the boy is the man in miniature; and that the distinguishing characteristics of each individual are the same, through the whole course of life. His favourites used to receive very liberal assistance from him; and such was the submission and deference with which he was treated, such the desire to obtain his regard, that three of the boys, of whom Mr. Hector was sometimes one, used to come in the morning as his humble attendants, and carry him to school. One in the middle stooped, while he sat upon his back, and one on each side supported him; and thus he was borne triumphant. Such a proof of the early predominance of intellectual vigour is very remarkable, and does honour to human nature. —Talking to me once himself of his being much distinguished at school, he told me, 'they never thought to raise me by comparing me to any one; they never said, Johnson is as good a scholar as such a one; but such a one is as good a scholar as Johnson; and this was said but of one, but of Lowe; and I do not think he was as good a scholar.'

5. After having resided for some time at the house of his uncle, Cornelius Ford, Johnson was, at the age of fifteen, removed to the school of Stourbridge, in Worcestershire, of which Mr. Wentworth was then master. This step was taken by the advice of his cousin, the Rev. Mr. Ford, a man in whom both talents and good dispositions were disgraced by licentiousness, but who was a very able judge of what was right. At this school he did not receive so much benefit as was expected. It has been said, that he acted in the capacity of an assistant to Mr. Wentworth, in teaching the younger boys. 'Mr. Wentworth (he told me) was a very able man, but an idle man, and to me very severe; but I cannot blame him much. I was then a big boy; he saw I did not reverence him; and that he should get no honour by me. I had brought enough with me, to carry me through; and all I should get at his school would be ascribed to my own labour, or to my former master. Yet he taught me a great deal.'

He thus discriminated, to Dr. Percy, Bishop of Dromore, his progress at his two grammar-schools: 'At one, I learned much in the school, but little from the master; in the other, I learnt much from the master, but little in the school.'

The next long step was to Oxford. Johnson entered Pembroke College in October 1728, and stayed thirteen months before lack of funds drove him back to Lichfield.

Financially, his going to Oxford in the first place had been something of an act of faith. His mother's cousin, Mrs Harriots of Trysull, Wolverhampton, had died in February 1727, leaving him £40—about enough for a year. Beyond that, he relied on the casually-given promise of Andrew Corbet, a well-to-do young man who had been, briefly, a school-fellow of his at Lichfield. Corbet, who was alone in the world and had money, took a fancy to the idea of sharing the experience of Oxford with Johnson, and offered him financial assistance. This assistance never materialized; when the £40 was spent, Johnson hung on until his fees were overdue and his clothes in rags, then returned to a failing business, a sick father, an anxiously nagging mother, and a brother of whom we know virtually nothing except that Johnson once described him as 'noisy'.

No wonder the Oxford months stood out as an oasis. Besides, Johnson liked the atmosphere of a university. In late life, talking to the statesman William Windham, who recorded the remark in his diary, he gave his reason for this liking with his usual economy and lucidity. 'The great advantage of a university is that a person lives in a place where his reputation depends upon his learning.'

Boswell, pumping Johnson for his undergraduate memories, got first a comic vignette of youthful insolence:

6. His tutor, Mr. Jorden, fellow of Pembroke, was not, it seems, a man of such abilities as we should conceive requisite for the instructor of Samuel Johnson, who gave me the following account of him. 'He was a very worthy man, but a very heavy man, and I did not profit much by his instructions. Indeed, I did not attend him much. The first day after I came to college, I waited upon him, and then staid away four. On the sixth, Mr. Jorden asked me why I had not attended. I answered, I had been sliding in Christ-Church meadow. And this I said with as much *nonchalance* as I am now talking to you. I had no notion that I was wrong or irreverent to my tutor.' Boswell. 'That, Sir, was great fortitude of mind.' Johnson. 'No, Sir, stark insensibility.'

A little later, Boswell is unearthing deeper feelings.

7. No man had a more ardent love of literature, or a higher respect for it, than Johnson. His apartment in Pembroke College was that upon the second floor over the gateway. The enthusiast of learning will ever contemplate it with veneration. One day, while he was sitting in it quite alone, Dr. Panting, then master of the College, whom he called 'a fine Jacobite fellow', overheard him uttering this soliloquy in his strong emphatic voice: 'Well, I have a mind to see what is done in other places of learning. I'll go and visit the Universities abroad. I'll go to France and Italy. I'll go to Padua.—And I'll mind my business. For an *Athenian* blockhead is the worst of all blockheads.'

Dr. Adams told me that Johnson, while he was at Pembroke College, 'was caressed and loved by all about him, was a gay and frolicsome fellow, and passed there the happiest part of his life'. But this is a striking proof of the fallacy of appearances, and how little any of us know of the real internal state even of those whom we see most frequently; for the truth is, that he was then depressed by poverty, and irritated by disease. When I mentioned to him this account as given me by Dr. Adams, he said, 'Ah, Sir, I was mad and violent. It was bitterness which they mistook for frolic. I was miserably poor, and I thought to fight my way by my literature and my wit; so I disregarded all power and all authority.'

Rebellious *vis-à-vis* authority, Johnson was a loyal son of the Muses; not merely learning, but imagination, and above all the art of poetry, called forth his deepest reverence. Boswell again:

8. Being himself a poet, Johnson was peculiarly happy in mentioning how many of the sons of Pembroke were poets; adding, with a smile of sportive triumph, 'Sir we are a nest of singing birds.'

Driven by poverty from the university, Johnson fell prey to melancholy and inertia. From 1729 to 1732 he lived at

Lichfield, sunk in depression and doing very little. His chief comfort during this time was the friendship and encouragement of Gilbert Walmsley, a well-to-do bachelor in his late forties who occupied the post of Registrar of the Ecclesiastical Court and lived in the splendid Bishop's Palace (still there but now a school-house). Walmsley, a cultivated and clever man, gave the young Johnson many a good dinner and, what he craved even more, many a good evening of wide-ranging talk. This friendship had begun before Johnson went up to Oxford; at Walmsley's house he had met the young David Garrick (q.v.) and the slightly older Robert James (q.v.); now, in his distress, he relied even more heavily on Walmsley's kindness and stimulus. In his *Lives of the Poets* (1779–81) he looked back across half a century to those evenings with Walmsley, and paid the man a noble tribute—not forgetting that Garrick and James were there too.

9. Of Gilbert Walmsley, thus presented to my mind, let me indulge myself in the remembrance. I knew him very early; he was one of the first friends that literature procured me, and I hope that at least my gratitude made me worthy of his notice.

He was of an advanced age, and I was only not a boy; yet he never received my notions with contempt. He was a Whig, with all the virulence and malevolence of his party; yet difference of opinion did not keep us apart. I honoured him, and he endured me.

He had mingled with the gay world without exemption from its vices or its follies, but had never neglected the cultivation of his mind; his belief of Revelation was unshaken; his learning preserved his principles: he grew first regular, and then pious.

His studies had been so various that I am not able to name a man of equal knowledge. His acquaintance with books was great; and what he did not immediately know he could at least tell where to find. Such was his amplitude of learning and such his copiousness of communication that it may be doubted whether a day now passes in which I have not some advantage from his friendship.

At this man's table I enjoyed many chearful and instructive hours, with companions such as are not often found: with one who has lengthened and one who has gladdened life; with Dr. James, whose skill in physic will be long remembered; and with David Garrick, whom I hoped to have gratified with this character of our common friend: but what are the hopes of man! I am disappointed by that stroke of death, which has eclipsed the gaiety of nations and impoverished the public stock of harmless pleasure.

> There followed a period in which Johnson tried desperately to establish himself in a schoolmastering post in his native Midlands. Two letters give us a glimpse of him. The first (10) shows his gratitude to Gregory Hickman for help in his (unsuccessful) application for the post of under-master or 'Usher' at Stourbridge Grammar School. Hickman, half-brother to Cornelius Ford, lived close to the Stourbridge school, and may have been instrumental in getting Johnson accepted as a pupil there after the virtual expulsion from Lichfield Grammar School which resulted from his long absence on that visit to Ford. He also appreciated Johnson's budding literary gifts, to the point of requesting some verses from him—a task from which Johnson in this letter gracefully excuses himself. The second letter (11) refers to the time when Johnson, in 1732, held briefly the post of schoolmaster at Market Bosworth. This was in the gift, and under the surveillance, of Sir Wolstan Dixie, a brutal and ignorant squire. Johnson's treatment by Dixie is not recorded in detail, but it was obviously irksome to him, and in applying for another job (again unsuccessfully!) he refers to his leaving Dixie's employ as *e carcere exire*, getting out of prison. This is the first surviving letter to John Taylor (q.v.), one of Johnson's most constant if most curmudgeonly friends.

10. Sir

I have so long neglected to return You thanks for the favours and Assistance I received from you at Stourbridge that I am afraid You have now done expecting it. I can indeed make no apology but by assuring you that this delay, whatever was the cause of it, proceeded neither from forgetfulness, disrespect, nor

Ingratitude; Time has not made the Sense of the Obligation less warm, nor the thanks I return less sincere. But while I am acknowledging one Favour I must beg another, that you would excuse the omission of the Verses You desired. be pleased to consider that versifying against ones inclination is the most disagreeable thing in the World, and that ones own disappointment is no inviting Subject, and that though the desire of gratifying You might have prevaild over my dislike of it, yet it proves upon reflection so barren that to attempt to write upon it, is to undertake to build without materials.

As I am yet unemploy'd, I hope You will, if anything should offer, remember and recommend

Sir Your humble Servant
Sam: Johnson

11. Dear Sir

I received a Letter last Night from Mr Corbett, who informs me of a Vacancy at Ashburne, I have no suspicion of any endeavours being wanting on Your Part to contribute to my success, and therefore do not ask for Your interest with the exactest Ceremony. I have sent this Messenger with letters to Mr Vernon, and Mr Corbett. Be pleas'd to favour me with Your Opinion of the means most proper to be used in this Matter. If there be any occasion for my coming to Ashburne, I shall readily do it. Mr Corbett has, I suppose, given You an account of my leaving Sir Woolstan's. It was really e Carcere exire.

I am Dear Sir, Your humble Servant, Sam: Johnson

Johnson was by now looking round for some way of making money by his pen. Edward Cave, owner and editor of the successful *Gentleman's Magazine*, pioneered that form of miscellaneous journalism. In a few years, Johnson was to be one of Cave's regular contributors and the *Gentleman's Magazine* was to be his chief source of income from his arrival in London in 1737 until his signing of the contract for the *Dictionary* in 1746. This preliminary ranging shot, in which Johnson for some reason calls himself 'S. Smith', produced no discernible result, though Cave methodically wrote 'Answered' on his copy of the letter.

12. Sir   *Novr 25th 1734*

As You appear no less sensible than your Readers of the defects
of your Poetical Article, you will not be displeased, if, in order
to the improvement of it, I communicate to You the Sentiments
of a person, who will undertake on reasonable terms sometimes
to fill a column.

His opinion is, that the Publick would not give You a bad
reception, if beside the current Wit of the Month, which a
critical examination would generally reduce to a narrow
Compass, You admitted not only Poems, Inscriptions &c never
printed before, which he will sometimes supply You with; but
likewise short literary Dissertations in Latin or English, Critical
Remarks on Authours Ancient or Modern, forgotten Poems
that deserve Revival, or loose pieces, like Floyers, worth preserving. By this Method your Literary Article, for so it might be
call'd, will, he thinks, be better recommended to the Publick,
than by low Jests, awkward Buffoonery, or the dull Scurrilities
of either Party.

If such a Correspondence will be agreable to You, be pleased
to inform me in two posts, what the Conditions are on which
You shall expect it. Your late offer gives me no reason to distrust
your Generosity. If You engage in any Literary projects beside
this Paper, I have other designs to impart if I could be secure
from having others reap the advantage of what I should hint.

Your letter, by being directed to S. Smith to be left at the
Castle in Birmingham, Warwickshire, will reach

Your humble Servant.

The 'Poetical Article' mentioned in the letter is the literary
section of the magazine, in which Cave published poetry
and criticism and offered prizes for poems on specific
subjects; for example, he had recently offered £50 for the
best poem on 'Life, Death, Judgment, Heaven and Hell'.

Johnson in 1735 got married to Elizabeth Jervis—a
matter which will be dealt with under the proper heading
—and set up the ill-fated 'academy' at Edial Hall which
lasted little more than a year.

Richard Congreve, a younger contemporary of Johnson's at Lichfield Grammar School, was at this time an

undergraduate of Christ Church, Oxford. He had spent some intervening time at Charterhouse, hence Johnson's request for the 'method' of that famous school.

13. . . . It is usual for Friends that have been long separated to entertain each other at their first meeting, with an account of that interval of Life which has pass'd since their last interview, a custom which I hope you will observe, but as little has happen'd to me that You can receive any pleasure from the relation of, I will not trouble you with an account of time not always very agreeably spent, but instead of past disappointments shall acquaint You with my present scheme of Life.

I am now going to furnish a House in the Country, and keep a private boarding-school for Young Gentlemen whom I shall endeavour to instruct in a method somewhat more rational than those commonly practised which you know there is no great vanity in presuming to attempt. Before I draw up my plan of Education, I shall attempt to procure an account of the different ways of teaching in use at the most celebrated Schools, and shall therefore hope You will favour me with the method of the Charterhouse, and procure me that of Westminster.

It may be written in a few lines by only mentioning under each class their Exercise and Authours.

You see I ask new favours before I have thank'd You for those I have receiv'd, but however I may neglect to express my gratitude, be assur'd I shall not soon forget my obligation either to Mr Reppington, or Yourself.

I am, Dear Sir, Your humble Servant, Sam: Johnson.

With the departure for London, Johnson's youth, or at any rate his 'early life', was over. He was in his twenty-eighth year, he had a wife to support, and he knew he must sink or swim. Lichfield saw him on one more visit, when he stayed for a time at the family house during the winter of 1740–1; after that, he came there no more until 1762, when he paid a five-day visit. During those twenty-one years, he was often homesick and nostalgic, but poverty and the ceaseless pressure of work kept him chained in London even when these fits were upon him. So perhaps

we may fittingly end this section with a rough translation
of the Latin poem he wrote in old age, perhaps on his last
visit to Lichfield in 1784. Looking back tenderly on those
times when his father had been not melancholy and withdrawn but kindly and participating, on the gentle water
and the long-felled trees, he shared his affectionate
memories by addressing his poem to a friend, Nisus to his
Euryalus; probably this was Edmund Hector, early
schoolfellow and constant friend, nephew (some authorities
say, son) of the George Hector who assisted at Johnson's
birth. The poem, *In Rivum a Mola Stoana Lichfeldiae
Diffluentem*, is given in the original Latin in all standard
editions of Johnson's poetry, including that of J. D.
Fleeman in Penguin Books (1971).

14. BY THE RIVER, AT STOWE MILL, LICHFIELD, WHERE
THE STREAMS FLOW TOGETHER

Clear as glass the stream still wanders through
green fields.
        Here, as a boy, I bathed
my tender limbs, unskilled, frustrated, while
with gentle voice my father from the bank
taught me to swim.
        The branches made
a hiding-place: the bending trees concealed
the water in a daytime darkness.
        Now
hard axes have destroyed those ancient shades:
the pool lies naked, even to distant eyes.

But the water, never tiring, still runs on
in the same channel: once hidden, now overt,
always flowing.
        Nisus, you too, what time
brings from outside, or wears away within
ignoring, do the things you have to do.

trans. J. W.

Chapter II

The Heat of the Day

Arrived in London, Johnson (1) tried Cave again. 'S. Smith' had died the death, and writing under his own name from Greenwich, where he had taken lodgings so as to be quiet and finish his tragedy *Irene*, Johnson addressed Cave with a specific proposal: to translate Father Paul Sarpi's *History of the Council of Trent*, using the recent well-annotated French version by Le Courayer. (Cave accepted the idea, but various snags arose and the book was never issued.)

1. Sir

Having observed in your papers very uncommon offers of encouragement to Men of Letters, I have chosen, being a Stranger in London, to communicate to you the following design, which I hope, if you join in it, will be of advantage to both of us.

The History of the council of Trent having been lately translated into French, and published with large Notes by Dr Le Courayer, The Reputation of that Book is so much revived in England, that it is presumed, a new translation of it from the Italian, together with Le Courayer's Notes from the French, could not fail of a favourable Reception.

If it be answered that the History is already in English, it must be remembred, that there was the same objection against Le Courayer's Undertaking, with this disadvantage, that the French had a version by one of their best translators, whereas you cannot read three Pages of the English History, without discovering that the Stile is capable of great Improvements, but whether those improvements are to be expected from this attempt, you must judge from the Specimen which, if you approve the Proposal, I shall submit to your examination.

Suppose the merit of the Versions equal, we may hope that the Addition of the Notes will turn the Ballance in our Favour, considering the Reputation of the Annotator.

Be pleas'd to favour me with a speedy Answer, if you are not willing to engage in this Scheme, and appoint me a day to wait upon you, if you are.

I am, Sir, Your humble Servant Sam: Johnson

Greenwich next door to the golden Heart, Church Street July 12th 1737

Having, presumably, met Cave, and got a toe in the door, Johnson returned to Staffordshire and persuaded his wife to accompany him back to London. We might date his final acceptance of the life of a London man of letters from this conjugal establishment; but I would prefer to date it slightly later. Johnson was still dreaming of the secure and peaceful life of a country schoolmaster; even after two years in London, years in which he produced memorable work and established regular employment with Cave, the news that the school in Appleby, in Leicestershire, was in need of a master was enough to send him hurrying back to the Midlands. Once again, his application failed, and when he returned after a prolonged absence, for he was in no hurry to leave his comfort and good company for the insecurity of London, it was with a final acceptance; his native heath did not see him again for over twenty years.

So the next series of letters to Cave, written during the interval between bringing Tetty to London and going in search of the job at Appleby, show Johnson's dealings with Cave in that intermediate period. We see him (2) bargaining with Cave on behalf of a fictitious third person, 'the author' whose poem he encloses. The poem is *London*, Johnson's first major work; he has already pleased Cave with a 'trifle'—doubtless the Latin poem in praise and defence of Cave, 'Ad Urbanum', which he contributed to the *Gentleman's Magazine* in March 1738.

2. Sir   *N° 6, Castle-street, Wednesday Morning.*

When I took the liberty of writing to you a few days ago, I did not expect a repetition of the same pleasure so soon; for a pleasure I shall always think it to converse in any manner with an ingenious and candid man; but having the inclosed poem in my hands to dispose of for the benefit of the author (of whose abilities I shall say nothing, since I send you his performance), I believed I could not procure more advantageous terms from any person than from you, who have so much distinguished yourself by your generous encouragement of poetry; and whose judgement of that art nothing but your commendation of my trifle can give me any occasion to call in question. I do not doubt but you will look over this poem with another eye, and reward it in a different manner, from a mercenary bookseller, who counts the lines he is to purchase, and considers nothing but the bulk. I cannot help taking notice, that, besides what the author may hope for on account of his abilities, he has likewise another claim to your regard, as he lies at present under very disadvantageous circumstances of fortune. I beg therefore that you will favour me with a letter to-morrow, that I may know what you can afford to allow him, that he may either part with it to you, or find out (which I do not expect) some other way more to his satisfaction.

I have only to add, that as I am sensible I have transcribed it very coarsely, which, after having altered it, I was obliged to do, I will, if you please to transmit the sheets from the press, correct it for you; and will take the trouble of altering any stroke of satire which you may dislike.

By exerting on this occasion your usual generosity, you will not only encourage learning, and relieve distress, but (though it be in comparison of the other motives of very small account) oblige in a very sensible manner, Sir,

Your very humble servant, Sam. Johnson.

In further letters about *London* Johnson suggests that 500 copies be printed, with a profit-and-loss agreement: any losses borne, or any profits collected, by the author. He is careful, for some reason, to point out that the poem will be longer than *Eugenio*, a poem recently issued by the

publisher Dodsley, with whom he and Cave are in negotiation; and insists that since *London* is an 'imitation' of
Juvenal's third satire, about Rome, the relevant passages
from Juvenal must be printed as footnotes.

In the next letter (3) he makes an apology to Cave for
some real or fancied negligence. Johnson was at this time
helping one Guthrie with the 'Debates in the Senate of
Magna Lilliputia', an ingenious series by which the
Gentleman's Magazine covered the proceedings in Parliament
while avoiding the otherwise inevitable prosecution for
breach of privilege. He has 'made fewer alterations than
usual' in Guthrie's copy, presumably because it will more
nearly do as it stands. He is also making selections, to
appear in the *G.M.*, from Du Halde's *Description of China*,
which he evidently does by 'folding down' the sheets to
expose the selected passages.

3. Sir

I did not care to detain your Servant while I wrote an answer
to your Letter, in which you seem to insinuate that I had
promised more than I am ready to perform. If I have raised
your Expectations by any thing that may have escap'd my
memory I am sorry, and if you remind me of it shall thank you
for the favour. If I made fewer alterations than usual in the
debates it was only because there appear'd, and still appears
to me to be less need of Alteration. The verses on Lady Fire-
brace may be had when you please, for you know that such a
subject neither deserves much thought nor requires it. The
Chinese Stories may be had folded down when you please to
send, in which I do not recollect that you desired any alterations
to be made.

An answer to another Query I am very willing to write and
had consulted with you about it last night, if there had been
time. For I think it the most proper way of inviting such a
correspondence, as may be an advantage to the Paper, not a
load upon it.

As to the prize verses a backwardness to determine their
degrees of merit, is nothing peculiar to me, you may, if you
please still have what I can say, but I shall engage with little

spirit in an affair, which I shall *hardly* end to my own satisfaction, and *certainly* not to the satisfaction of the parties
concerned.

As to Father Paul, I have not yet been just to my proposal,
but have met with impediments which I hope, are now at an
end, and if you find the Progress hereafter not such as you
have a right to expect, you can easily stimulate a negligent
Translator.

If any or all these have contributed to your discontent, I will
endeavour to remove it. And desire you to propose the Question
to which you wish for an answer.

    I am Sir Your humble Servant, Sam: Johnson.
Wednesday

> Then comes the extended visit to the Midlands, autumn
> 1739 to spring 1740. In trying for the post at Appleby he
> had the support of Lord Gower of Trentham, who, though
> not personally acquainted with him, knew his reputation
> as a good scholar. Gower, in the letter printed here (4),
> is sounding out the possibility of Johnson's being awarded
> an honorary degree from Trinity College, Dublin, and
> writes to an Irish friend asking if Dean Swift (then at the
> height of his fame) will give any help in this quarter. (Swift
> appears to have made no response.) The phrase about
> 'choosing rather to die upon the road, than be starved to
> death in translating for booksellers', might well have come
> to Gower's ears from Johnson's own talk.

4. Sir,
Mr. Samuel Johnson (authour of London, a satire, and some
other poetical pieces) is a native of this country, and much
respected by some worthy gentlemen in his neighbourhood,
who are trustees of a charity-school now vacant; the certain
salary is sixty pounds a year, of which they are desirous to
make him master; but, unfortunately, he is not capable of
receiving their bounty, which *would make him happy for life*, by
not being *a Master of Arts*; which, by the statutes of this school,
the master of it must be.

Now these gentlemen do me the honour to think that I have

interest enough in you, to prevail upon you to write to Dean Swift, to persuade the University of Dublin to send a diploma to me, constituting this poor man Master of Arts in their University. They highly extol the man's learning and probity; and will not be persuaded that the University will make any difficulty of conferring such a favour upon a stranger, if he is recommended by the Dean. They say, he is not afraid of the strictest examination, though he is of so long a journey; and will venture it, if the Dean thinks it necessary; choosing rather to die upon the road, *than be starved to death in translating for booksellers*; which has been his only subsistence for some time past.

I fear there is more difficulty in this affair, than those good-natured gentlemen apprehended; especially as their election cannot be delayed longer than the 11th of next month. If you see this matter in the same light that it appears to me, I hope you will burn this, and pardon me for giving you so much trouble about an impracticable thing; but, if you think there is a probability of obtaining the favour asked, I am sure your humanity, and propensity to relieve merit in distress, will incline you to serve the poor man, without my adding any more to the trouble I have already given you, than assuring you that I am, with great truth, Sir,

Your faithful servant,
GOWER.

Trentham, Aug. 1, 1739.

Despite his failure at Appleby, Johnson enjoyed his stay in the country. He was the guest of his life-long (and well-off) friend John Taylor, and he moved, for the first time, in the better society of the district, among the cultivated squirearchy; the Meynells, the Boothbys, the Astons. During this period he met Miss Hill Boothby, sister of Sir Brooke Boothby of Ashbourne, and grand-daughter of Sir William Boothby who had been an enthusiastic customer of his father's in the 1680s. She became one of his closest and most admired friends, the only woman with whom he corresponded regularly. He also met, and evidently fell in love with, Miss Mary ('Molly') Aston, daughter of a local baronet, a beauty, a wit and a Whig. No wonder Tetty Johnson was jealous! Left alone by her husband in comfortless lodgings in London, she finally wrote to tell him, no doubt with perfect truth, that she had fallen and injured herself, and that it was about time he came back. His guilt-stricken reply, his only surviving letter to her, is given in its proper place (V, 6).

Next, a business letter. Having failed to find employment, and returning empty-handed to semi-starvation in London, Johnson had to raise what money he could on his one remaining asset, the house in Lichfield occupied by his mother, her companion Catherine Chambers, and Tetty's daughter Lucy Porter. He therefore obtained a loan of £80 from Theophilus Levet, town clerk of Lichfield, at $4\frac{1}{2}\%$ interest and with the house as collateral security. This is why he can urge Tetty to engage the best surgeons, and not fear to part with a guinea, for he can let her have twenty more. He did not return to Lichfield for twenty years, and the letter to Levet, dating from 1743, shows him taking upon himself a debt for which Levet might otherwise have dunned Sarah Johnson, 'my dear Mother', whom he was never to see again.

5. Sir

I am extremely sorry that We have encroached so much upon your Forbearance with respect to the Interest, which a great Perplexity of affairs hindred me from thinking of with that attention that I ought, and which I am not immediately able to remit to you, but will pay it (I think twelve pounds) in two Months. I look upon this and on the future Interest of that Mortgage as my own Debt, and beg that You will be pleased to give me directions how to pay it, and not mention it to my dear Mother. If it be necessary to pay this in less time I believe I can do it, but I take two Months for certainty, and beg an answer whether You can allow me so much time. I think myself very much obliged by your Forbearance, and shall esteem it a great happiness to be able to serve You. I have great opportunities for dispersing anything that you may think proper to make public. I will give you a Note for the Money payable at the time mentioned to any one here that you shall appoint.

Your most obedient and most humble Servant Sir
Sam: Johnson

These were hard, grinding years. Johnson was working as hard as he could, and slowly building up a solid reputation; but he was a poor man, and poor men have often to swallow insults from people they know to be their inferiors but who happen to have better-lined pockets. As Johnson feelingly put it in his poem *London*:

Fate never wounds more deep the gen'rous Heart,
Than when a Blockhead's Insult points the Dart.

Some insulting blockheads, however, got their deserts. Osborne forgot his manners one day and was speedily taught to remember them. Mrs Thrale heard the story years later:

6. Of the truth of stories which ran currently about the town concerning Dr. Johnson, it was impossible to be certain, unless one asked him himself; and what he told, or suffered to be told before his face without contradicting, has every possible mark I think of real and genuine authenticity. I made one day very minute enquiries about the tale of his knocking down the famous Tom Osborne with his own Dictionary in the man's own house. And how was that affair, in earnest? do tell me, Mr. Johnson? 'There is nothing to tell, dearest Lady, but that he was insolent and I beat him, and that he was a blockhead and told of it, which I should never have done; so the blows have been multiplying, and the wonder thickening for all these years, as Thomas was never a favourite with the Public. I have beat many a fellow, but the rest had the wit to hold their tongues.'

(*Anecdotes*, 1786)

These tasks were just lucrative enough to keep Johnson's chin above water. But clearly something more solid had to be forthcoming. Fortunately, it was. Let Boswell break the news.

7. How long this immense undertaking had been the object of his contemplation, I do not know. I once asked him by what means he had attained to that astonishing knowledge of our language, by which he was enabled to realize a design of such extent and accumulated difficulty. He told me, that 'it was not the effect of particular study; but that it had grown up in his mind insensibly'. I have been informed by Mr. James Dodsley, that several years before this period, when Johnson was one day sitting in his brother Robert's shop, he heard his brother suggest to him, that a Dictionary of the English Language would be a work that would be well received by the public; that Johnson seemed at first to catch at the proposition, but, after a pause, said, in his abrupt decisive manner, 'I believe I shall not undertake it.' That he, however, had bestowed much thought upon the subject, before he published his 'Plan', is evident from the enlarged, clear, and accurate views which it exhibits; and we find him mentioning in that tract, that many of the writers whose testimonies were to be produced as authorities, were selected by Pope; which proves that he had been furnished, probably by Mr. Robert Dodsley, with whatever hints that eminent poet had contributed towards a great literary project, that had been the subject of important consideration in a former reign.

The booksellers who contracted with Johnson, single and un-aided, for the execution of a work, which in other countries has not been effected but by the co-operating exertions of many, were Mr. Robert Dodsley, Mr. Charles Hitch, Mr. Andrew Millar, the two Messieurs Longman, and the two Messieurs Knapton. The price stipulated was fifteen hundred and seventy-five pounds.

The group of seven booksellers who employed Johnson on this gigantic task had to begin by providing the material circumstances in which the work would be possible. They handed over an advance sufficient to enable the Johnsons to rent a fine, large house—17, Gough Square, now famous to London sightseers as 'Dr Johnson's House'. Here, in 1747, Johnson set to work with a team of six amanuenses. But before starting work on the details, he issued a masterly statement, the *Plan of a Dictionary of the English Language.*

To please Dodsley, who had done so much to bring the venture to birth, Johnson agreed that this *Plan* should be dedicated to Philip Dormer, Earl of Chesterfield, Secretary of State and a polished, literate man. The *Plan* combined courteous, if markedly unservile, compliments to the grand aristocrat with a statement of aims that shows how deeply Johnson had meditated on the art and science of lexicography.

8. My Lord,

When first I undertook to write an English Dictionary, I had no expectation of any higher patronage than that of the proprietors of the copy, nor prospect of any other advantage than the price of my labour. I knew that the work in which I engaged is generally considered as drudgery for the blind, as the proper toil of artless industry; a task that requires neither the light of learning, nor the activity of genius, but may be successfully performed without any higher quality than that of bearing burdens with dull patience, and beating the track of the alphabet with sluggish resolution.

Whether this opinion, so long transmitted, and so widely propagated, had its beginning from truth and nature, or from accident and prejudice; whether it be decreed by the authority of reason or the tyranny of ignorance, that, of all the candidates for literary praise, the unhappy lexicographer holds the lowest place, neither vanity nor interest incited me to inquire. It appeared that the province allotted me was, of all the regions of learning, generally confessed to be the least delightful, that it was believed to produce neither fruits nor flowers; and that, after a long and laborious cultivation, not even the barren laurel had been found upon it.

Yet on this province, my Lord, I entered, with the pleasing hope, that, as it was low, it likewise would be safe. I was drawn forward with the prospect of employment, which, though not splendid, would be useful; and which, though it could not make my life envied, would keep it innocent; which would awaken no passion, engage me in no contention, nor throw in my way any temptation to disturb the quiet of others by censure, or my own by flattery.

I had read, indeed, of times, in which princes and statesmen thought it part of their honour to promote the improvement of their native tongues; and in which dictionaries were written under the protection of greatness. To the patrons of such undertakings I willingly paid the homage of believing that they, who were thus solicitous for the perpetuity of their language, had reason to expect that their actions would be celebrated by posterity, and that the eloquence which they promoted would be employed in their praise. But I considered such acts of beneficence as prodigies, recorded rather to raise wonder than expectation; and, content with the terms that I had stipulated, had not suffered my imagination to flatter me with any other encouragement, when I found that my design had been thought by your Lordship of importance sufficient to attract your favour.

How far this unexpected distinction can be rated among the happy incidents of life, I am not yet able to determine. Its first effect has been to make me anxious, lest it should fix the attention of the public too much upon me; and, as it once happened to an epic poet of France, by raising the reputation of the attempt, obstruct the reception of the work. I imagine what the world will expect from a scheme, prosecuted under your Lordship's influence; and I know that expectation, when her wings are once expanded, easily reaches heights which performance never will attain; and when she has mounted the summit of perfection, derides her follower, who dies in the pursuit.

Not, therefore, to raise expectation, but to repress it, I here lay before your Lordship the plan of my undertaking, that more may not be demanded than I intend; and that, before it is too far advanced to be thrown into a new method, I may be advertised of its defects or superfluities. Such informations I may justly hope, from the emulation with which those, who desire the praise of elegance or discernment, must contend in the promotion of a design that you, my Lord, have not thought unworthy to share your attention with treaties and with wars.

In the first attempt to methodise my ideas I found a difficulty, which extended itself to the whole work. It was not easy to determine by what rule of distinction the words of this dictionary were to be chosen. The chief intent of it is to preserve the purity, and ascertain the meaning of our English idiom; and

33

this seems to require nothing more than that our language be considered, so far as it is our own; that the words and phrases used in the general intercourse of life, or found in the works of those whom we commonly style polite writers, be selected, without including the terms of particular professions; since, with the arts to which they relate, they are generally derived from other nations, and are very often the same in all the languages of this part of the world. This is, perhaps, the exact and pure idea of a grammatical dictionary; but in lexicography, as in other arts, naked science is too delicate for the purposes of life. The value of a work must be estimated by its use; it is not enough that a dictionary delights the critic, unless, at the same time, it instructs the learner; as it is to little purpose that an engine amuses the philosopher by the subtilty of its mechanism, if it requires so much knowledge in its application as to be of no advantage to the common workman.

*　　*　　*

This, my Lord, is my idea of an English dictionary; a dictionary by which the pronunciation of our language may be fixed, and its attainment facilitated; by which its purity may be preserved, its use ascertained, and its duration lengthened. And though, perhaps, to correct the language of nations by books of grammar, and amend their manners by discourses of morality, may be tasks equally difficult, yet, as it is unavoidable to wish, it is natural likewise to hope, that your Lordship's patronage may not be wholly lost; that it may contribute to the preservation of ancient, and the improvement of modern writers; that it may promote the reformation of those translators, who, for want of understanding the characteristical difference of tongues, have formed a chaotic dialect of heterogeneous phrases; and awaken to the care of purer diction some men of genius, whose attention to argument makes them negligent of style, or whose rapid imagination, like the Peruvian torrents, when it brings down gold, mingles it with sand.

When I survey the Plan which I have laid before you, I cannot, my Lord, but confess, that I am frighted at its extent, and, like the soldiers of Cæsar, look on Britain as a new world, which it is almost madness to invade. But I hope, that though

I should not complete the conquest, I shall, at least, discover the coast, civilize part of the inhabitants, and make it easy for some other adventurer to proceed further, to reduce them wholly to subjection, and settle them under laws.

Of Johnson's other works during the 1740s, the most important is the *Life of Savage*, but I give no extract, for it would have to be printed entire, and is unfortunately too long to be included here. Savage was a strange, gifted psychopath who made friends with Johnson, shared poverty and neglect with him, and died in a debtor's prison in 1743. Johnson worked with feverish concentration on a *Life* of his friend, and brought it out the following year. The *Life of Savage* is a deeply personal work, though it is the story of another man's misfortunes and there is hardly more than a sentence or two in the whole book that relates directly to Johnson himself. In the depth of his sympathy with Savage's troubles, in the strength of his understanding of the man's nature, Johnson reveals much about himself and about his own situation in the 1740s. Feelings which he kept stoically buttoned up when he faced his own difficulties could issue freely when he faced those of his dead friend. Incapable of self-pity, he could feel a burning pity for one whose fate in so many ways was like his own. But the beautiful, intensely glowing work does not submit to snipping-up, and since Johnson included it among his *Lives of the Poets* nearly thirty years later, it has been frequently reprinted and is, by comparison with most of Johnson's early work, easy to get hold of.

A work of a very different nature saw the light soon after Johnson began work on the *Dictionary*. Johnson's friend and ex-pupil, David Garrick, took over the management of Drury Lane Theatre in 1747 and asked Johnson for a verse prologue to be spoken on the opening night. Johnson responded with the resounding 'Prologue' which gave a round-up of English theatrical history from Shakespeare's day to his own, and also expressed the new and lofty theatrical ethic that was to underlie Garrick's idealism and energy. Not much more than a year later, in February

1749, Garrick handsomely repaid Johnson's efforts by staging, at lavish expense and with an important cast, Johnson's thirteen-year-old tragedy *Irene*. The audience was unenthusiastic, but Garrick dragged the play through nine nights in order that Johnson should get his three nights' benefit, and *Irene* did in fact make Johnson more money than any of his works up to that time (£195 7s, plus a further £100 from the publisher Dodsley for the sale of the copyright).

Plainly, however, Johnson's career as a playwright was over, and it was back to his desk, away from the bright lights and animated crowds. The nine years' work on the *Dictionary* was hard and unremitting; yet it is entirely characteristic of Johnson that he should have undertaken another task, to run concurrently, and that this task should have been serious and weighty enough to occupy the entire attention of most writers. This was *The Rambler*, a series of essays on life and conduct which Johnson wrote at the rate of two a week for two years, 1750–2.

Extract 9 shows Johnson addressing the Scottish publisher James Elphinston, who brought out an edition of the essays timed to run just behind the London dates and to cost less. Elphinston was a good man of business who also respected Johnson as a writer, and the tone of Johnson's letters to him is markedly warm and friendly.

9. Sir

I have for a long time intended to answer the Letter which You were pleased to send me, and know not why I have delayed it so long but that I had nothing particular either of enquiry or information to send You, and the same reason might still have the same consequence, but that I find in my recluse kind of Life, that I am not likely to have much more to say at one time than at another, and that therefore I may endanger by an appearance of neglect long continued, the loss of such an Acquaintance as I know not where to supply.

I therefore write now to assure you how sensible I am of the kindness you have always expressed to me, and how much I desire the cultivation of that Benevolence which perhaps nothing but the distance between us has hindred from ripening before this time into Friendship. Of myself I have very little to say, and of any body else less, let me however be allowed one thing and that in my own favour that I am

Dear Sir Your most humble servant

Sam : Johnson

April 20th 1749.

> The next letter takes us to the *Dictionary*. In so laborious an undertaking it is understandable that Johnson should now and then fall behind schedule. The sense of his letter to Strahan, the printer of the work, is evidently that the 'gentlemen partners' who are backing the enterprise are threatening to cut off supplies. Johnson was paid at the rate of a guinea a sheet, i.e. as much copy as would make up a printed sheet. Out of this he had to pay his amanuenses. Presumably he did so weekly, and his ultimatum to Strahan is that unless the 'partners' relent and send some money, he will disband his staff 'to-morrow evening', i.e. Saturday.

10. Dearest Sir.   *Novr 1. 1751*
The message which You sent me by Mr Stuart I do not consider as at all your own, but if you were contented to be the deliverer of it to me, you must favour me so far as to return my answer, which I have written down to spare you the unpleasing office of doing it in your own words. You advise me to write, I know with very kind intentions, nor do I intend to treat your counsel with any disregard when I declare that in the present state of the matter 'I shall *not* write'—otherwise than the words following—

'That my Resolution has long been, and is *not* now altered, and is now *less* likely to be altered, that I shall *not* see the Gentlemen Partners till the first volume is in the press which they may forward or retard by dispensing or not dispensing with the last Message.'

Be pleased to lay this my determination before them this morning, for I shall think of taking my measures accordingly to morrow evening, only this that I mean no harm, but that my citadel shall not be taken by storm while I can defend it, and that if a blockade is intended, the country is under the command of my batteries, I shall think of laying it under contribution to morrow Evening.

I am, Sir, Your most obliged, most obedient, and most humble Servant, Sam: Johnson

> A little later, in a hasty, undated letter, he is writing to Strahan that he 'knows not how to manage':

11. Dear Sir

I must desire you to add to your other civilities this one, to go to Mr Millar and represent to him our manner of going on, and inform him that I know not how to manage, I pay three and twenty shillings a week to my assistants, in truth without having much assistance from them, but they tell me they shall be able to fall better in method, as indeed I intend they shall. The point is to get two Guineas for Your humble Servant Sam: Johnson

> Matters were patched up and the work continued. Letter 12 cannot be understood without knowing Johnson's method of procedure. His staff were not collaborators, only copyists. He himself decided what words were to be included, and provided each one with a definition and an etymology. This part of the work he wrote down with his own hand, allowing two or three words to a column and two columns to a large sheet. Then came the illustrative quotations. Since Johnson was trying to set a standard of clear and correct usage, he used quotations not as they are used in the *Oxford Dictionary*, to plot the word's history, but to demonstrate how the word should be used by a writer aiming at the best English. He chose the quotations in hundreds of hours of reading, confining himself to what he considered the classic period of English usage; when he found a particularly apt use of a word, he underlined it in pencil, wrote its initial letter in the margin, and indicated by vertical lines the limits of the quotation to be copied out. The amanuenses copied out the indicated passages on to slips of paper, which they then pasted on to the sheets. If they cut out these slips as neatly and economically as possible, the result was cleaner copy for the printer, but it appears from this letter that normal human inefficiency

obtained in Gough Square as everywhere else. Frank
Stuart, who died before the *Dictionary* was completed, had
evidently been willing to 'clip close', but the rest were
careless, and 'one cannot always be on the watch'.

12. Sir
I have often suspected that it is as you say, and have told Mr
Dodsley of it. It proceeds from the haste of the amanuensis to
get to the end of his day's work. I have desired the passages to be
clipped close, and then perhaps for two or three leaves it is
done. But since poor Stuart's time I could never get that part
of the work into regularity, and perhaps never shall. I will try
to take some more care but can promise nothing; when I am
told there is a sheet or two I order it away. You will find it
sometimes close; when I make up any myself, which never
happens but when I have nobody with me, I generally clip it
close, but one cannot always be on the watch.

I am, Sir, Your most. &c. Sam : Johnson.

During these years of multifarious activity, Johnson came
into contact with many writers and scholars: Samuel
Richardson, Charlotte Lennox, Arthur Murphy, and,
perhaps most notably of all, Joseph Warton and his
younger brother Thomas.

The Wartons were the sons of a poet, Joseph Warton
('the elder'), and both were poets as well as scholars.
Joseph was headmaster of Winchester; Thomas, a Fellow
of Trinity College, Oxford, twice holder of the Professor-
ship of Poetry, Poet Laureate in later life, a formidable
scholar and a convivial, easy-going man. Both were good
friends to Johnson; Thomas, in particular, was of service
to him at a crucial time, for it was largely by his efforts
that the University was led to bestow the honorary degree
of Master of Arts on Johnson, in time for it to appear on the
title-page of the *Dictionary*. ('I will keep back the titlepage
for such an insertion as you seem to promise me.')

In his letters to the Wartons, Johnson several times
mentions their common friend the poet William Collins
(1721–1759), whom Johnson had known in early London
days. Collins had already fallen under the shadow of that

incurable insanity that accompanied him to his early grave. Johnson wonders (14) whether a letter would cheer him up, but if he did write to Collins the letter has not survived —tragically, for such a letter from Johnson would be wonderfully revealing of his delicacy of feeling and dignity of style.

13. Sir

It is but an ill return for the book with which you were pleased to favour me, to have delayed my thanks for it till now. I am too apt to be negligent but I can never deliberately show any disrespect to a man of your character, and I now pay you a very honest acknowledgement for the advancement of the literature of our native Country. You have shown to all who shall hereafter attempt the study of our ancient authours the way to success, by directing them to the perusal of the books which those authours had read. Of this method Hughes and Men much greater than Hughes seem never to have thought. The Reason why the authours which are yet read of the sixteenth Century are so little understood is that they are read alone, and no help is borrowed from those who lived with them or before them. Some part of this ignorance I hope to remove by my book which now draws towards its end, but which I cannot finish to my mind without visiting the Libraries of Oxford which I therefore hope to see in about a fortnight. I know not how long I shall stay or where I shall lodge, but shall be sure to look for you at my arrival, and we shall easily settle the rest.

I am Dear Sir Your most obedient and most humble servant
July 16. 1754   Sam : Johnson

14. Dear Sir

I am extremely obliged to you and to Mr Wise, for the uncommon care which you have taken of my interest, if you can accomplish your kind design, I shall certainly take me a little habitation among you.

The Books which I promised to Mr Wise I have not yet been able to procure, but I shall send him a *Finnick Dictionary* the only copy perhaps in England which was presented me by a learned Swede, but I keep it back that it may make a set of my own Books of the new edition with which I shall accompany it more welcome. You will assure him of my gratitude.

Poor dear Collins—would a letter give him any pleasure: I have a mind to write.

I am glad of your hindrance in your Spenserian design, yet I would not have it delayed. Three hours a day stolen from sleep and amusement will produce it, let a servitour transcribe the quotations and interleave them with references to save time. This will shorten the work and lessen the fatigue.

Can I do anything to promoting the diploma—? I would not be wanting to cooperate with your kindness, of which whatever be the effect I shall be

Dear Sir, Your most obliged and most humble servant
Nov 28. 1754   Sam: Johnson

> At last the *Dictionary* was published, and in its famous Preface Johnson gives a moving and memorable self-portrait as a man wearied by toil, saddened by the blows of life and the deaths of those he loves, but confident that he has found honourable work to do in the world ('the chief glory of every nation arises from its authors') and that he has performed this part of his life's work faithfully and well.

15.   PREFACE TO THE ENGLISH DICTIONARY.
It is the fate of those, who toil at the lower employments of life, to be rather driven by the fear of evil, than attracted by the prospect of good; to be exposed to censure, without hope of praise; to be disgraced by miscarriage, or punished for neglect, where success would have been without applause, and diligence without reward.

Among these unhappy mortals is the writer of dictionaries; whom mankind have considered, not as the pupil, but the slave of science, the pioneer of literature, doomed only to remove rubbish and clear obstructions from the paths, through which Learning and Genius press forward to conquest and glory, without bestowing a smile on the humble drudge that facilitates their progress. Every other author may aspire to praise; the lexicographer can only hope to escape reproach, and even this negative recompense has been yet granted to very few.

I have, notwithstanding this discouragement, attempted a Dictionary of the English language, which, while it was employed in the cultivation of every species of literature, has itself been hitherto neglected; suffered to spread, under the direction of chance, into wild exuberance; resigned to the tyranny of time and fashion; and exposed to the corruptions of ignorance, and caprices of innovation.

When I took the first survey of my undertaking, I found our speech copious without order, and energetic without rules: wherever I turned my view, there was perplexity to be disentangled, and confusion to be regulated; choice was to be made out of boundless variety, without any established principle of selection; adulterations were to be detected, without a settled test of purity; and modes of expression to be rejected or received, without the suffrages of any writers of classical reputation or acknowledged authority.

Having, therefore, no assistance but from general grammar, I applied myself to the perusal of our writers; and, noting whatever might be of use to ascertain or illustrate any word or phrase, accumulated in time the materials of a dictionary, which, by degrees, I reduced to method, establishing to myself, in the progress of the work, such rules as experience and analogy suggested to me: experience, which practice and observation were continually increasing; and analogy, which, though in some words obscure, was evident in others.

*   *   *

A large work is difficult, because it is large, even though all its parts might singly be performed with facility; where there are many things to be done, each must be allowed its share of time and labour, in the proportion only which it bears to the whole; nor can it be expected, that the stones which form the dome of a temple, should be squared and polished like the diamond of a ring.

Of the event of this work, for which, having laboured it with so much application, I cannot but have some degree of parental fondness, it is natural to form conjectures. Those who have been persuaded to think well of my design, will require that it should fix our language, and put a stop to those alterations which time and chance have hitherto been suffered to make in it without opposition. With this consequence I will confess that I flattered myself for a while; but now begin to fear, that I have indulged expectation which neither reason nor experience can justify. When we see men grow old and die at a certain time one after another, from century to century, we laugh at the elixir that promises to prolong life to a thousand years; and with equal justice may the lexicographer be derided, who being able to produce no example of a nation that has preserved their words and phrases from mutability, shall imagine that his dictionary can embalm his language, and secure it from corruption and decay, that it is in his power to change sublunary nature, and clear the world at once from folly, vanity and affectation.

With this hope, however, academies have been instituted, to guard the avenues of their languages, to retain fugitives, and repulse intruders; but their vigilance and activity have hitherto been vain; sounds are too volatile and subtile for legal restraints; to enchain syllables, and to lash the wind, are equally the undertakings of pride, unwilling to measure its desires by its strength. The French language has visibly changed under the inspection of the academy; the style of Amelot's translation of father Paul is observed by Le Courayer to be *un peu passé*; and no Italian will maintain, that the diction of any modern writer is not perceptibly different from that of Boccace, Machiavel, or Caro.

Total and sudden transformations of a language seldom happen; conquests and migrations are now very rare; but there are other causes of change, which, though slow in their operation, and invisible in their progress, are, perhaps, as much superiour to human resistance, as the revolutions of the sky, or intumescence of the tide. Commerce, however necessary, however lucrative, as it depraves the manners, corrupts the language; they that have frequent intercourse with strangers, to whom they endeavour to accommodate themselves, must in time learn a mingled dialect, like the jargon which serves the traffickers on the Mediterranean and Indian coasts. This will not always be confined to the exchange, the warehouse, or the port, but will be communicated by degrees to other ranks of the people, and be at last incorporated with the current speech.

43

There are likewise internal causes equally forcible. The language most likely to continue long without alteration, would be that of a nation raised a little, and but a little, above barbarity, secluded from strangers, and totally employed in procuring the conveniencies of life; either without books, or, like some of the Mahometan countries, with very few: men thus busied and unlearned, having only such words as common use requires, would, perhaps, long continue to express the same notions by the same signs. But no such constancy can be expected in a people polished by arts, and classed by subordination, where one part of the community is sustained and accommodated by the labour of the other. Those who have much leisure to think, will always be enlarging the stock of ideas; and every increase of knowledge, whether real or fancied, will produce new words, or combinations of words. When the mind is unchained from necessity, it will range after convenience; when it is left at large in the fields of speculation, it will shift opinions; as any custom is disused, the words that expressed it must perish with it; as any opinion grows popular, it will innovate speech in the same proportion as it alters practice.

As by the cultivation of various sciences, a language is amplified, it will be more furnished with words deflected from their original sense; the geometrician will talk of a 'courtier's zenith, or the eccentric virtue of a wild hero'; and the physician of 'sanguine expectations and phlegmatic delays'. Copiousness of speech will give opportunities to capricious choice, by which some words will be preferred, and others degraded; vicissitudes of fashion will enforce the use of new, or extend the signification of known terms. The tropes of poetry will make hourly encroachments, and the metaphorical will become the current sense: pronunciation will be varied by levity or ignorance, and the pen must at length comply with the tongue; illiterate writers will, at one time or other, by public infatuation, rise into renown, who, not knowing the original import of words, will use them with colloquial licentiousness, confound distinction, and forget propriety. As politeness increases, some expressions will be considered as too gross and vulgar for the delicate, others as too formal and ceremonious for the gay and airy; new phrases are, therefore, adopted, which must, for the same reasons, be in time dismissed. Swift, in his petty treatise on the English language, allows that new words must sometimes be introduced, but proposes that none should be suffered to become obsolete. But what makes a word obsolete, more than general agreement to forbear it? and how shall it be continued, when it conveys an offensive idea, or recalled again into the mouths of mankind, when it has once become unfamiliar by disuse, and unpleasing by unfamiliarity?

There is another cause of alteration more prevalent than any other, which yet in the present state of the world cannot be obviated. A mixture of two languages will produce a third distinct from both; and they will always be mixed, where the chief part of education, and the most conspicuous accomplishment, is skill in ancient or in foreign tongues. He that has long cultivated another language, will find its words and combinations crowd upon his memory; and haste and negligence, refinement and affectation, will obtrude borrowed terms and exotic expressions.

The great pest of speech is frequency of translation. No book was ever turned from one language into another, without imparting something of its native idiom; this is the most mischievous and comprehensive innovation; single words may enter by thousands, and the fabric of the tongue continue the same; but new phraseology changes much at once; it alters not the single stones of the building, but the order of the columns. If an academy should be established for the cultivation of our style; which I, who can never wish to see dependance multiplied, hope the spirit of English liberty will hinder or destroy, let them, instead of compiling grammars and dictionaries, endeavour, with all their influence, to stop the license of translators, whose idleness and ignorance, if it be suffered to proceed, will reduce us to babble a dialect of France.

If the changes, that we fear, be thus irresistible, what remains but to acquiesce with silence, as in the other insurmountable distresses of humanity? It remains that we retard what we cannot repel, that we palliate what we cannot cure. Life may be lengthened by care, though death cannot be ultimately defeated: tongues, like governments, have a natural tendency to degeneration; we have long preserved our constitution, let us make some struggles for our language.

45

In hope of giving longevity to that which its own nature forbids to be immortal, I have devoted this book, the labour of years, to the honour of my country, that we may no longer yield the palm of philology, without a contest, to the nations of the continent. The chief glory of every people arises from its authors: whether I shall add any thing by my own writings to the reputation of English literature, must be left to time: much of my life has been lost under the pressures of disease; much has been trifled away; and much has always been spent in provision for the day that was passing over me; but I shall not think my employment useless or ignoble, if, by my assistance, foreign nations, and distant ages, gain access to the propagators of knowledge, and understand the teachers of truth; if my labours afford light to the repositories of science, and add celebrity to Bacon, to Hooker, to Milton, and to Boyle.

When I am animated by this wish, I look with pleasure on my book, however defective, and deliver it to the world with the spirit of a man that has endeavoured well. That it will immediately become popular I have not promised to myself: a few wild blunders, and risible absurdities, from which no work of such multiplicity was ever free, may, for a time, furnish folly with laughter, and harden ignorance into contempt; but useful diligence will at last prevail, and there never can be wanting some who distinguish desert; who will consider that no dictionary of a living tongue ever can be perfect, since, while it is hastening to publication, some words are budding, and some falling away; that a whole life cannot be spent upon syntax and etymology, and that even a whole life would not be sufficient; that he, whose design includes whatever language can express, must often speak of what he does not understand; that a writer will sometimes be hurried by eagerness to the end, and sometimes faint with weariness under a task, which Scaliger compares to the labours of the anvil and the mine; that what is obvious is not always known, and what is known is not always present; that sudden fits of inadvertency will surprise vigilance, slight avocations will seduce attention, and casual eclipses of the mind will darken learning; and that the writer shall often in vain trace his memory, at the moment of need, for that which yesterday he knew with intuitive readiness, and which will come uncalled into his thoughts to-morrow.

In this work, when it shall be found that much is omitted, let it not be forgotten that much likewise is performed; and though no book was ever spared out of tenderness to the author, and the world is little solicitous to know whence proceeded the faults of that which it condemns; yet it may gratify curiosity to inform it, that the English Dictionary was written with little assistance of the learned, and without any patronage of the great; not in the soft obscurities of retirement, or under the shelter of academic bowers, but amidst inconvenience and distraction, in sickness and in sorrow. It may repress the triumph of malignant criticism to observe, that if our language is not here fully displayed, I have only failed in an attempt, which no human powers have hitherto completed. If the lexicons of ancient tongues, now immutably fixed, and comprised in a few volumes, be yet, after the toil of successive ages, inadequate and delusive; if the aggregated knowledge, and co-operating diligence of the Italian academicians, did not secure them from the censure of Beni; if the embodied critics of France, when fifty years had been spent upon their work, were obliged to change its economy, and give their second edition another form, I may surely be contented without the praise of perfection, which, if I could obtain, in this gloom of solitude, what would it avail me? I have protracted my work till most of those, whom I wished to please, have sunk into the grave, and success and miscarriage are empty sounds: I, therefore, dismiss it with frigid tranquillity, having little to fear or hope from censure or from praise.

Johnson was indeed, at this time, a very weary man. The immense effort of concentration needed to compile the *Dictionary*, continued as it had been for nine years, had brought him into a state of debility and irritation which must partly account for the savage feelings one senses clearly behind the stately phrases of his famous letter to Lord Chesterfield. This important peer, Secretary of State and a well-known patron of literature, had accepted the Dedication in 1747 of the Plan of the Dictionary, and was in a position to do the work some good by his interested support.

47

But he had neglected Johnson for years during which the work was doggedly pushed on 'without one act of assistance, one word of encouragement, or one smile of favour'—and Johnson was not going to forgive him now. Hearing that publication was imminent, Chesterfield wrote two essays in a fashionable periodical, the *World*, in which he commended it. 'I have sailed a long and painful voyage round the world of the English language,' Johnson growled, 'and does he now send out two cock-boats to tow me into harbour?'

16. My Lord   *February 1755*
I have been lately informed by the proprietor of The World that two Papers in which my Dictionary is recommended to the Public were written by your Lordship. To be so distinguished is an honour which, being very little accustomed to favours from the Great, I know not well how to receive, or in what terms to acknowledge.

When upon some slight encouragement I first visited your Lordship I was overpowered like the rest of Mankind by the enchantment of your adress, and could not forbear to wish that I might boast myself Le Vainqueur du Vainqueur de la Terre, that I might obtain that regard for which I saw the world contending, but I found my attendance so little incouraged, that neither pride nor modesty would suffer me to continue it. When I had once adressed your Lordship in public, I had exhausted all the art of pleasing which a retired and uncourtly Scholar can possess. I had done all that I could, and no Man is well pleased to have his all neglected, be it ever so little.

Seven years, My Lord, have now past since I waited in your outward Rooms or was repulsed from your Door, during which time I have been pushing on my work through difficulties of which It is useless to complain, and have brought it at last to the verge of Publication without one Act of assistance, one word of encouragement, or one smile of favour. Such treatment I did not expect, for I never had a Patron before.

The Shepherd in Virgil grew at last acquainted with Love, and found him a Native of the Rocks. Is not a Patron, My Lord, one who looks with unconcern on a Man struggling for Life in the water and when he has reached ground encumbers him with help. The notice which you have been pleased to take of my Labours, had it been early, had been kind; but it has been delayed till I am indifferent and cannot enjoy it, till I am solitary and cannot impart it, till I am known and do not want it.

I hope it is no very cinical asperity not to confess obligation where no benefit has been received, or to be unwilling that the Public should consider me as owing that to a Patron, which Providence has enabled me to do for myself.

Having carried on my work thus far with so little obligation to any Favourer of Learning I shall not be disappointed though I should conclude it, if less be possible, with less, for I have been long wakened from that Dream of hope, in which I once boasted myself with so much exultation, My lord Your Lordship's Most humble Most Obedient Servant,

Sam: Johnson

The *Dictionary* made Johnson famous. But it did not put him above the reach of want. He still had to spend most of his time in provision for the day that was passing over him. Even after such heroic toil and honourable fame, he was still only a few steps from the pavement. In view of the fate that awaited the debtor in eighteenth-century prisons, it is with a shock that we learn from the hurried note to Richardson, (17) that Johnson was under arrest for a debt of £5 18s.

17. Sir

I am obliged to entreat your assistance, I am now under an arrest for five pounds eighteen shillings. Mr Strahan from whom I should have received the necessary help in this case is not at home, and I am afraid of not finding Mr Millar, if you will be so good as to send me this sum, I will very gratfully repay You, and add it to all former obligations.

I am Sir, Your most obedient and most humble Servant
Gough Square March 16   Sam: Johnson

The years in which Johnson had to earn his bread from day to day by the drudging and uncertain trade of writing —drudging and uncertain at any time, but especially so in the earlier eighteenth century—were hard, merciless years. No wonder the act of writing was associated in his mind with back-breaking work, undertaken for survival. Boswell remarks, under the year 1776, that Johnson 'uniformly adhered to that strange opinion which his indolent disposition made him utter: "No man but a blockhead ever wrote, except for money."' He gives no date for this remark, representing it merely as a consistent opinion of Johnson's. So it was, but to attribute it simply to Johnson's 'indolent disposition' is a simplification, such as Boswell was not often guilty of. Johnson kept his mind very active in later years, when he had no need to write for money; he studied, he meditated, he travelled. But writing, the physical act of driving his pen across the paper, was never much of a pleasure to him, nor the literary character, *per se*, glamorous or enviable. Work, to him, was the curse of Adam, a consequence of man's fallen nature, and he was always firm with what he considered the cant of those who maintained that it was a pleasure. So, as a coda to this section, here is Boswell's report of a short conversation about work and its delights; Boswell having remarked that trade gave pleasure 'by its furnishing occupation to such numbers of mankind':

18. JOHNSON. 'Why, Sir, you cannot call that pleasure to which all are averse, and which none can begin but with the hope of leaving off; a thing which men dislike before they have tried it, and when they have tried it.' BOSWELL. 'But, Sir, the mind must be employed, and we grow weary when idle.' JOHNSON. 'That is, Sir, because, others being busy, we want company; but if we were all idle, there would be no growing weary; we should all entertain one another. There is, indeed, this in trade:—it gives men an opportunity of improving their situation. If there were no trade, many who are poor would always remain poor. But no man loves labour for itself.' BOSWELL. 'Yes, Sir, I know a person who does. He is a very laborious Judge, and he loves the labour.' JOHNSON. 'Sir, that is because he loves respect and distinction. Could he have them without labour, he would like it less.' BOSWELL. 'He tells me he likes it for itself.'—'Why, Sir, he fancies so, because he is not accustomed to abstract.'

Chapter III

'The Public has no Further Claim Upon Me'

The seven years 1755–62 are a kind of interregnum in Johnson's life. His fame is established; he is Dictionary Johnson, 'our English Lexiphanes', the Rambler, a lawgiver in moral as well as stylistic matters. But he still is a poor man, condemned to unceasing toil, one jump ahead of bailiffs and creditors. During these hard-pressed years, a great deal of miscellaneous work flows from his pen; he also undertakes a labour almost as great as that of the *Dictionary*, a labour that was to be his last sustained effort on the grand scale.

In 1758 Johnson began a new series of periodical essays, *The Idler*, similar to *The Rambler* but lighter in tone, and running for a similar life-span, about two years. In the following year his mother died; needing to pay some small debts she had left, he wrote and published *The Prince of Abissinia, a Tale in Two Volumes*—generally known, and hereinafter referred to, as *Rasselas*. This short, compressed fable was written at almost incredible speed—in the evenings of one week, according to Johnson's entirely reliable word—but, as usual with him, the act of writing was a rapid crystallization of material that had long been forming in his mind. The issues dealt with in *Rasselas* had been deeply meditated for more than twenty years; the form, an 'Eastern tale' with an exotic setting and overtly symbolic overtones, was one that Johnson had used before both in *Irene* and in The Vision of Theodore the Hermit (1748). So that when Johnson (1) talks lightly of *Rasselas*

51

as 'a little story book' it is as well to remember his habitual modesty and his lifelong refusal to overprice his own achievements.

Meanwhile his work as a journalist continued. We catch a welcome glimpse of Johnson with the tea-pot perpetually at his side, from a passage (2) from his review in the *Literary Magazine* of Jonas Hanway's *Journal of Eight Days' Journey*, in which he turns aside to contest Hanway's ardent propaganda against the habit of tea-drinking. A couple of years later he contributed to the same magazine one of his finest pieces of writing, instinct with a fierce irony and a noble indignation, his famous review of *A Free Enquiry into the Nature and Origin of Evil* by Soame Jenyns. The unfortunate Jenyns had advanced a theory which derived ultimately from Leibnitz and maintained that every form of life had its place in the grand scheme of the Creator; a scorpion or an influenza germ had its appointed function, as did a man; if we could see the whole design we would grasp the benevolent nature of the presiding Mind. Formally, Johnson would have little enough quarrel with this, but he was angered by a certain complacency which Jenyns had allowed to creep into his tone. Writing from the comfortable point of view of a leisured man, Jenyns spoke a little too placidly of the sufferings of the poor, the diseased, even the insane; and he permitted himself the speculation that a race of beings higher up on the Great Chain might even derive amusement from the spectacle of the struggles and sufferings of lower beings, including ourselves. Such trifling appeared to Johnson to show a lack of ordinary human compassion, and he went after Jenyns in no uncertain manner. I give below (3) an extract from the review at its most characteristic: not because it is, strictly speaking, a personal utterance that relates to Johnson himself, but because it is the statement of a passionately held attitude towards life and experience. Johnson is writing at white heat from the very centre of his nature, and what he has to say is personal even if it is not autobiographical or self-regarding.

The extract from *Rasselas* (not the only one in this book,

see VII, 1) is more nearly personal in that the character of Imlac, the philosopher, is clearly intended to be in some ways a surrogate for the author. Once again, the extracts show up less well in isolation than in their context; in this densely organized work, the moral reflections take on colour and weight which depend to some extent on their place in the narrative. But, as representing an opinion very central to Johnson, we may single out the encounter with the hermit (Chapter XXI), which expresses Johnson's suspicion of the cloistered life as an infallible route to piety and virtue.

As a final document of this phase of Johnson's life, we have (5) the last number of *The Idler*, which appeared in Easter week 1760 and found Johnson in solemn mood. It is his farewell to periodical writing; though he went on to contribute a number of papers to a publication called *The Adventurer*, he never again took sole responsibility for a periodical.

1. Sir

When I was with you last night I told you of a thing which I was preparing for the press. The title will be

The choice of Life

or

The History of —— Prince of Abissinia

It will make about two volumes like little Pompadour that is about one middling volume. The bargain which I made with Mr Johnston was seventy five pounds (or guineas) a volume, and twenty five pounds for the second Edition. I will sell this either at that price or for sixty the first edition of which he shall himself fix the number, and the property then to revert to me, or for forty pounds, and share the profit that is retain half the copy. I shall have occasion for thirty pounds on Monday night when I shall deliver the book which I must entreat you upon such delivery to procure me. I would have it offered to Mr Johnston, but have no doubt of selling it, on some of the terms mentioned.

I will not print my name, but expect it to be known.

I am Dear Sir Your most humble Servant

Jan. 20. 1759   Sam: Johnson

Get me the money if you can.

'A hardened and shameless Tea-drinker.'

2. We have already given in our collections one of the letters, in which Mr. Hanway endeavours to show, that the consumption of Tea is injurious to the interest of our country. We shall now endeavour to follow him regularly through all his observations on this modern luxury; but it can scarcely be candid, not to make a previous declaration, that he is to expect little justice from the author of this extract, a hardened and shameless Tea-drinker, who has for twenty years diluted his meals with only the infusion of this fascinating plant, whose kettle has scarcely time to cool, who with Tea amuses the evening, with Tea solaces the midnight, and with Tea welcomes the morning.

3. Having thus despatched the consideration of particular evils, he comes at last to a general reason for which *evil* may be said to be *our good*. He is of opinion that there is some inconceivable benefit in pain abstractedly considered; that pain, however inflicted or wherever felt, communicates some good to the general system of being, and that every animal is some way or other the better for the pain of every other animal. This opinion he carried so far as to suppose that there passes some principle of union through all animal life, as attraction is communicated to all corporeal nature, and that the evils suffered on this globe may, by some inconceivable means, contribute to the felicity of the inhabitants of the remotest planet.

How the origin of evil is brought nearer to human conception by any *inconceivable* means, I am not able to discover. We believed that the present system of creation was right, though we could not explain the adaptation of one part to the other, or for the whole succession of causes and consequences. Where has this enquirer added to the little knowledge that we had before? He has told us of the benefits of evil, which no man feels, and relations between distant parts of [the] universe, which he cannot himself conceive. There was enough in this question inconceivable before, and we have little advantage from a new inconceivable solution.

I do not mean to reproach this author for not knowing what

is equally hidden from learning and from ignorance. The shame is to impose words for ideas upon ourselves or others; to imagine that we are going forward when we are only turning round; to think that there is any difference between him that gives no reason, and him that gives a reason which by his own confession cannot be conceived.

But that he may not be thought to conceive nothing but things inconceivable, he has at last thought on a way by which human sufferings may produce good effects. He imagines that as we have not only animals for food, but choose some for our diversion, the same privilege may be allowed to some beings above us, *who may deceive, torment, or destroy us for the ends only of their own pleasure or utility.* This he again finds impossible to be conceived, *but that impossibility lessens not the probability of the conjecture, which by analogy is so strongly confirmed.*

I cannot resist the temptation of contemplating this analogy, which I think he might have carried further very much to the advantage of his argument. He might have shown that these *hunters whose game is man* have many sports analogous to our own. As we drown whelps and kittens, they amuse themselves now and then with sinking a ship, and stand round the fields of Blenheim or the walls of Prague as we encircle a cock-pit. As we shoot a bird flying, they take a man in the midst of his business or pleasure, and knock him down with an apoplexy. Some of them, perhaps, are virtuosi, and delight in the operations of an asthma, as a human philosopher in the effects of the air pump. To swell a man with a tympany is as good sport as to blow a frog. Many a merry bout have these frolic beings at the vicissitudes of an ague, and good sport it is to see a man tumble with an epilepsy, and revive and tumble again, and all this he knows not why. As they are wiser and more powerful than we, they have more exquisite diversions, for we have no way of procuring any sport so brisk and so lasting as the paroxysms of the gout and stone which undoubtedly must make high mirth, especially if the play be a little diversified with the blunders and puzzles of the blind and deaf. We know not how far their sphere of observation may extend. Perhaps now and then a merry being may place himself in such a situation as to enjoy at once all the varieties of an epidemical disease, or amuse his leisure with the tossings and contortions of every possible pain exhibited together.

One sport the merry malice of these beings has found means of enjoying to which we have nothing equal or similar. They now and then catch a mortal proud of his parts, and flattered either by the submission of those who court his kindness, or the notice of those who suffer him to court theirs. A head thus prepared for the reception of false opinions and the projection of vain designs, they easily fill with idle notions, till in time they make their plaything an author : their first diversion commonly begins with an ode or an epistle, then rises perhaps to a political irony, and is at last brought to its height by a treatise of philosophy. Then begins the poor animal to entangle himself in sophisms, and flounder in absurdity, to talk confidently of the scale of being, and to give solutions which himself confesses impossible to be understood. Sometimes, however, it happens that their pleasure is without much mischief. The author feels no pain, but while they are wondering at the extravagance of his opinion and pointing him out to one another as a new example of human folly, he is enjoying his own applause, and that of his companions, and perhaps is elevated with the hope of standing at the head of a new sect.

Many of the books which now crowd the world may be justly suspected to be written for the sake of some invisible order of beings, for surely they are of no use to any of the corporeal inhabitants of the world. Of the productions of the last bounteous year, how many can be said to serve any purpose of use or pleasure. The only end of writing is to enable the readers better to enjoy life, or better to endure it : and how will either of those be put more in our power by him who tells us that we are puppets, of which some creature not much wiser than ourselves manages the wires : that a set of beings, unseen and unheard, are hovering about us, trying experiments upon our sensibility, putting us in agonies to see our limbs quiver, torturing us to madness that they may laugh at our vagaries ; sometimes obstructing the bile, that they may see how a man looks when he is yellow, sometimes breaking a traveller's bones to try how he will get home, sometimes wasting a man to a skeleton, and sometimes killing him fat for the greater elegance of his hide?

This is an account of natural evil which though, like the rest, not quite new is very entertaining, though I know not how much it may contribute to patience. The only reason why we should contemplate evil is that we may bear it better, and I am afraid nothing is much more placidly endured for the sake of making others sport.

4. *CHAPTER XXI* The happiness of solitude. The hermit's history

They came on the third day, by the direction of the peasants, to the hermit's cell: it was a cavern in the side of a mountain, overshadowed with palm-trees, at such a distance from the cataract that nothing more was heard than a gentle uniform murmur, such as composed the mind to pensive meditation, especially when it was assisted by the wind whistling among the branches. The first rude essay of nature had been so much improved by human labour that the cave contained several apartments, appropriated to different uses, and often afforded lodging to travellers whom darkness or tempests happened to overtake.

The hermit sat on a bench at the door to enjoy the coolness of the evening. On one side lay a book with pens and papers, on the other mechanical instruments of various kinds. As they approached him unregarded, the princess observed that he had not the countenance of a man that had found, or could teach, the way to happiness.

They saluted him with great respect, which he repaid like a man not unaccustomed to the forms of courts. 'My children', said he, 'if you have lost your way, you shall be willingly supplied with such conveniences for the night as this cavern will afford. I have all that nature requires, and you will not expect delicacies in a hermit's cell.'

They thanked him, and, entering, were pleased with the neatness and regularity of the place. The hermit set flesh and wine before them, though he fed only upon fruits and water. His discourse was cheerful without levity, and pious without enthusiasm. He soon gained the esteem of his guests, and the princess repented of her hasty censure.

At last Imlac began thus: 'I do not now wonder that your reputation is so far extended; we have heard at Cairo of your wisdom, and came hither to implore your direction for this young man and maiden in the *choice of life.*'

'To him that lives well,' answered the hermit, 'every form of life is good; nor can I give any other rule for choice than to remove from all apparent evil.'

'He will remove most certainly from evil,' said the prince, 'who shall devote himself to that solitude which you have recommended by your example.'

'I have indeed lived fifteen years in solitude,' said the hermit, 'but have no desire that my example should gain any imitators. In my youth I professed arms, and was raised by degrees to the highest military rank. I have traversed wide countries at the head of my troops, and seen many battles and sieges. At last, being disgusted by the preferment of a younger officer, and finding my vigour beginning to decay, I resolved to close my life in peace, having found the world full of snares, discord, and misery. I had once escaped from the pursuit of the enemy by the shelter of this cavern, and therefore chose it for my final residence. I employed artificers to form it into chambers, and stored it with all that I was likely to want.

'For some time after my retreat, I rejoiced like a tempest-beaten sailor at his entrance into the harbour, being delighted with the sudden change of the noise and hurry of war to stillness and repose. When the pleasure of novelty went away, I employed my hours in examining the plants which grow in the valley and the minerals which I collected from the rocks. But that enquiry is now grown tasteless and irksome. I have been for some time unsettled and distracted: my mind is disturbed with a thousand perplexities of doubt and vanities of imagination which hourly prevail upon me, because I have no opportunities of relaxation or diversion. I am sometimes ashamed to think that I could not secure myself from vice but by retiring from the practice of virtue, and begin to suspect that I was rather impelled by resentment, than led by devotion, into solitude. My fancy riots in scenes of folly, and I lament that I have lost so much and have gained so little. In solitude, if I escape the example of bad men, I want likewise the counsel and conversation of the good. I have been long comparing the evils with the advantages of society, and resolve to return into the world tomorrow. The life of a solitary man will be certainly miserable, but not certainly devout.'

They heard his resolution with surprise, but, after a short pause, offered to conduct him to Cairo. He dug up a considerable treasure which he had hid among the rocks, and accompanied them to the city, on which, as he approached it, he gazed with rapture.

5. Much of the pain and pleasure of mankind arises from the conjectures which every one makes of the thoughts of others; we all enjoy praise which we do not hear, and resent contempt which we do not see. The Idler may therefore be forgiven, if he suffers his imagination to represent to him what his readers will say or think, when they are informed that they have now his last paper in their hands.

Value is more frequently raised by scarcity than by use. That which lay neglected when it was common, rises in estimation as its quantity becomes less. We seldom learn the true want of what we have, till it is discovered that we can have no more.

This essay will, perhaps, be read with care even by those who have not yet attended to any other; and he that finds this late attention recompensed, will not forbear to wish that he had bestowed it sooner.

Though the Idler and his readers have contracted no close friendship, they are perhaps both unwilling to part. There are few things not purely evil, of which we can say, without some emotion of uneasiness, *this is the last.* Those who never could agree together, shed tears when mutual discontent has determined them to final separation; of a place which has been frequently visited, though without pleasure, the last look is taken with heaviness of heart; and the Idler, with all his chillness of tranquillity, is not wholly unaffected by the thought that his last essay is now before him.

This secret horrour of the last is inseparable from a thinking being, whose life is limited, and to whom death is dreadful. We always make a secret comparison between a part and the whole; the termination of any period of life reminds us that life itself has likewise its termination; when we have done any thing for the last time, we involuntarily reflect that a part of the days allotted us is past, and that as more is past there is less remaining.

It is very happily and kindly provided, that in every life there are certain pauses and interruptions, which force consideration upon the careless, and seriousness upon the light; points of time where one course of action ends, and another begins; and by vicissitudes of fortune, or alteration of employment, by change of place or loss of friendship, we are forced to say of something, *this is the last.*

An even and unvaried tenour of life always hides from our apprehension the approach of its end. Succession is not perceived but by variation; he that lives to-day as he lived yesterday, and expects that as the present day is such will be the morrow, easily conceives times as running in a circle and returning to itself. The uncertainty of our duration is impressed commonly by dissimilitude of condition; it is only by finding life changeable that we are reminded of its shortness.

This conviction, however forcible at every new impression, is every moment fading from the mind; and partly by the inevitable incursion of new images, and partly by voluntary exclusion of unwelcome thoughts, we are again exposed to the universal fallacy; and we must do another thing for the last time, before we consider that the time is nigh when we shall do no more.

As the last *Idler* is published in that solemn week which the Christian world has always set apart for the examination of the conscience, the review of life, the extinction of earthly desires, and the renovation of holy purposes; I hope that my readers are already disposed to view every incident with seriousness, and improve it by meditation; and that, when they see this series of trifles brought to a conclusion, they will consider that, by outliving the Idler, they have passed weeks, months, and years, which are no longer in their power; that an end must in time be put to every thing great as to every thing little; that to life must come its last hour, and to this system of being its last day, the hour at which probation ceases, and repentance will be vain; the day in which every work of the hand, and imagination of the heart, shall be brought to judgment, and an everlasting futurity shall be determined by the past.

> Since at this point we take our leave of Johnson the hard-pressed professional journalist, it is legitimate to co-opt a passage from a much later work, the *Life of Milton*, which puts into memorable form an opinion that must have been matured during these years. Every journalist comes into contact, in one way or another, with censorship; we all speak of the freedom of the press as an ideal, but there are some insistent underlying questions, such as freedom to do what? To make the newspapers and books merely the mouthpiece of the ruling power, as happens in totalitarian countries, is obviously a bad thing; but if we remove all restraints of every kind from everyone able to hold a pen (or, in our days, manipulate any of the media) are we really serving the best interests of society? This question Johnson considers not yet solved in his time; has it been solved in ours?

6. He published about the same time his *Areopagitica, a Speech of Mr.* John Milton *for the liberty of unlicensed Printing.* The danger of such unbounded liberty, and the danger of bounding it, have produced a problem in the science of Government, which human understanding seems hitherto unable to solve. If nothing may be published but what civil authority shall have previously approved, power must always be the standard of truth; if every dreamer of innovations may propagate his projects, there can be no settlement; if every murmurer at government may diffuse discontent, there can be no peace; and if every sceptic in theology may teach his follies, there can be no religion. The remedy against these evils is to punish the authors; for it is yet allowed that every society may punish, though not prevent, the publication of opinions, which that society shall think pernicious; but this punishment, though it may crush the author, promotes the book; and it seems not more reasonable, to leave the right of printing unrestrained because writers may be afterwards censured, than it would be to sleep with doors unbolted, because by our laws we can hang a thief.

By the time he wrote that last *Idler*, Johnson was already four years deep into his last labour of Hercules, the edition of Shakespeare. Back in the 1740s, he had been eager to produce an edition of Shakespeare in which he would sort out textual problems and explain difficulties; the scheme had been blocked at that time by the publisher Tonson, who took advantage of the confused state of copyright law to claim that he owned copyright in the Bard's works. Johnson's publisher, Cave, had been frightened by the thought of a legal battle with so mighty an antagonist, and dropped the idea. Now, however, it was possible to go on. Johnson's reputation was such that the idea of his editing Shakespeare would receive general support. Accordingly, he put out a pamphlet in 1756, setting out Proposals for the edition; this was to attract subscribers who sent in cash with their orders.

When Johnson undertook to write the *Dictionary*, his friends were staggered at the Herculean self-confidence he showed. But he had meditated long and deeply on the nature of the work and the method, he knew his own powers, and while his original estimate of the time it would take—three years—was wildly optimistic, in the end he got through it in nine. In 1779, when Boswell remarked to him, 'You did not know what you were undertaking', Johnson replied, 'Yes, Sir, I knew very well what I was undertaking,—and very well how to do it,—and have done it very well.' We can hear the deep, slow, emphatic voice, charged with justifiable self-satisfaction. In the same spirit, he announced in 1756 that the edition of Shakespeare would be out by Christmas 1757. When that time came, he said he would publish in March 1758; in March, he said it would be 'before summer'. After that he seems to have given up publicly announcing a date. Meanwhile subscriptions were coming in, though people who knew Johnson understandably held on to their money as the only means of making him get on with the job: 'he never thinks of working if he has a couple of guineas in his pocket', wrote Dr Grainger to Bishop Percy, counselling him to hold back at least part of the subscription until Johnson was in want of it.

Ultimately Johnson's failure to produce became something of a scandal. The satiric poet Charles Churchill brought out in 1762 a poem called *The Ghost*, in which Johnson is ridiculed under the name of '*Pomposo*'; naturally, the business of the subscribed cash and the non-existent work was too good to miss:

> He for subscribers baits his hook
> And takes their cash—but where's the book?
> No matter where—wise fear, we know,
> Forbids the robbing of a foe;
> But what, to serve our private ends,
> Forbids the cheating of our friends?

This well-deserved caning appears to have had no effect on Johnson. Since he never thought of working when he had a couple of guineas in his pocket, it was unfortunate for the Shakespeare project that the Government of George III chose this moment (July 1762) to award him a pension. The wonder is that he did not down tools immediately. (Perhaps he would have done had he not, by his own admission, lost the piece of paper on which the names of subscribers were entered; since the money could not be refunded, it would just have to be earned.) At last, in October 1765, the edition issued from the press. It was at once seen to be worth the twenty years of thought that Johnson had given to Shakespeare since the publication of his original, abortive 'Proposals' in 1745. The noble Preface alone would justify Johnson's entire existence.

In the selections that follow, we see Johnson (7) outlining, in the Proposals of 1756, the historical method that he means to follow in elucidating Shakespeare; writing to his old collaborator Thomas Birch (8) to request the loan of works by Shakespeare's 'contemporaries or ancestors'; recommending his edition to the encouragement of David Garrick, as the star actor-manager of his day (9); and,

after the edition is at last published, writing to Joseph
Warton (10), 'I . . . am well enough pleased that the public
has no further claim on me.'

**7. PROPOSALS FOR PRINTING THE DRAMATIC WORKS OF
WILLIAM SHAKESPEARE**

[issued June 1756]

When the works of *Shakespeare* are, after so many editions, again
offered to the Public, it will doubtless be inquired, why *Shakespeare* stands in more need of critical assistance than any other
of the *English* writers, and what are the deficiencies of the late
attempts, which another editor may hope to supply?

The business of him that republishes an ancient book is, to
correct what is corrupt, and to explain what is obscure. To have
a text corrupt in many places, and in many doubtful, is, among
the authors that have written since the use of types, almost
peculiar to *Shakespeare*. Most writers, by publishing their own
works, prevent all various readings, and preclude all conjectural
criticism. Books indeed are sometimes published after the death
of him who produced them; but they are better secured from
corruption than these unfortunate compositions. They subsist
in a single copy, written or revised by the author; and the faults
of the printed volume can be only faults of one descent.

But of the works of *Shakespeare* the condition has been far
different: he sold them, not to be printed, but to be played.
They were immediately copied for the actors, and multiplied
by transcript after transcript, vitiated by the blunders of the
penman, or changed by the affectation of the player; perhaps
enlarged to introduce a jest, or mutilated to shorten the representation; and printed at last without the concurrence of the
author, without the consent of the proprietor, from compila-
tions made by chance or by stealth out of the separate parts
written for the theatre: and thus thrust into the world surrep-
titiously and hastily, they suffered another depravation from
the ignorance and negligence of the printers, as every man
who knows the state of the press in that age will readily
conceive.

It is not easy for invention to bring together so many causes
concurring to vitiate a text. No other author ever gave up his

works to fortune and time with so little care: no books could be left in hands so likely to injure them, as plays frequently acted, yet continued in manuscript: no other transcribers were likely to be so little qualified for their task as those who copied for the stage, at a time when the lower ranks of the people were universally illiterate: no other editions were made from fragments so minutely broken, and so fortuitously reunited; and in no other age was the art of printing in such unskilful hands.

With the causes of corruption that make the revisal of *Shakespeare*'s dramatic pieces necessary, may be enumerated the causes of obscurity, which may be partly imputed to his age, and partly to himself.

When a writer outlives his contemporaries, and remains almost the only unforgotten name of a distant time, he is necessarily obscure. Every age has its modes of speech, and its cast of thought; which, though easily explained when there are many books to be compared with each other, become sometimes unintelligible and always difficult, when there are no parallel passages that may conduce to their illustration. *Shakespeare* is the first considerable author of sublime or familiar dialogue in our language. Of the books which he read, and from which he formed his style, some perhaps have perished, and the rest are neglected. His imitations are therefore unnoted, his allusions are undiscovered, and many beauties, both of pleasantry and greatness, are lost with the objects to which they were united, as the figures vanish when the canvass has decayed.

It is the great excellence of *Shakespeare*, that he drew his scenes from nature, and from life. He copied the manners of the world then passing before him, and has more allusions than other poets to the traditions and superstitions of the vulgar; which must therefore be traced before he can be understood.

He wrote at a time when our poetical language was yet unformed, when the meaning of our phrases was yet in fluctuation, when words were adopted at pleasure from the neighbouring languages, and while the *Saxon* was still visibly mingled in our diction. The reader is therefore embarrassed at once with dead and with foreign languages, with obsoleteness and innovation. In that age, as in all others, fashion produced phraseology, which succeeding fashion swept away before its meaning was generally known, or sufficiently authorized: and in that age, above all others, experiments were made upon our language, which distorted its combinations, and disturbed its uniformity.

If *Shakespeare* has difficulties above other writers, it is to be imputed to the nature of his work, which required the use of the common colloquial language, and consequently admitted many phrases allusive, elliptical, and proverbial, such as we speak and hear every hour without observing them; and of which, being now familiar, we do not suspect that they can ever grow uncouth, or that, being now obvious, they can ever seem remote.

These are the principal causes of the obscurity of *Shakespeare*; to which might be added that fulness of idea, which might sometimes load his words with more sentiment than they could conveniently convey, and that rapidity of imagination which might hurry him to a second thought before he had fully explained the first. But my opinion is, that very few of his lines were difficult to his audience, and that he used such expressions as were then common, though the paucity of contemporary writers makes them now seem peculiar.

*　　*　　*

He that undertakes an edition of *Shakespeare*, has all these difficulties to encounter, and all these obstructions to remove.

The corruptions of the text will be corrected by a careful collation of the oldest copies, by which it is hoped that many restorations may yet be made: at least it will be necessary to collect and note the variations as materials for future critics; for it very often happens that a wrong reading has affinity to the right.

*　　*　　*

It has been long found, that very specious emendations do not equally strike all minds with conviction, nor even the same mind at different times; and therefore, though perhaps many alterations may be proposed as eligible, very few will be obtruded as certain. In a language so ungrammatical as the *English*, and so licentious as that of *Shakespeare*, emendatory criticism is always hazardous; nor can it be allowed to any man who is not particularly versed in the writings of that age, and particularly studious of his author's diction. There is danger lest peculiarities should be mistaken for corruptions, and passages rejected as unintelligible, which a narrow mind happens not to understand.

* * *

With regard to obsolete or peculiar diction, the editor may perhaps claim some degree of confidence, having had more motives to consider the whole extent of our language than any other man from its first formation. He hopes that, by comparing the works of *Shakespeare* with those of writers who lived at the same time, immediately preceded, or immediately followed him, he shall be able to ascertain his ambiguities, disentangle his intricacies, and recover the meaning of words now lost in the darkness of antiquity.

When therefore any obscurity arises from an allusion to some other book, the passage will be quoted. When the diction is entangled, it will be cleared by a paraphrase or interpretation. When the sense is broken by the suppression of part of the sentiment in pleasantry or passion, the connexion will be supplied. When any forgotten custom is hinted, care will be taken to retrieve and explain it. The meaning assigned to doubtful words will be supported by the authorities of other writers, or by parallel passages of *Shakespeare* himself.

The observation of faults and beauties is one of the duties of an annotator, which some of *Shakespeare*'s editors have attempted, and some have neglected. For this part of his task, and for this only, was Mr. *Pope* eminently and indisputably qualified; nor has Dr. *Warburton* followed him with less diligence or less success. But I have never observed that mankind was much delighted or improved by their asterisks, commas, or double commas; of which the only effect is, that they preclude the pleasure of judging for ourselves, teach the young and ignorant to decide without principles; defeat curiosity and discernment, by leaving them less to discover; and at last show the opinion of the critic, without the reasons on which it was founded, and without affording any light by which it may be examined.

The editor, though he may less delight his own vanity, will probably please his reader more, by supposing him equally able with himself to judge of beauties and faults, which require no previous acquisition of remote knowledge. A description of the obvious scenes of nature, a representation of general life, a sentiment of reflection or experience, a deduction of conclusive argument, a forcible eruption of effervescent passion, are to be considered as proportionate to common apprehension, un-assisted by critical officiousness; since, to conceive them, nothing more is requisite than acquaintance with the general state of the world, and those faculties which he must always bring with him who would read *Shakespeare*.

But when the beauty arises from some adaptation of the sentiment to customs worn out of use, to opinions not univer-sally prevalent, or to any accidental or minute particularity, which cannot be supplied by common understanding, or com-mon observation, it is the duty of a commentator to lend his assistance.

The notice of beauties and faults thus limited, will make no distinct part of the design, being reducible to the explana-tion of obscure passages.

The editor does not however intend to preclude himself from the comparison of *Shakespeare*'s sentiments or expression with those of ancient or modern authors, or from the display of any beauty not obvious to the students of poetry; for as he hopes to leave his author better understood, he wishes likewise to procure him more rational approbation.

The former editors have affected to slight their predecessors: but in this edition all that is valuable will be adopted from every commentator, that posterity may consider it as including all the rest, and exhibiting whatever is hitherto known of the great father of the *English* drama.

8. Sir

Being, as you will find by the proposal, engaged in a work which requires the concurrence of my friends to make it of much benefit to me, I have taken the liberty of recommending six receipts to your care, and do not doubt of your endeavour to dispose of them.

I have likewise a further favour to beg. I know you have been long a curious collector of books. If therefore you have any of the contemporaries or Ancestors of Shakespeare, it will be of great use to lend me them for a short time; my stock of those authours is yet but curta supellex.

I am Sir Your obliged humble servant

June 22. 1756.   Sam: Johnson

9. Dear Sir

I know that great regard will be had to your opinion of an Edition of Shakespeare. I desire therefore to secure an honest prejudice in my favour by securing your suffrage, and that this prejudice may really be honest, I wish you would name such plays as you would see, and they shall be sent you by

Sir Your most humble servant

May 18. 1765   Sam: Johnson

10. Dear Sir,   Oct. 9th, 1765.

Mrs. Warton uses me hardly in supposing that I could forget so much kindness and civility as she showed me at Winchester. I remember likewise our conversation about St. Cross. The desire of seeing her again will be one of the motives that will bring me into Hampshire.

I have taken care of your book; being so far from doubting your subscription, that I think you have subscrib'd twice: you once paid your guinea into my own hand in the garret in Gough Square. When you light on your receipt, throw it on the fire; if you find a second receipt, you may have a second book.

To tell the truth, as I felt no solicitude about this work, I receive no great comfort from its conclusion; but yet am well enough pleased that the public has no further claim upon me. I wish you would write more frequently to,

Dear Sir, Your affectionate humble servant, Sam. Johnson.

The great Edition itself presents us with our usual problems of definition. Obviously, it is not a personal utterance; its aim is to illuminate Shakespeare and to package his work for the eighteenth-century reader. On the other hand, there are points at which the opinion expressed is so centrally Johnsonian that it has the flavour (almost) of a page from a diary or notebook. The opening pages of the Preface, in which Johnson succinctly gives his reasons for believing in Shakespeare's greatness; the closing pages, where he muses on the usefulness or otherwise of notes (this, after spending nine years writing footnotes!), seem personal by any definition; so do some of the notes on particular passages, where Shakespeare's words have started a train of thought in Johnson's own mind, or jogged into expression some deeply-held conviction, such as that actors are inordinately vain or that vivisection is cruel.

The Romantic critics of two generations later, who habitually expressed themselves in soaring rapture and conscious hyperbole, dismissed Johnson as a Shakespearian critic (there is hardly a reference to him by Coleridge, for example, that is anything but contemptuous). Their attitude seems to have been that Johnson merely sat in judgment on Shakespeare without deeply responding to the emotional and imaginative power of his work. That fallacy hardly needs correction today, yet it is still interesting to recall how fundamental and lifelong was the hold of Shakespeare over Johnson's mind and heart, and to this end we begin the section with Hester Thrale's touching little anecdote of his childish reading of *Hamlet* by the kitchen fire.

11. I have heard him relate another odd thing of himself too, but it is one which every body has heard as well as I : how, when he was about nine years old, having got the play of Hamlet in his hand, and reading it quietly in his father's kitchen, he kept on steadily enough, till coming to the Ghost scene, he suddenly hurried up stairs to the street door that he might see people about him.

12. PREFACE TO SHAKESPEARE

(1765)

That praises are without reason lavished on the dead, and that the honours due only to excellence are paid to antiquity, is a complaint likely to be always continued by those, who, being able to add nothing to truth, hope for eminence from the heresies of paradox; or those, who, being forced by disappointment upon consolatory expedients, are willing to hope from posterity what the present age refuses, and flatter themselves that the regard which is yet denied by envy, will be at last bestowed by time.

Antiquity, like every other quality that attracts the notice of mankind, has undoubtedly votaries that reverence it, not from reason, but from prejudice. Some seem to admire indiscriminately whatever has been long preserved, without considering that time has sometimes co-operated with chance; all perhaps are more willing to honour past than present excellence; and the mind contemplates genius through the shades of age, as the eye surveys the sun through artificial opacity. The great contention of criticism is to find the faults of the moderns, and the beauties of the ancients. While an authour is yet living we estimate his powers by his worst performance, and when he is dead, we rate them by his best.

*   *   *

Shakespeare is above all writers, at least above all modern writers, the poet of nature; the poet that holds up to his readers a faithful mirror of manners and of life. His characters are not modified by the customs of particular places, unpractised by the rest of the world; by the peculiarities of studies or professions, which can operate but upon small numbers; or by the accidents of transient fashions or temporary opinions: they are the genuine progeny of common humanity, such as the world will always supply, and observation will always find. His persons act and speak by the influence of those general passions and principles by which all minds are agitated, and the whole system of life is continued in motion. In the writings of other poets a character is too often an individual; in those of *Shakespeare* it is commonly a species.

It is from this wide extension of design that so much instruction is derived. It is this which fills the plays of *Shakespeare* with practical axioms and domestic wisdom. It was said of *Euripides*, that every verse was a precept; and it may be said of *Shakespeare*, that from his works may be collected a system of civil and oeconomical prudence. Yet his real power is not shewn in the splendour of particular passages, but by the progress of his fable, and the tenour of his dialogue; and he that tries to recommend him by select quotations, will succeed like the pedant in *Hierocles*, who, when he offered his house to sale, carried a brick in his pocket as a specimen.

It will not easily be imagined how much *Shakespeare* excells in accommodating his sentiments to real life, but by comparing him with other authours. It was observed of the ancient schools of declamation, that the more diligently they were frequented, the more was the student disqualified for the world, because he found nothing there which he should ever meet in any other place. The same remark may be applied to every stage but that of *Shakespeare*. The theatre, when it is under any other direction, is peopled by such characters as were never seen, conversing in a language which was never heard, upon topics which will never arise in the commerce of mankind. But the dialogue of this authour is often so evidently determined by the incident which produces it, and is pursued with so much ease and simplicity, that it seems scarcely to claim the merit of fiction, but to have been gleaned by diligent selection out of common conversation, and common occurrences.

*   *   *

Notes are often necessary, but they are necessary evils. Let him, that is yet unacquainted with the powers of *Shakespeare*, and who desires to feel the highest pleasure that the drama can give, read every play from the first scene to the last, with utter negligence of all his commentators. When his fancy is once on the wing, let it not stoop at correction or explanation. When his attention is strongly engaged, let it disdain alike to turn aside to the name of *Theobald* and of *Pope*. Let him read on through brightness and obscurity, through integrity and corruption; let him preserve his comprehension of the dialogue and his interest in the fable. And when the pleasures of novelty have ceased, let him attempt exactness, and read the commentators.

Particular passages are cleared by notes, but the general effect of the work is weakened. The mind is refrigerated by interruption; the thoughts are diverted from the principal subject; the reader is weary, he suspects not why; and at last throws away the book, which he has too diligently studied.

Parts are not to be examined till the whole has been surveyed;

there is a kind of intellectual remoteness necessary for the com-prehension of any great work in its full design and its true pro-portions; a close approach shews the smaller niceties, but the beauty of the whole is discerned no longer. . . .

13. MEASURE FOR MEASURE, ACT III, SCENE I

> Thou hast nor youth, nor age;
> But as it were an after dinner's sleep,
> Dreaming on both.

This is exquisitely imagined. When we are young we busy ourselves in forming schemes for succeeding time, and miss the gratifications that are before us; when we are old we amuse the languor of age with the recollection of youthful pleasures or performances; so that our life, of which no part is filled with the business of the present time, resembles our dreams after dinner, when the events of the morning are mingled with the designs of the evening.

KING JOHN, ACT III, SCENE 4

> CONSTANCE. Had you such a loss as I,
> I could give better comfort than you do.

This is a sentiment which great sorrow always dictates. Who-ever cannot help himself casts his eyes on others for assistance, and often mistakes their inability for coldness.

HENRY IV PART 2

. . . But *Falstaff* unimitated, unimitable *Falstaff*, how shall I describe thee? Thou compound of sense and vice; of sense which may be admired but not esteemed, of vice which may be despised, but hardly detested. *Falstaff* is a character loaded with faults, and with those faults which naturally produce contempt. He is a thief, and a glutton, a coward, and a boaster, always ready to cheat the weak, and prey upon the poor; to terrify the timorous and insult the defenceless. At once obsequious and malignant, he satirises in their absence those whom he lives by flattering. He is familiar with the prince only as an agent of vice, but of this familiarity he is so proud as not only to be super-cilious and haughty with common man, but to think his interest of importance to the duke of *Lancaster*. Yet the man thus

73

corrupt, thus despicable, makes himself necessary to the prince
that despises him, by the most pleasing of all qualities, perpetual
gaiety, by an unfailing power of exciting laughter, which is the
more freely indulged, as his wit is not of the splendid or ambitious
kind, but consists in easy escapes and sallies of levity, which make
sport but raise no envy. It must be observed that he is stained
with no enormous or sanguinary crimes, so that his licentiousness is not so offensive but that it may be borne for his mirth.

The moral to be drawn from this representation is, that no
man is more dangerous than he that with a will to corrupt, hath
the power to please; and that neither wit nor honesty ought to
think themselves safe with such a companion when they see
Henry seduced by *Falstaff*.

HENRY V, ACT II, SCENE 4

Such is the end of *Falstaff*, from whom *Shakespeare* had
promised us in his epilogue to *Henry* IV that we should receive
more entertainment. It happened to *Shakespeare* as to other
writers, to have his imagination crowded with a tumultuary
confusion of images, which, while they were yet unsorted and
unexamined, seemed sufficient to furnish a long train of incidents, and a new variety of merriment, but which, when he
was to produce them to view, shrunk suddenly from him, or
could not be accommodated to his general design. That he
once designed to have brought *Falstaff* on the scene again, we
know from himself; but whether he could contrive no train of
adventures suitable to his character, or could match him with
no companions likely to quicken his humour, or could open
no new vein of pleasantry, and was afraid to continue the same
strain lest it should not find the same reception, he has here
for ever discarded him, and made haste to dispatch him, perhaps for the same reason for which *Addison* killed Sir *Roger*,
that no other hand might attempt to exhibit him.

Let meaner authors learn from this example, that it is
dangerous to sell the bear which is not yet hunted, to promise
to the public what they have not written.

KING LEAR

The Tragedy of *Lear* is deservedly celebrated among the
dramas of *Shakespeare*. There is perhaps no play which keeps

the attention so strongly fixed; which so much agitates our passions and interests our curiosity. The artful involutions of distinct interests, the striking opposition of contrary characters, the sudden changes of fortune, and the quick succession of events, fill the mind with a perpetual tumult of indignation, pity, and hope. There is no scene which does not contribute to the aggravation of the distress or conduct of the action, and scarce a line which does not conduce to the progress of the scene. So powerful is the current of the poet's imagination, that the mind, which once ventures within it, is hurried irresistibly along.

On the seeming improbability of *Lear*'s conduct it may be observed, that he is represented according to histories at that time vulgarly received as true. And perhaps if we turn our thoughts upon the barbarity and ignorance of the age to which this story is referred, it will appear not so unlikely as while we estimate *Lear*'s manners by our own. Such preference of one daughter to another, or resignation of dominion on such conditions, would be yet credible, if told of a petty prince of *Guinea* or *Madagascar*. *Shakespeare*, indeed, by the mention of his Earls and Dukes, has given us the idea of times more civilised, and of life regulated by softer manners; and the truth is, that though he so nicely discriminates, and so minutely describes the characters of men, he commonly neglects and confounds the characters of ages, by mingling customs ancient and modern, *English* and foreign.

My learned friend Mr. *Warton*, who has in the *Adventurer* very minutely criticised this play, remarks, that the instances of cruelty are too savage and shocking, and that the intervention of *Edmund* destroys the simplicity of the story. These objections may, I think, be answered, by repeating, that the cruelty of the daughters is an historical fact, to which the poet has added little, having only drawn it into a series by dialogue and action. But I am not able to apologise with equal plausibility for the extrusion of *Gloucester*'s eyes, which seems an act too horrid to be endured in dramatic exhibition, and such as must always compel the mind to relieve its distress by incredulity. Yet let it be remembered that our author well knew what would please the audience for which he wrote.

The injury done by *Edmund* to the simplicity of the action is abundantly recompensed by the addition of variety, by the

75

art with which he is made to co-operate with the chief design, and the opportunity which he gives the poet of combining perfidy with perfidy, and connecting the wicked son with the wicked daughters, to impress this important moral, that villany is never at a stop, that crimes lead to crimes, and at last terminate in ruin.

But though this moral be incidentally enforced, *Shakespeare* has suffered the virtue of *Cordelia* to perish in a just cause, contrary to the natural ideas of justice, to the hope of the reader, and, what is yet more strange, to the faith of chronicles. Yet this conduct is justified by the Spectator, who blames *Tate* for giving *Cordelia* success and happiness in his alteration, and declares, that, in his opinion, *the tragedy has lost half its beauty*. *Dennis* has remarked, whether justly or no, that, to secure the favourable reception of *Cato, the town was poisoned with much false and abominable criticism*, and that endeavours had been used to discredit and decry poetical justice. A play in which the wicked prosper, and the virtuous miscarry, may doubtless be good, because it is a just representation of the common events of human life: but since all reasonable beings naturally love justice, I cannot easily be persuaded, that the observation of justice makes a play worse; or, that if other excellencies are equal, the audience will not always rise better pleased from the final triumph of persecuted virtue.

In the present case the public has decided. *Cordelia*, from the time of *Tate*, has always retired with victory and felicity. And, if my sensations could add anything to the general suffrage, I might relate, that I was many years ago so shocked by *Cordelia*'s death, that I know not whether I ever endured to read again the last scenes of the play till I undertook to revise them as an editor.

CYMBELINE, Act I, Scene 5

QUEEN.   I will try the forces
Of these thy compounds on such creatures as
We count not worth the hanging, but none human, . . .

CORNELIUS.   Your Highness
Shall from this practice but make hard your heart.

There is in this passage nothing that much requires a note,

yet I cannot forbear to push it forward into observation. The thought would probably have been more amplified, had our author lived to be shocked with such experiments as have been published in later times, by a race of men that have practised tortures without pity, and related them without shame, and are yet suffered to erect their heads among human beings.

Cape saxa manu, cape robora, pastor.

> Back now to the Pension. Johnson was momentarily embarrassed at the offer of £300 a year from the Crown, since pensions were so often associated with party services and he wanted no part of any such horse-trading. His friends, notably Reynolds, assured him that a pension to him would be universally seen as the recompense of his magnificent work in literature and moral instruction. This satisfied Johnson, and he accepted the pension in a magnificent letter (14) to the responsible Minister, Lord Bute. At the same time, his response to the pension generally is quiet and guarded. He makes very few references to it. On the very same day as his lapidary epistle of acknowledgment and thanks to Bute, he writes to his friend Joseph Baretti and, though the letter is intended to convey his personal news, says nothing of the pension. Only to Lucy Porter (15) did he, four days later, tell the news of his financial independence; as his step-daughter, she had a right to know his circumstances.

14. My Lord

When the bills were yesterday delivered to me by Mr. Wedderburne, I was informed by him of the future favours which his Majesty has, by your Lordship's recommendation, been induced to intend for me.

Bounty always receives part of its value from the manner in which it is bestowed; your Lordship's kindness includes every circumstance that can gratify delicacy, or enforce obligation. You have conferred your favours on a man who has neither alliance nor interest, who has not merited them by services, nor courted them by officiousness; you have spared him the shame of solicitation, and the anxiety of suspense.

77

What has been thus elegantly given, will, I hope, not be reproachfully enjoyed; I shall endeavour to give your Lordship the only recompense which generosity desires,—the gratification of finding that your benefits are not improperly bestowed. I am, my Lord,

Your Lordship's most obliged, most obedient, and most humble Servant,

July 20, 1762. Sam: Johnson

15. Dear Madam

If I write but seldom to you, it is because it seldom happens that I have any thing to tell you that can give you pleasure, but last Monday I was sent for by the chief Minister the Earl of Bute, who told me that the King had empowered him to do something for me, and let me know that a pension was granted me of three hundred a year. Be so kind as to tell Kitty.

I am Dearest Madam Your most affectionate

July 24. 1762. Sam: Johnson

The pension came just in time. In 1758 Johnson had been under arrest for debt a second time, for £40 (nearly a thousand in modern money), and he had never yet known a day without some anxiety about money in the background of his mind. Now, that was over. For the rest of his life, more than twenty years, he could improve his mind at leisure, and pass on the fruits of his meditation to other people by means of that incomparable talk on which so great a part of his fame must always rest.

Chapter IV

Characters

Most of the personalities in Johnson's life were friends. He had, it is true, a few enemies. Some of them were people who had fallen out with him on some definite issue, like James Macpherson, the translator-cum-fabricator of 'Ossian', who felt (19) his own interests to be directly threatened by Johnson's entirely justified scepticism about what he was offering to the public. Other adversaries were simply people who disapproved of Johnson's literary influence. The poet Cowper, reading Johnson's less than adulatory *Life of Milton*, is said to have exclaimed in a fit of annoyance, 'I could thrash his old jacket till his pension jingled in his pocket!' Cowper, however, never attacked Johnson in print. Others were not so forgiving. A 'Club of Caledonian Wits' (the description is that of the Shakespearean scholar George Steevens) concocted in 1782 a pamphlet called *Deformities of Dr. Samuel Johnson, Selected from his Works*, which sought to show Johnson as a pernicious influence on English style.

Johnson never paid any attention to these attacks. His attitude, in any case, was that of any veteran in the literary world—that an attack is as good as a boost, any publicity being good publicity. In his personal relationships he never brooded over wrongs and slights, preferring to delight in the company of those who were fond of him. Friendship was a vitally important element in his life. Once he had made a friend of anyone, he stuck to him (or her) for life. More, he was ready, from youth right up to extreme old age, to form new friendships. One of his most celebrated remarks, made to Sir Joshua Reynolds and recorded by

Boswell under 1755, is, 'If a man does not make new acquaintance as he advances through life, he will soon find himself alone. A man, Sir, should keep his friendship *in constant repair.*' And to Fanny Burney, who was speaking dismissively about someone who wanted to be her friend but of whom she had no great opinion, he said simply, 'Cling to those who cling to you.' She never forgot his words.

To have been the friend of his youth, or even to date from a good number of years ago, was a great recommendation in Johnson's eyes. He felt it to be wrong, almost a freakish offence against nature, to let go of the past. What a man lived through was in some important ways one of his inalienable possessions, and to throw the accumulation of experience on the scrap-heap was to him a grave mistake. Memories should be taken out and polished; the lessons of life should be pondered, and how can that be unless they are kept in order? So it is with a kind of revulsion that he runs across Charles Congreve, one of his early acquaintances (see I, 13), and finds him in later life careless of memories of fact and date.

1. Charles Congreve is here, in an ill state of health, for advice. How long he has been here I know not. He sent to me one that attends him as an humble friend, and she left me a direction. He told me he knew not how to find me. He is in his own opinion recovering, but has the appearance of a man much broken. He talked to me of theological points, and is going to print a sermon, but I thought he appeared neither very acute nor very knowing. His room was disordered and oppressive, he has the appearance of a man wholly sunk into that sordid self-indulgence which disease, real or imaginary, is apt to dictate. He has lived, as it seems, with no great frequency of recollection. He asked me, and told me he had forgot, whether I was bred at Oxford or at Cambridge. The mind that leaves things so fast behind it, ought to have gone forward at no common rate. I believe he is charitable, yet he seems to have money much in his thoughts; he told me that this ilness would cost him fifty pound, and told it with some appearance of discontent: he seemed glad to see me, and I intend to visit him

again. I rather wonder that he sent to me. I mentioned Hector to him whom I saw about ten weeks ago, but he heard the name without emotion or enquiry, nor has ever spoken of any old companions or past occurrences. Is not this an odd frame of understanding? I asked him how long it was since we had seen one another, and he answered me roundly, fifty years.

Many people feel this in later life, but with Johnson it appears to have been already developed during his vigorous middle years. In November 1756, only a few weeks into his forty-eighth year, he is writing to his old friend Edmund Hector of Birmingham:

2. Dear Sir

I was very much gratified by your last letter, do not let us again intermit our correspondence. What changes time makes in the mind. A letter from an old friend raises in me emotions very different from those which I felt when we used to talk to one another formerly by every post or carrier. As we come forward into life we naturally turn back now and then upon the past. I now think more upon my Schooldays than I did when I had just broken loose from a Master. Happy is he that can look back upon the past with pleasure. Of those happy Beings have you known many? I long to sit with you for some days in some retreat and compare the ⟨   ?   ⟩ which experience has given me with those which we once formed upon conjecture. Shall we like each other when we meet as we liked once? let neither form too great expectations and there will be less danger of disappointment.

I sincerely thank you for the readiness with which you undertake my subscription. I hope all my old friends will be persuaded to help me. As you receive three or four Guineas send them to my Mother, she may want them.

I should be glad to hear of any of our common friends, with whom we sometimes spent our time at Birmingham, for every body whose memory stands in my mind connected with Yours has some claim to the kindness of,

Dear Sir, Your most affectionate

Nov. 11. 1756 Sam: Johnson

This matter of continuing old friendships must have been
in his mind during that autumnal month, because we
find him only a week later writing to John Taylor of
Ashbourne:

3. When you come to town let us contrive to see one another
more frequently at least once a week. We have both lived long
enough to bury many friends, and have therefore learned to set
a value on those who are left. Neither of us now can find many
whom he has known so long as we have known each other. Do
not let us lose our intimacy at a time when we ought rather to
think of encreasing it. We both stand almost single in the world,
I have no brother, and with your sister you have little correspondence.

Having begun to think of the relationship between Taylor
and his sister, Johnson goes on to give his friend some
heartfelt advice: if they are drifting away from each other,
let him be the first to make an effort to draw their lives
together.

But if you will take my advice, you will make some overtures
of reconciliation to her. If you have been to blame, you know
it is your duty first to seek a renewal of kindness. If she has been
faulty, you have an opportunity to exercise the virtue of forgiveness. You must consider that of her faults and follies no
very great part is her own. Much has been the consequence of
her education, and part may be imputed to the neglect with
which you have sometimes treated her. Had you endeavoured
to gain her kindness and her confidence you would have had
more influence over her. I hope that, before I shall see you, she
will have had a visit or a letter from you. The longer you delay
the more you will sometime repent. When I am musing alone,
I feel a pang for every moment that any human being has by
my peevishness or obstinacy spent in uneasiness. I know not
how I have fallen upon this, I had no thought of it, when I
began the letter, ⟨yet⟩ am glad that I have written it.

　　　　　I am, Dearest Sir, Your most affectionate
Novr 18 1756　　　　　　　　　　　　Saml: Johnson

Clearly enough, Johnson 'fell upon' this topic because the whole question of loneliness and estrangement was so much in his thoughts. Life is so often cold and hostile, its problems insoluble, its consolations few; why make it worse by turning away from sources of kindness and warmth that are to be had for the asking? Especially since moral guilt attaches to the one who does the turning away, and Johnson's phenomenally active conscience gave him 'a pang' at the most distant approach of wrong-doing.

Since we have paused over John Taylor, we may conveniently take his case as the archetype or diagram of one kind of Johnsonian friendship, the friendship based on length of acquaintance and therefore by definition becoming tougher, though not necessarily deeper, as the years go by. Taylor was a man with whom Johnson had very little in common. Bred to the law, he became a clergyman for what seem to have been entirely worldly reasons; taking full advantage of the lax eighteenth-century attitude towards pluralism, he pulled in a large income which he invested mainly in thoroughbred cattle, becoming a notable breeder on his land at Ashbourne. Johnson's visits there were a comedy in themselves; the urban Johnson and the bucolic Taylor had scarcely a subject of conversation in common; Johnson must have felt like Falstaff in the Shallow and Silence scenes of Shakespeare's *Henry IV*. He duly interests himself in everything that is going forward, several times mentioning 'the great bull' that must have been the pride of Taylor's farmyard, passing on with a dry humour such items of news as arose in a quiet country life, as when he writes to Hester Thrale (6 October 1777), 'Taylor is now going to have a Ram, and then after aries and taurus we shall have gemini. His oats are now in the wet, here is a deal of rain. Mr Langdon bought at Nottingham fair fifteen tun of Cheese, which at an ounce apiece will suffice after dinner for 480,000 men. This is all the news that the place affords.'

On his last visit to Ashbourne, a few months before his death, Johnson wrote to Boswell (26 July 1784) a description of Taylor's way of life at that time.

4. On the 20th, I came hither, and found a house half-built, of very uncomfortable appearance; but my own room has not been altered. That a man worn with diseases, in his seventy-second or third year, should condemn part of his remaining life to pass among ruins and rubbish, and that no inconsiderable part, appears to me very strange.—I know that your kindness makes you impatient to know the state of my health, in which I cannot boast of much improvement. I came through the journey without much inconvenience, but when I attempt self-motion I find my legs weak, and my breath very short; this day I have been much disordered. I have no company; the Doctor is busy in his fields, and goes to bed at nine, and his whole system is so different from mine, that we seem formed for different elements; I have, therefore, all my amusement to seek within myself.

Yet it never occurred to Johnson to drop Taylor, bored as he was both by Taylor's company and his non-company. Taylor had been his companion at school and at college; that in itself would be enough; but then, in his usual way, Johnson set about searching out the man's redeeming features. Commonplace as he was, Taylor threw himself into life with zest; he did not sit in a chair and mope about his troubles, which were real ones; Johnson once applied to him a couplet from Dryden's *Absalom and Achitophel*,

> Blest madman, who could every hour employ
> With something new to wish or to enjoy.

'Dr Taylor', Johnson writes to Hester Thrale, 'desires always to have his compliments sent. He is, in his usual way very busy,—getting a Bull to his cows and a Dog to his bitches. His waterfall runs very well. Old Shakespeare is dead and he wants to buy another horse for his mares. He is one of those who finds every hour *something new to wish or to enjoy*.'

One of the most tangible of Taylor's misfortunes was the quarrel with his wife that led to their separation. Johnson, on learning that Mrs Taylor had left the connubial home, wrote Taylor a letter of such sound common-sense that, though it does not refer to himself, it deserves a place in any collection of Johnson's personal writings, so fully does it reveal the *Johnsonius ipsissimus*:

5. Dear Sir

You may be confident that what I can do for you either by help or counsel in this perplexity shall not be wanting, and I take it as a proof of friendship that you have recourse to me on this strange revolution of your domestic life.

I do not wonder that the commotion of your mind made it difficult for you to give me a particular account, but while my knowledge is only general, my advice must be general too.

Your first care must be of yourself and your own quiet. do not let this vexation take possession of your thoughts, or sink too deeply into your heart. To have an unsuitable or unhappy marriage happens every day to multitudes, and you must endeavour to bear it like your fellow sufferers by diversion at one time and reflection at another. The happiness of conjugal life cannot be ascertained or secured either by sense or by virtue, and therefore its miseries may be numbered among those evils which we cannot prevent and must only labour to endure with patience, and palliate with judgement. If your condition is known I should ⟨think⟩ it best to come from the place, that you may not be a gazing stock to idle people who have nobody but you to talk of. You may live privately in a thousand places till the novelty of the transaction is worn away. I shall be glad to contribute to your peace by any amusement in my power.

With respect to the Lady I so little understand her paper that I know not what to propose. Did she go with [with] a male or female companion? With what money do you believe her provided? To whom do you imagine she will recur for shelter? What is the abuse of her person which she mentions? What is ⟨the⟩ danger which she resolves never again to incur? The tale of Hannah I suppose to be false, not that if it be true it will justify her violence and precipitation, but it will give her cause great superiority in the publick opinion and in the courts of Justice, and it will be better for you to endure hard conditions than bring your character into a judicial disquisition.

I know you never lived very well together but I suppose that an outrage like this must have been preceded by some uncommon degrees of discord from which you might have prognosticated some odd design, or that some preparations for this excursion must have been made of which the recollection may give you some direction what to conjecture, and how to proceed.

You know that I have never advised you to any thing tyrannical or violent, and in the present case it is of great importance to keep yourself in the right, and not injure your own right by any intemperance of resentment or eagerness of reprisal. For the present I think it prudent to forbear all persuit, and all open inquiry, to wear an appearance of complete indifference, and calmly wait the effects of time, of necessity, and of shame. I suppose she cannot live long without your money, and the confession of her want will probably humble her. Whether you will inform her brother, I must leave to your discretion who know his character and the terms on which you have lived. If you write to him, write like a man ill-treated but neither dejected nor enraged.

I do not know what more I can say without more knowledge of the case, only I repeat my advice that you keep yourself chearful, and add that I would have ⟨you⟩ contribute nothing to the publication of your own misfortune. I wondered to see the note transcribed by a hand which I did not know.

I am Dear Sir Your most affectionate

August 13. 1763   Sam : Johnson.

Johnson's letters, as we noted in the Introduction, vary in tone from one correspondent to another. To an extent unguessed at by anyone who knows Johnson only from his caricature reputation, a stiff bundle of comical prejudices and inflexible opinions, he shows himself a different person with different people. For this reason, his letters all complement each other in building up the grand portrait. We can be grateful to Taylor for his very conventionality and ordinariness. For these qualities in his recipient led Johnson to write very plainly, to spell out his opinions beyond all possibility of misinterpretation. Thus it is that we find in a letter to Taylor (21 January 1783) a very explicit statement of Johnson's political views, at least as regard England's internal politics. His distrust of the nascent force of popular democracy was never more clearly expressed, even in his hard-hitting pamphlet *The False Alarm* (1770).

6. Dear Sir

I am glad that your friends are not among the promoters of equal representation, which I consider as specious in theory but dangerous in experiment, as equitable in itself, but above human wisdom to be equitably adjusted, and which is now proposed only to distress the government.

An equal representation can never form a constitution because it can have no stability, for whether you regulate the representation by numbers or by property, that which is equal today, will be unequal in a week.

To change the constituent parts of Government must be always dangerous, for who can tell where changes will stop. A new representation will want the reverence of antiquity, and the firmness of Establishment. The new senate will be considered as Mushrooms which springing in a day may be blasted in a night.

What will a parliament chosen in any new manner, whether more or less numerous, do which is not done by such parliaments as we have? Will it be less tumultuous if we have more, or less mercenary if we have fewer? There is no danger that the parliament as now chosen should betray any of our important rights, and that is all that we can wish.

If the scheme were more reasonable this is not a time for innovation. I am afraid of a civil war. The business of every wise man seems to be now to keep his ground.

I am very glad you are coming.

I am &c.

Jan. 21, 1783   Sam: Johnson.

As well as clinging to old friends like Taylor and Edmund Hector, Johnson of course formed a larger circle of friends, with whom he kept in more regular contact, during the years of his fame. Most of these were within the ranks of 'the Club', that association of free and equal spirits that gathered about Johnson as its nucleus, beginning in the winter of 1762/3. In twenty years the Club doubled its size, and came to include a high proportion of the most brilliant men of that brilliant age, but even at its inception the founder-members included Burke, Reynolds and Goldsmith. These men were celebrities, living in the public eye, as was Johnson himself from about 1760 onwards; their letters were scrupulously preserved, their conversations often recorded in diaries and letters. It is all the more interesting to go back slightly before Johnson's career entered its full meridian, and before he met Boswell in May 1763 and came under the scrutiny of his biographer's loving and attentive eye, never afterwards to leave it. A friend of an earlier vintage than those of the Club, a friend of pre-Boswell days, was the Italian scholar Giuseppe Baretti (q.v.). In 1761, when Baretti was making a prolonged visit to his native land, Johnson bestirred himself sufficiently to write 'my Baretti', as he affectionately called him, a letter which wonderfully captures the flavour of his life in that period immediately before the award of the Pension: a life largely monotonous, varied by excursions into social converse and entertainment, undertaken largely as an escape from melancholy (Johnson goes often to the theatre, but only 'to escape from myself').

7. You reproach me very often with parsimony of writing: but you may discover by the extent of my paper, that I design to recompense rarity by length. A short letter to a distant friend is, in my opinion, an insult like that of a slight bow or cursory salutation;—a proof of unwillingness to do much, even where there is a necessity of doing something. Yet it must be remembered, that he who continues the same course of life in the same place, will have little to tell. One week and one year are very like another. The silent changes made by time are not always perceived; and if they are not perceived, cannot be recounted. I have risen and lain down, talked and mused, while you have roved over a considerable part of Europe; yet I have not envied my Baretti any of his pleasures, though perhaps I have envied others his company; and I am glad to have other nations made acquainted with the character of the English, by a traveller who has so nicely inspected our manners, and so successfully studied our literature. I received your kind letter from Falmouth, in which you gave me notice of your departure for Lisbon; and another from Lisbon, in which you told me, that you were to leave Portugal in a few days. To either of these how could any answer be returned? I have had a third from Turin, complaining that I have not answered the former. Your English stile still continues in its purity and vigour. With vigour your genius will supply it; but its purity must be continued by close attention. To use two languages familiarly, and without contaminating one by the other, is very difficult; and to use more than two, is hardly to be hoped. The praises which some have received for their multiplicity of languages, may be sufficient to excite industry, but can hardly generate confidence.

I know not whether I can heartily rejoice at the kind reception which you have found, or at the popularity to which you are exalted. I am willing that your merit should be distinguished; but cannot wish that your affections may be gained. I would have you happy wherever you are; yet I would have you wish to return to England. If ever you visit us again, you will find the kindness of your friends undiminished. To tell you how many enquiries are made after you would be tedious or if not tedious, would be vain; because you may be told in a very few words, that all who knew you wish you well; and that all that you embraced at your departure, will caress you at your return: therefore do not let Italian academicians nor Italian ladies drive us from your thoughts. You may find among us what you will leave behind, soft smiles and easy sonnets. Yet I shall not wonder if all our invitations should be rejected: for there is a pleasure in being considerable at home, which is not easily resisted.

By conducting Mr. Southwell to Venice, you fulfilled, I know, the original contract: yet I would wish you not wholly to lose him from your notice, but to recommend him to such acquaintance as may best secure him from suffering by his own follies, and to take such general care both of his safety and his interest as may come within your power. His relations will thank you for any such gratuitous attention: at least they will not blame you for any evil that may happen, whether they thank you or not for any good.

You know that we have a new King and a new Parliament. Of the new Parliament Fitzherbert is a member. We were so weary of our old King, that we are much pleased with his successor; of whom we are so much inclined to hope great things, that most of us begin already to believe them. The young man is hitherto blameless; but it would be unreasonable to expect much from the immaturity of juvenile years, and the ignorance of princely education. He has been long in the hands of the Scots, and has already favoured them more than the English will contentedly endure. But perhaps he scarcely knows whom he has distinguished, or whom he has disgusted.

The Artists have instituted a yearly exhibition of pictures and statues, in imitation, as I am told, of foreign Academies. This year was the second exhibition. They please themselves much with the multitude of spectators, and imagine that the English school will rise in reputation. Reynolds is without a rival, and continues to add thousands to thousands, which he deserves, among other excellencies, by retaining his kindness for Baretti. This exhibition has filled the heads of the Artists and lovers of art. Surely life, if it be not long, is tedious, since we are forced to call in the assistance of so many trifles to rid us of our time, of that time which never can return.

I know my Baretti will not be satisfied with a letter in which I give him no account of myself: yet what account shall I give him? I have not, since the day of our separation, suffered or done any thing considerable. The only change in my way of life is, that I have frequented the theatre more than in former seasons. But I have gone thither only to escape from myself. We have had many new farces, and the comedy called *The Jealous Wife*, which, though not written with much genius, was yet so well adapted to the stage, and so well exhibited by the actors, that it was crowded for near twenty nights. I am digressing from myself to the play-house; but a barren plan must be filled with episodes. Of myself I have nothing to say, but that I have hitherto lived without the concurrence of my own judgment; yet I continue to flatter myself, that, when you return, you will find me mended. I do not wonder that, where the monastick life is permitted, every order finds votaries, and every monastery inhabitants. Men will submit to any rule, by which they may be exempted from the tyranny of caprice and of chance. They are glad to supply by external authority their own want of constancy and resolution, and court the government of others, when long experience has convinced them of their own inability to govern themselves. If I were to visit Italy, my curiosity would be more attracted by convents than by palaces; though I am afraid that I should find expectation in both places equally disappointed, and life in both places supported with impatience, and quitted with reluctance. That it must be so soon quitted, is a powerful remedy against impatience; but what shall free us from reluctance? Those who have endeavoured to teach us to die well, have taught few to die willingly; yet I cannot but hope that a good life might end at last in a contented death.

You see to what a train of thought I am drawn by the mention of myself. Let us now turn my attention upon you. I hope you take care to keep an exact journal, and to register all occurrences and observations; for your friends here expect such a book of travels as has not been often seen. You have given us good specimens in your letters from Lisbon. I wish you had staid longer in Spain, for no country is less known to the rest of Europe; but the quickness of your discernment must make amends for the celerity of your motions. He that knows which way to direct his view, sees much in a little time.

Write to me very often, and I will not neglect to write to you; and I may perhaps in time get something to write: at least, you will know by my letters, whatever else they may have or want, that I continue to be

Your most affectionate friend, Samuel Johnson
London, June 10, 1761.

Just over a year later he is writing to Baretti again, and this letter too contains a vivid sketch of himself, this time on a visit to Lichfield; but he does not mention the most important recent event in his life, the award of the Pension.

8. Sir

However justly you may accuse me for want of punctuality in correspondence, I am not so far lost in negligence, as to omit the opportunity of writing to you, which Mr. Beauclerk's passage through Milan affords me.

I suppose you received the Idlers, and I intend that you shall soon receive Shakespeare, that you may explain his works to the ladies of Italy, and tell them the story of the editor, among the other strange narratives with which your long residence in this unknown region has supplied you.

As you have now been long away, I suppose your curiosity may pant for some news of your old friends. Miss Williams and I live much as we did. Miss Cotterel still continues to cling to Mrs. Porter, and Charlotte is now big of the fourth child. Mr. Reynolds gets six thousand a year. Levet is lately married, not without much suspicion that he has been wretchedly cheated in his match. Mr. Chambers is gone this day, for the first time, the circuit with the Judges. Mr. Richardson is dead of an apoplexy, and his second daughter has married a merchant.

My vanity, or my kindness, makes me flatter myself, that you would rather hear of me than of those whom I have mentioned; but of myself I have very little which I care to tell. Last winter I went down to my native town, where I found the streets much narrower and shorter than I thought I had left them, inhabited by a new race of people, to whom I was very little known. My play-fellows were grown old, and forced me to suspect, that I was no longer young. My only remaining friend has changed his principles, and was become the tool of the predominant faction. My daughter-in-law, from whom I expected most, and whom I met with sincere benevolence, has lost the beauty and gaiety of youth, without having gained much of the wisdom of age. I wandered about for five days, and took the first convenient opportunity of returning to a place, where, if there is not much happiness, there is at least such a diversity of good and evil, that slight vexations do not fix upon the heart.

I think in a few weeks to try another excursion; though to what end? Let me know, my Baretti, what has been the result of your return to your own country: whether time has made

any alteration for the better, and whether, when the first rap-
tures of salutation were over, you did not find your thoughts
confessed their disappointment.

Moral sentences appear ostentatious and tumid, when they
have no greater occasions than the journey of a wit to his own
town: yet such pleasures and such pains make up the general
mass of life; and as nothing is little to him that feels it with
great sensibility, a mind able to see common incidents in their
real state, is disposed by very common incidents to very serious
contemplations. Let us trust that a time will come, when the
present moment shall be no longer irksome; when we shall not
borrow all our happiness from hope, which at last is to end in
disappointment.

I beg that you will shew Mr. Beauclerk all the civilities which
you have in your power; for he has always been kind to me.

I have lately seen Mr. Stratico, Professor of Padua, who has
told me of your quarrel with an Abbot of the Celestine Order;
but had not the particulars very ready in his memory. When
you write to Mr. Marsili, let him know that I remember him
with kindness.

May you, my Baretti, be very happy at Milan, or some other
place nearer to, Sir,

Your most affectionate humble servant,

Sam: Johnson

Among the original members of the Club, Topham Beauclerk and Bennet Langton represented that younger
generation with whom Johnson delighted to keep in touch,
the generation that provided him with Boswell, whom in
fact he first met in this same year of 1763. Later, Boswell
was elected to the Club, as were such notable men as
Gibbon the historian and Sir William Jones the orientalist.

David Garrick, too, was of this later vintage. It may
seem strange that Garrick did not belong to the Club from
the beginning. He was one of Johnson's earliest acquaintances; his father, Captain Garrick, had lived within a
street or two of the Johnsons' home during Sam's youth;
since Garrick was eight years Johnson's junior, they had
not been close in boyhood, but they had often met, and

Johnson was probably among the audience for Garrick's first appearance on the stage, a performance of Farquhar's *The Beaux' Stratagem* put on by a Lichfield group in the 1720s; a few years later the Garrick brothers were among the pupils at Johnson's short-lived boarding school at nearby Edial. When the school broke up, Johnson and Garrick journeyed to London together and were largely in one another's company during their first few weeks in the capital. All this ought to have forged a bond between them, and certainly in some ways it did. Garrick was always a loyal friend to Johnson, and was indeed demonstratively affectionate. Johnson's attitude was more ambivalent. When he spoke of Garrick, it was sometimes in measured praise, but just as often he could say things that were rather cutting. With all this, he had a proprietary attitude towards the famous actor that caused his friends some amusement. So that Boswell tells us (17 April 1778),

> Sir Joshua Reynolds observed, with great truth, that Johnson considered Garrick to be as it were his *property*. He would allow no man either to blame or to praise Garrick in his presence, without contradicting him.

Hester Thrale once said to Johnson that he would allow no one to abuse Garrick but himself. On this occasion Johnson parried with, 'Why, madam. . . . I will allow no man to speak ill of David that he does not deserve.' The last five words give the flavour. Johnson believed, or acted as if he believed, that Garrick needed a more or less constant cutting down to size. The younger man's success had been so resplendent, he had leapt to fame and riches while Johnson was still toiling bravely upward step by step, and moreover Garrick's success had not been, like a success in business or politics, outside the orbit of Johnson's own life; he had taken the world by storm as an actor, and Johnson was ambitious to write for the theatre; and as first and foremost a Shakespearean actor, and Johnson was a critic and editor of Shakespeare. In spite of the warmth that existed between them, there was evidently something about

Garrick that disturbed Johnson; he seems to have felt crowded and diminished by the ebullient little man: as the Soothsayer warns Antony in Shakespeare's play (*Antony and Cleopatra*, II, iii),

> thy lustre thickens
> When he shines by: I say again, thy spirit
> Is all afraid to govern thee near him,
> But he away, 'tis noble.

Certainly Johnson was very quick to pounce on any chance expression of Garrick's that seemed to indicate conceit or arrogance. When the Club was first formed, and Garrick heard of it, he said good-humouredly to Reynolds, 'I like it much; I think I shall be of you.' When Johnson heard this, he was incensed. 'He'll be of us? How does he know we will permit him? The first Duke in England has no right to hold such language.' On the other hand, there is no support for the story, told both by Sir John Hawkins and Hester Thrale, that Johnson actively opposed Garrick's membership of the Club. The outburst had been a momentary one, as Johnson's outbursts against Garrick generally were.

Two diary entries, which follow (9 and 10), illustrate the way Johnson habitually referred to Garrick in conversation. The first is from the young Fanny Burney, the second from Hester Thrale's voluminous family chronicle, 'Thraliana'.

9.   After this, they talked of Mr. Garrick and his late exhibition before the King, to whom and to the Queen and Royal Family he read Lethe *in character, c'est à dire*, in different voices, and theatrically.[1] Mr. Seward gave us an account of a Fable, which Mr. Garrick had written, by way of prologue or Introduction, upon the occasion. In this he says, that a blackbird, grown old and feeble, droops his wings &c. &c., and gives up singing; but being called upon by the eagle, his voice recovers its powers,

---

[1] A farce of Garrick's own writing, in which he had been used to act more than one part.

his spirits revive, he sets age at defiance, and sings better than ever. The application is obvious.

'There is not', said Dr. Johnson, 'much of the spirit of *fabulosity* in this Fable; for the *call* of an eagle never yet had much tendency to restore the voice of a *black-bird*! 'Tis true that the fabulists frequently make the *wolves* converse with the *lambs*; but, when the conversation is over, the *lambs* are sure to be eaten! And so the *eagle* may entertain the *black-bird*; but the entertainment always ends in a feast for the *eagle*.'

'They say', cried Mrs. Thrale, 'that Garrick was extremely hurt at the coolness of the King's applause, and did not find his reception such as he expected.'

'He has been so long accustomed', said Mr. Seward, 'to the thundering approbation of the Theatre, that a mere "*Very well*," must necessarily and naturally disappoint him.'

'Sir,' said Dr. Johnson, 'he should not, in a Royal apartment, expect the hallowing and clamour of the One Shilling Gallery. The King, I doubt not, gave him as much applause, as was rationally his due; and, indeed, great and uncommon as is the merit of Mr. Garrick, no man will be bold enough to assert he has not had his just proportion both of fame and profit. He has long reigned the unequalled favourite of the public; and therefore nobody will mourn his hard fate, if the King and the Royal Family were not transported into rapture, upon hearing him read Lethe. Yet Mr. Garrick will complain to his friends, and his friends will lament the King's want of feeling and taste;— and then Mr. Garrick will kindly *excuse* the King. He will say that His Majesty might be thinking of something else; that the affairs of America might occur to him; or some subject of more importance than Lethe; but, though he will say this himself, he will not forgive his friends, if they do not contradict him!'

But, now that I have written this satire, it is but just both to Mr. Garrick and to Dr. Johnson, to tell you what he said of him afterwards, when he discriminated his character with equal candour and humour.

'Garrick', said he, 'is accused of vanity; but few men would have borne such unremitting prosperity with greater, if with equal moderation. He is accused, too, of avarice; but, were he not, he would be accused of just the contrary; for he now lives rather as *a prince* than an actor; but the frugality he practised, when he first appeared in the world, and which, even then was perhaps beyond his necessity, has marked his character ever since; and now, though his table, his equipage, and manner of living, are all the most expensive, and equal to those of a noble-man, yet the original stain still blots his name! Though, had he not fixed upon himself the charge of avarice, he would long since have been reproached with luxury and with living beyond his station in magnificence and splendour.'

Another time he said of him, 'Garrick never enters a room, but he regards himself as the object of general attention, from whom the entertainment of the company is expected; and true it is, that he seldom disappoints them; for he has infinite humour, a very just proportion of wit, and more convivial pleasantry, than almost any other man. But then *off*, as well as *on* the Stage, he is always an Actor; for he thinks it so incumbent upon him to be sportive, that his gaiety becomes mechanical through being habitual, and he can exert his spirits at all times alike, without consulting his real disposition to hilarity.'

10. Garrick was one night coming on the Stage in Lear as I remember, when Johnson laughing or arguing behind the scenes made such a Noise that the little Man was teized by it—and said at last—do have done with all this Rattle.—it spoyls my Thoughts, it destroys my Feelings—No No Sir returns the other—(loud enough for all the players to hear him)—I know better things—*Punch* has no *feelings*.

At this point, our selection might become unmanageably extensible. Johnson was, as we remarked earlier, to some extent a different person when writing to different people, and his letters to one friend differ in tone from those to another. Virtually every letter that he wrote that was not a mere business letter (and even some of them), could be cited as a document of Johnson on Johnson. Since a line must be drawn somewhere—and since, further, Johnson's letters to women, in which he tended to reveal his inner feelings more than to men, are used in our next section—

I give below a selection from the letters to only one person. And who else but James Boswell?

From their first meeting in the back parlour of Tom Davies's bookshop in May 1763—a meeting described by Boswell in one of the most vivid and amusing passages of the *Life*—to their last meeting on 30 June 1784, also memorably described in Boswell's pages, their relationship was warm, explosive, funny, affectionate, exasperated. Boswell, who could keep nothing back and who was sufficiently a man of the generation of Rousseau to think it a sin to keep anything back, poured into Johnson's ear the story of his conflicts, backslidings, depressions and quirks. Johnson gave him warm affection and sage counsel; he enjoyed Boswell's frisking energy and gravely admonished him to turn it to good use if he could. He must have enjoyed Boswell's company, because he often said so, and he must have enjoyed getting letters from him, indeed in his last letter to Boswell (18) he complains, with the querulousness of age and illness, that Boswell does not write often enough. The only trouble with getting letters is that it puts the ball in one's court to answer them; Johnson often defends himself against Boswell's charge that he is a bad correspondent, but one virtue of a good correspondent was so far out of his reach that he never aspired to it: the virtue of not merely exchanging letter for letter, but actually *answering* the other person, engaging in a dialogue. Boswell wrote ruefully to Johnson on 24 June 1774, 'Neither can I prevail with you to *answer* my letters, though you honour me with *returns*.' In the selection of Johnson's letters to Boswell that follow we see something of the range of their relationship, a relationship that throws light on both their characters. A few months after getting to know Johnson, Boswell set out on an extended visit to the Continent, as part of his legal studies (and of much else); Johnson's first letter to him, addressed to Utrecht (11), contains a vivid sketch of Boswell's own character— for of course Boswell is the 'gentleman' who 'thought that all appearance of diligence would deduct something from the reputation of genius', and hoped to acquire knowledge

and skills easily and quickly 'amidst all the ease of carelessness and all the tumult of diversion.' Some years later still,
Johnson is irritated by Boswell's emotional need for continued protestations of affection between them—'there
ought to be no need of reiterated professions' (14). Sometimes the letters are amusingly irascible, as in 15; at other
times, gravely wise. Our selection ends with that last surviving note, importuning more letters to cheer an old man
in his terminal illness.

11. Dear Sir

You are not to think yourself forgotten, or criminally neglected, that you have had yet no letter from me. I love to see
my friends, to hear from them, to talk to them, and to talk of
them; but it is not without a considerable effort of resolution
that I prevail upon myself to write. I would not, however,
gratify my own indolence by the omission of any important
duty, or any office of real kindness.

To tell you that I am or am not well, that I have or have not
been in the country, that I drank your health in the room in
which we sat last together, and that your acquaintance continue to speak of you with their former kindness, topicks with
which those letters are commonly filled which are written only
for the sake of writing, I seldom shall think worth communicat-
ing; but if I can have it in my power to calm any harassing
disquiet, to excite any virtuous desire, to rectify any important
opinion, or fortify any generous resolution, you need not doubt
but I shall at least wish to prefer the pleasure of gratifying a
friend much less esteemed than yourself, before the gloomy
calm of idle vacancy. Whether I shall easily arrive at an exact
punctuality of correspondence, I cannot tell. I shall, at present,
expect that you will receive this in return for two which I have
had from you. The first, indeed, gave me an account so hopeless of the state of your mind, that it hardly admitted or
deserved an answer; by the second I was much better pleased;
and the pleasure will still be increased by such a narrative of
the progress of your studies, as may evince the continuance of
an equal and rational application of your mind to some useful
enquiry.

You will, perhaps, wish to ask, what study I would recommend. I shall not speak of theology, because it ought not to be considered as a question whether you shall endeavour to know the will of God.

I shall, therefore, consider only such studies as we are at liberty to pursue or to neglect; and of these I know not how you will make a better choice, than by studying the civil law, as your father advises, and the ancient languages, as you had determined for yourself; at least resolve, while you remain in any settled residence, to spend a certain number of hours every day amongst your books. The dissipation of thought, of which you complain, is nothing more than the vacillation of a mind suspended between different motives, and changing its direction as any motive gains or loses strength. If you can but kindle in your mind any strong desire, if you can but keep predominant any wish for some particular excellence or attainment, the gusts of imagination will break away, without any effect upon your conduct, and commonly without any traces left upon the memory.

There lurks, perhaps, in every human heart a desire of distinction, which inclines every man first to hope, and then to believe, that Nature has given him something peculiar to himself. This vanity makes one mind nurse aversions, and another actuate desires, till they rise by art much above their original state of power; and as affectation, in time, improves to habit, they at last tyrannise over him who at first encouraged them only for show. Every desire is a viper in the bosom, who, while he was chill, was harmless; but when warmth gave him strength, exerted it in poison. You know a gentleman, who, when first he set his foot in the gay world, as he prepared himself to whirl in the vortex of pleasure, imagined a total indifference and universal negligence to be the most agreeable concomitants of youth, and the strongest indication of an airy temper and a quick apprehension. Vacant to every object, and sensible of every impulse, he thought that all appearance of diligence would deduct something from the reputation of genius; and hoped that he should appear to attain, amidst all the ease of carelessness and all the tumult of diversion, that knowledge and those accomplishments which mortals of the common fabrick obtain only by mute abstraction and solitary drudgery. He tried this scheme of life awhile, was made weary of it by his sense and his virtue, he then wished to return to his studies; and finding long habits of idleness and pleasure harder to be cured than he expected, still willing to retain his claim to some extraordinary prerogatives, resolved the common consequences of irregularity into an unalterable decree of destiny, and concluded that Nature had originally formed him incapable of rational employment.

Let all such fancies, illusive and destructive, be banished henceforward from your thoughts for ever. Resolve, and keep your resolution; choose, and pursue your choice. If you spend this day in study, you will find yourself still more able to study to-morrow; not that you are to expect that you shall at once obtain a complete victory. Depravity is not very easily overcome. Resolution will sometimes relax, and diligence will sometimes be interrupted; but let no accidental surprize or deviation, whether short or long, dispose you to despondency. Consider these failings as incident to all mankind. Begin again where you left off, and endeavour to avoid the seducements that prevailed over you before.

This, my dear Boswell, is advice which, perhaps, has been often given you, and given you without effect. But this advice, if you will not take from others, you must take from your own reflections, if you purpose to do the duties of the station to which the bounty of Providence has called you.

Let me have a long letter from you as soon as you can. I hope you continue your journal, and enrich it with many observations upon the country in which you reside. It will be a favour if you can get me any books in the Frisick language, and can enquire how the poor are maintained in the Seven Provinces.

I am, dear Sir, Your most affectionate servant,
London, Dec. 8, 1763.   Sam: Johnson

12. My dear Boswell,

I am surprized that, knowing as you do the disposition of your countrymen to tell lies in favour of each other, you can be at all affected by any reports that circulate among them. Macpherson never in his life offered me the sight of any original or of any evidence of any kind, but thought only of intimidating me by noise and threats, till my last answer,—that I would not be deterred from detecting what I thought a cheat, by the menaces of a ruffian,—put an end to our correspondence.

The state of the question is this. He, and Dr. Blair, whom I consider as deceived, say, that he copied the poem from old manuscripts. His copies, if he had them, and I believe him to have none, are nothing. Where are the manuscripts? They can be shown if they exist, but they were never shown. *De non existentibus et non apparentibus*, says our law, *eadem est ratio*. No man has a claim to credit upon his own word, when better evidence, if he had it, may be easily produced. But, so far as we can find, the Erse language was never written till very lately for the purposes of religion. A nation that cannot write, or a language that was never written, has no manuscripts.

But whatever he has, he never offered to show. If old manuscripts should now be mentioned, I should, unless there were more evidence than can be easily had, suppose them another proof of Scotch conspiracy in national falsehood.

Do not censure the expression; you know it to be true.

Dr. Memis's question is so narrow as to allow no speculation; and I have no facts before me but those which his advocate has produced against you.

I consulted this morning the President of the London College of Physicians, who says, that with us, *Doctor of Physick* (we do not say *Doctor of Medicine*) is the highest title that a practicer of physick can have; that *Doctor* implies not only *Physician*, but teacher of physick; that every *Doctor* is legally a *Physician*, but no man, not a *Doctor*, can *practice physick* but by *licence* particularly granted. The Doctorate is a licence of itself. It seems to us a very slender cause of prosecution.

Your love of publication is offensive and disgusting, and will end, if it be not reformed, in a general distrust among all your friends.

I am now engaged, but in a little time I hope to do all you would have. My compliments to Madam and Veronica.

I am, Sir, Your most humble servant,

February 7, 1775.   Sam. Johnson

13. Dear Sir

I had great pleasure in hearing that you are at last on good terms with your father. Cultivate his kindness by all honest and manly means. Life is but short; no time can be afforded but for the indulgence of real sorrow, or contests upon questions seriously momentous. Let us not throw any of our days away upon useless resentment, or contend who shall hold out longest in stubborn malignity. It is best not to be angry, and best, in the next place, to be quickly reconciled. May you and your father pass the remainder of your time in reciprocal benevolence!

* * *

Do you ever hear from Mr. Langton? I visit him sometimes, but he does not talk. I do not like his scheme of life; but, as I am not permitted to understand it, I cannot set any thing right that is wrong. His children are sweet babies.

I hope my irreconcileable enemy, Mrs. Boswell, is well. Desire her not to transmit her malevolence to the young people. Let me have Alexander, and Veronica, and Euphemia, for my friends.

Mrs. Williams, whom you may reckon as one of your well-wishers, is in a feeble and languishing state, with little hope of growing better. She went for some part of the autumn into the country, but is little benefited; and Dr. Lawrence confesses that his art is at an end. Death is, however, at a distance; and what more than that can we say of ourselves? I am sorry for her pain, and more sorry for her decay. Mr. Levett is sound, wind and limb.

I was some weeks this autumn at Brighthelmston. The place was very dull, and I was not well: the expedition to the Hebrides was the most pleasant journey that I ever made. Such an effort annually would give the world a little diversification.

Every year, however, we cannot wander, and must therefore endeavour to spend our time at home as well as we can. I believe it is best to throw life into a method, that every hour may bring its employment, and every employment have its hour. Xenophon observes, in his 'Treatise of Oeconomy', that if every thing be kept in a certain place, when any thing is worn out or consumed, the vacuity which it leaves will shew what is wanting; so if every part of time has its duty, the hour will call into remembrance its proper engagement.

I have not practised all this prudence myself, but I have suffered much for want of it; and I would have you, by timely recollection and steady resolution, escape from those evils which have lain heavy upon me. I am, my dearest Boswell, Your most humble servant,

Bolt-court, Nov. 16, 1776.   Sam. Johnson

14. Dear Sir,

I have received two letters from you, of which the second complains of the neglect shown to the first. You must not tye your friends to such punctual correspondence. You have all possible assurances of my affection and esteem; and there ought to be no need of reiterated professions. When it may happen that I can give you either counsel or comfort, I hope it will never happen to me that I should neglect you; but you must not think me criminal or cold if I say nothing, when I have nothing to say.

You are now happy enough. Mrs. Boswell is recovered; and I congratulate you upon the probability of her long life. If general approbation will add any thing to your enjoyment, I can tell you that I have heard you mentioned as *a man whom every body likes*. I think life has little more to give.

——has gone to his regiment. He has laid down his coach, and talks of making more contractions of his expence: how he will succeed I know not. It is difficult to reform a household gradually; it may be better done by a system totally new. I am afraid he has always something to hide. When we pressed him to go to——, he objected the necessity of attending his navigation; yet he could talk of going to Aberdeen, a place not much nearer his navigation. I believe he cannot bear the thought of living at——in a state of diminution; and of appearing among the gentlemen of the neighbourhood *shorn of his beams*. This is natural, but it is cowardly. What I told him of the encreasing expence of a growing family seems to have struck him. He certainly had gone on with very confused views, and we have, I think, shown him that he is wrong; though, with the common deficience of advisers, we have not shown him how to do right.

I wish you would a little correct or restrain your imagination, and imagine that happiness, such as life admits, may be had at other places as well as London. Without asserting Stoicism, it may be said, that it is our business to exempt ourselves as much as we can from the power of external things. There is but one solid basis of happiness; and that is, the reasonable hope of a happy futurity. This may be had every where.

I do not blame your preference of London to other places, for it is really to be preferred, if the choice is free; but few have the choice of their place, or their manner of life; and mere pleasure ought not to be the prime motive of action.

Mrs Thrale, poor thing, has a daughter. Mr. Thrale dislikes the times, like the rest of us. Mrs. Williams is sick; Mrs. Desmoulins is poor. I have miserable nights. Nobody is well but Mr. Levett.

I am, dear Sir, Your most, &c.

London, July 3, 1778.   Sam. Johnson.

15. Dear Sir,

Why should you importune me so earnestly to write? Of what importance can it be to hear of distant friends, to a man who finds himself welcome wherever he goes, and makes new friends faster than he can want them? If, to the delight of such universal kindness of reception, any thing can be added by knowing that you retain my good-will, you may indulge yourself in the full enjoyment of that small addition.

I am glad that you made the round of Lichfield with so much success: the oftener you are seen, the more you will be liked. It was pleasing to me to read that Mrs. Aston was so well; and that Lucy Porter was so glad to see you.

In the place where you now are, there is much to be observed; and you will easily procure yourself skilful directors. But what will you do to keep away the *black dog* that worries you at home? If you would, in compliance with your father's advice, enquire into the old tenures, and old charters of Scotland, you would certainly open to yourself many striking scenes of the manners of the middle ages. The feudal system, in a country half barbarous, is naturally productive of great anomalies in civil life. The knowledge of past times is naturally growing less in all cases not of publick record; and the past time of Scotland is so unlike the present, that it is already difficult for a Scotchman to image the œconomy of his grandfather. Do not be tardy, nor negligent; but gather up eagerly what can yet be found.

We have, I think, once talked of another project, a History of the late insurrection in Scotland, with all its incidents. Many falsehoods are passing into uncontradicted history. Voltaire, who loved a striking story, has told what we could not find to be true.

You may make collections for either of these projects, or for both, as opportunities occur, and digest your materials at leisure. The great direction which Burton has left to men disordered like you, is this, *Be not solitary; be not idle*: which I would thus modify;—If you are idle, be not solitary; if you are solitary, be not idle.

There is a letter for you, from

Your humble servant,

London, Oct. 27, 1779.   Sam. Johnson.

16. Dear Sir

The earnestness and tenderness of your letter is such, that I cannot think myself shewing it more respect than it claims by sitting down to answer it the day on which I received it.

This year has afflicted me with a very irksome and severe disorder. My respiration has been much impeded, and much blood has been taken away. I am now harrassed by a catarrhous cough, from which my purpose is to seek relief by change of air; and I am, therefore, preparing to go to Oxford.

Whether I did right in dissuading you from coming to London this spring, I will not determine. You have not lost much by missing my company; I have scarcely been well for a single week. I might have received comfort from your kindness; but you would have seen me afflicted, and, perhaps, found me peevish. Whatever might have been your pleasure or mine, I know not how I could have honestly advised you to come hither with borrowed money. Do not accustom yourself to consider debts only as an inconvenience; you will find it a calamity. Poverty takes away so many means of doing good, and produces so much inability to resist evil, both natural and moral, that it is by all virtuous means to be avoided. Consider a man whose fortune is very narrow; whatever be his rank by birth, or whatever his reputation by intellectual excellence, what good can he do? or what evil can he prevent? That he cannot help the needy is evident, he has nothing to spare. But, perhaps, his advice or admonition may be useful. His poverty will destroy his influence: many more can find that he is poor, than that he is wise; and few will reverence the understanding that is of so little advantage to its owner. I say nothing of the personal wretchedness of a debtor, which, however, has passed into a proverb. Of riches, it is not necessary to write the praise. Let it, however, be remembered, that he who has money to spare, has it always in his power to benefit others; and of such power a good man must always be desirous.

I am pleased with your account of Easter. We shall meet, I hope, in autumn, both well and both chearful; and part each the better for the other's company.

Make my compliments to Mrs. Boswell, and to the young charmers. I am, &c.

London, June 3, 1782.   Sam. Johnson.

17. Dear Sir

I have struggled through this year with so much infirmity of body, and such strong impressions of the fragility of life, that death, wherever it appears, fills me with melancholy; and I cannot hear without emotion, of the removal of any one, whom I have known, into another state.

Your father's death had every circumstance that could enable you to bear it; it was at a mature age, and it was expected; and as his general life had been pious, his thoughts had doubtless for many years past been turned upon eternity. That you did not find him sensible must doubtless grieve you; his disposition towards you was undoubtedly that of a kind, though not of a fond father. Kindness, at least actual, is in our power, but fondness is not; and if by negligence or imprudence you had extinguished his fondness, he could not at will rekindle it. Nothing then remained between you but mutual forgiveness. of each other's faults, and mutual desire of each other's happiness.

107

I shall long to know his final disposition of his fortune.

You, dear Sir, have now a new station, and have therefore new cares, and new employments. Life, as Cowley seems to say, ought to resemble a well ordered poem; of which one rule generally received is, that the exordium should be simple, and should promise little. Begin your new course of life with the least show, and the least expence possible; you may at pleasure encrease both, but you cannot easily diminish them. Do not think your estate your own, while any man can call upon you for money which you cannot pay; therefore, begin with timorous parsimony. Let it be your first care not to be in any man's debt.

When the thoughts are extended to a future state, the present life seems hardly worthy of all those principles of conduct, and maxims of prudence, which one generation of men has transmitted to another; but upon a closer view, when it is perceived how much evil is produced, and how much good is impeded by embarrassment and distress, and how little room the expedients of poverty leave for the exercise of virtue; it grows manifest that the boundless importance of the next life, enforces some attention to the interests of this.

Be kind to the old servants, and secure the kindness of the agents and factors; do not disgust them by asperity, or unwelcome gaiety, or apparent suspicion. From them you must learn the real state of your affairs, the characters of your tenants, and the value of your lands.

Make my compliments to Mrs. Boswell; I think her expectations from air and exercise are the best that she can form. I hope she will live long and happily.

I forget whether I told you that Rasay has been here; we dined cheerfully together. I entertained lately a young gentleman from Corrichatachin.

I received your letters only this morning. I am, dear Sir, yours, &c.

London, Sept. 7, 1782.   Sam. Johnson.

18. Dear Sir

I have this summer sometimes amended and sometimes relapsed, but upon the whole, have lost ground very much.

My legs are extremely weak, and my breath very short, and the water is now encreasing upon me. In this uncomfortable state your letters used to relieve; what is the reason that I have them no longer? Are you sick, or are you sullen? Whatever be the reason, if it be less than necessity, drive it away, and of the short life that we have, make the best use for yourself and for your friends ****** I am sometimes afraid that your omission to write has some real cause, and shall be glad to know that you are not sick, and that nothing ill has befallen dear Mrs. Boswell, or any of your family. I am, Sir, your, &c.
Lichfield, Nov. 3, 1784.   Sam. Johnson.

The controversy over Macpherson, referred to in 12, concerned the latter's famous literary imposture. In the early days of romantic and scholarly enthusiasm for folklore and oral tradition, Macpherson claimed to have discovered an impressive body of epic poetry, preserved by bardic tradition in the Highlands of Scotland. Being himself a Highlander with some command of Gaelic, he was able to give some colour to these assertions at first, but when he rapidly produced a large body of work which he claimed to have translated from the ancient bard Oisin or 'Ossian', scepticism was at once aroused, and unfortunately Macpherson made it all worse by claiming that he had in his possession a large number of manuscripts which he obstinately refused to let anyone see. As Johnson reasonably remarked to Boswell, 'If he had not talked unskilfully of *manuscripts*, he might have fought with oral tradition much longer.' Macpherson, aware of the importance of Johnson's testimony, tried to silence him by expostulation, and when this failed was so foolish as to threaten Johnson with a beating. Macpherson was a big man, and much the younger of the two, but Johnson's dismissive reply is what might be expected from one who, whatever his metaphysical terrors, was a stranger to bodily fear. In a worldly sense, Macpherson could be said to have had the better of this argument; his successful career continued quite unchecked, and he is buried quite close to Johnson in Westminster Abbey.

19. Mr James Macpherson—I received your foolish and impudent note. Whatever insult is offered me I will do my best to repel, and what I cannot do for myself the law will do for me. I will not desist from detecting what I think a cheat, from any fear of the menaces of a Ruffian.

You want me to retract. What shall I retract? I thought your book an imposture from the beginning, I think it upon yet surer reasons an imposture still. For this opinion I give the publick my reasons which I here dare you to refute.

But however I may despise you, I reverence truth and if you can prove the genuineness of the work I will confess it. Your rage I defy, your abilities since your Homer are not so formidable, and what I have heard of your morals disposes me to pay regard not to what you shall say, but to what you can prove.

You may print this if you will.

Jan. 20. 1775   Sam : Johnson

Johnson had many and various ways of expressing his response to the characters with whom he came into contact: in letters, in conversations, in reminiscence both written and spoken, in fervent and compassionate intercession for them in his prayers. As a periodical writer, he now and then inserted a portrait into his majestic series of moral reflections. In the *Rambler*, the portraits are few and are heavily subordinated to the moral reflections which are the *raison d'être* of the essay. In the *Idler*, Johnson's tone is lighter; the moral reflections are still there, of course ('It is always a writer's duty to make the world better') but the portraiture has a deftness that is often amusing in the way that Addison and Steele can be amusing, or the contemporary novelists.

Interestingly, Johnson twice introduced himself as a character in the *Idler* series. 'Sober', the man afflicted with idleness in *Idler* 31, is Johnson's rueful sketch of certain features of his own nature; while *Idler* 75, the Eastern tale about 'Gelaleddin', though not directly about Johnson himself, contains a melancholy paragraph or two that seem to reflect his own situation after coming down from

Oxford in December 1729. The whole piece is worth inclusion, not only for that glance at his own early experience, but for the centrally Johnsonian message: a writer and scholar is usually respected mainly by other writers and scholars, and when he leaves that circle he commands attention only if he has some easily recognizable mark of success, such as money ('the dull . . . wondered why any man should take pains to obtain so much knowledge which would never do him good'). The brief summary of Gelaleddin's fortunes among the great who might have been his patrons reminds us that Johnson's brush with Chesterfield was still a recent memory.

We have Johnson's word for it, to Hester Thrale, that these two papers were to some extent autobiographical. 'He told me,' she writes in her *Anecdotes*, 'that the character of Sober in the *Idler* was by himself intended as his own portrait; and that he had his own outset into life in his eye when he wrote the eastern story of Gelaleddin.'

20. NO. 31. SATURDAY, NOVEMBER 18, 1758.

DISGUISES OF IDLENESS. SOBER'S CHARACTER.

Many moralists have remarked, that pride has, of all human vices, the widest dominion, appears in the greatest multiplicity of forms, and lies hid under the greatest variety of disguises; of disguises which, like the moon's *veil of brightness*, are both its *lustre and its shade*, and betray it to others though they hide it from ourselves.

It is not my intention to degrade pride from this pre-eminence of mischief; yet I know not whether idleness may not obtain a very doubtful and obstinate competition.

There are some that profess idleness in its full dignity, who call themselves, the *Idle*, as Busiris, in the play, calls himself the *Proud*; who boast that they do nothing, and thank their stars that they have nothing to do; who sleep every night till they can sleep no longer, and rise only that exercise may enable them to sleep again; who prolong the reign of darkness by double curtains, and never see the sun but to *tell him how they hate his beams*; whose whole labour is to vary the posture of indulgence, and whose day differs from their night but as a couch or chair differs from a bed.

These are the true and open votaries of idleness, for whom she weaves the garlands of poppies, and into whose cup she pours the waters of oblivion; who exist in a state of unruffled stupidity, forgetting and forgotten; who have long ceased to live, and at whose death the survivors can only say, that they have ceased to breathe.

But idleness predominates in many lives where it is not suspected; for, being a vice which terminates in itself, it may be enjoyed without injury to others; and it is therefore not watched like fraud, which endangers property; or like pride, which naturally seeks its gratifications in another's inferiority. Idleness is a silent and peaceful quality, that neither raises envy by ostentation, nor hatred by opposition: and therefore nobody is busy to censure or detect it.

As pride sometimes is hid under humility, idleness is often covered by turbulence and hurry. He that neglects his known duty and real employment, naturally endeavours to crowd his mind with something that may bar out the remembrance of his own folly, and does any thing but what he ought to do with eager diligence, that he may keep himself in his own favour.

Some are always in a state of preparation, occupied in previous measures, forming plans, accumulating materials, and providing for the main affair. These are certainly under the secret power of idleness. Nothing is to be expected from the workman whose tools are for ever to be sought. I was once told by a great master, that no man ever excelled in painting, who was eminently curious about pencils and colours.

There are others to whom idleness dictates another expedient, by which life may be passed unprofitably away, without the tediousness of many vacant hours. The art is, to fill the day with petty business, to have always something in hand, which may raise curiosity, but not solicitude, and keep the mind in a state of action, but not of labour.

This art has for many years been practised by my old friend Sober with wonderful success. Sober is a man of strong desires and quick imagination, so exactly balanced by the love of ease, that they can seldom stimulate him to any difficult undertaking; they have, however, so much power, that they will not suffer him to lie quite at rest; and though they do not make him sufficiently useful to others, they make him at least weary of himself.

Mr. Sober's chief pleasure is conversation: there is no end of his talk or his attention; to speak or to hear is equally pleasing; for he still fancies that he is teaching or learning something, and is free for the time from his own reproaches.

But there is one time at night when he must go home, that his friends may sleep; and another time in the morning, when all the world agrees to shut out interruption. These are the moments of which poor Sober trembles at the thought. But the misery of these tiresome intervals he has many means of alleviating. He has persuaded himself that the manual arts are undeservedly overlooked: he has observed in many trades the effects of close thought, and just ratiocination. From speculation he proceeded to practice, and supplied himself with the tools of a carpenter, with which he mended his coal-box very successfully, and which he still continues to employ, as he finds occasion.

He has attempted at other times the crafts of shoemaker, tinman, plumber, and potter; in all these arts he has failed, and resolves to qualify himself for them by better information. But his daily amusement is chemistry. He has a small furnace, which he employs in distillation, and which has long been the solace of his life. He draws oils and waters, and essences and spirits, which he knows to be of no use; sits and counts the drops as they come from his retort, and forgets that whilst a drop is falling, a moment flies away.

Poor Sober! I have often teized him with reproof, and he has often promised reformation; for no man is so much open to conviction as the Idler, but there is none on whom it operates so little. What will be the effect of this paper I know not; perhaps he will read it and laugh, and light the fire in his furnace; but my hope is, that he will quit his trifles, and betake himself to rational and useful diligence.

21. NO. 75. SATURDAY, SEPTEMBER 22, 1759.

GELALEDDIN OF BASSORA.

In the time when Bassora was considered as the school of Asia, and flourished by the reputation of its professors and the confluence of its students, among the pupils that listened round the chair of Albumazar was Gelaleddin, a native of Tauris, in Persia, a young man amiable in his manners and beautiful in his form, of boundless curiosity, incessant diligence, and irresistible genius, of quick apprehension and tenacious memory, accurate without narrowness, and eager for novelty without inconstancy.

No sooner did Gelaleddin appear at Bassora, than his virtues and abilities raised him to distinction. He passed from class to class, rather admired than envied by those whom the rapidity of his progress left behind; he was consulted by his fellow-students as an oraculous guide, and admitted as a competent auditor to the conferences of the sages.

After a few years, having passed through all the exercises of probation, Gelaleddin was invited to a professor's seat, and entreated to increase the splendour of Bassora. Gelaleddin affected to deliberate on the proposal, with which, before he considered it, he resolved to comply; and next morning retired to a garden planted for the recreation of the students, and entering a solitary walk, began to meditate upon his future life.

'If I am thus eminent', said he, 'in the regions of literature, I shall be yet more conspicuous in any other place; if I should now devote myself to study and retirement, I must pass my life in silence, unacquainted with the delights of wealth, the influence of power, the pomp of greatness, and the charms of elegance, with all that man envies and desires, with all that keeps the world in motion, by the hope of gaining or the fear of losing it. I will therefore depart to Tauris, where the Persian monarch resides in all the splendour of absolute dominion: my reputation will fly before me, my arrival will be congratulated by my kinsmen and my friends; I shall see the eyes of those who predict my greatness, sparkling with exultation, and the faces of those that once despised me clouded with envy, or countereiting kindness by artificial smiles. I will show my wisdom by my discourse, and my moderation by my silence; I will instruct the modest with easy gentleness, and repress the ostentatious by seasonable superciliousness. My apartments will be crowded by the inquisitive and the vain, by those that honour and those that rival me; my name will soon reach the court; I shall stand before the throne of the emperor; the judges of the law will confess my wisdom, and the nobles will contend to heap gifts upon me. If I shall find that my merit, like that of others, excites malignity, or feel myself tottering on the seat of elevation, I may at last retire to academical obscurity, and become, in my lowest state, a professor of Bassora.'

Having thus settled his determination, he declared to his friends his design of visiting Tauris, and saw with more pleasure than he ventured to express, the regret with which he was dismissed. He could not bear to delay the honours to which he was destined, and therefore hastened away, and in a short time entered the capital of Persia. He was immediately immersed in the crowd, and passed unobserved to his father's house. He entered, and was received, though not unkindly, yet without any excess of fondness or exclamations of rapture. His father had, in his absence, suffered many losses, and Gelaleddin was considered as an additional burden to a falling family.

When he recovered from his surprise, he began to display his acquisitions, and practised all the arts of narration and disquisition: but the poor have no leisure to be pleased with eloquence; they heard his arguments without reflection, and his pleasantries without a smile. He then applied himself singly to his brothers and sisters, but found them all chained down by invariable attention to their own fortunes, and insensible of any other excellence than that which could bring some remedy for indigence.

It was now known in the neighbourhood that Gelaleddin was returned, and he sat for some days in expectation that the learned would visit him for consultation, or the great for entertainment. But who will be pleased or instructed in the mansions of poverty? He then frequented places of public resort, and endeavoured to attract notice by the copiousness of his talk. The sprightly were silenced, and went away to censure in some other place his arrogance and his pedantry; and the dull listened quietly for a while, and then wondered why any man should take pains to obtain so much knowledge which would never do him good.

He next solicited the visiers for employment, not doubting but his service would be eagerly accepted. He was told by one that there was no vacancy in his office; by another, that his merit was above any patronage but that of the emperor; by a third, that he would not forget him; and by the chief visier, that he did not think literature of any great use in public business. He was sometimes admitted to their tables, where he exerted his wit and diffused his knowledge; but he observed, that where, by endeavour or accident, he had remarkably excelled, he was seldom invited a second time.

He now returned to Bassora, wearied and disgusted, but confident of resuming his former rank, and revelling again in satiety of praise. But he who had been neglected at Tauris, was not much regarded at Bassora; he was considered as a fugitive, who returned only because he could live in no other place; his companions found that they had formerly over-rated his abilities, and he lived long without notice or esteem.

Johnson's last major work was the magnificent series of *Lives of the Poets*, commissioned by a group of booksellers to serve as introductory material for a collection of the corpus of English poetry that was chiefly in demand at that time. The *Lives* were published in two groups, in 1779 and 1781. Johnson wrote them quickly and fluently, drawing on the reading and experience of a lifetime; dealing mostly with poets who had lived and worked in the century before he wrote the work, he had occasion to deal with the lives of many poets he had known, distantly or intimately. Many of the minor characters, too, people who appear for a paragraph or two in the story, had been acquaintances of his. The beautiful and tender sketch of Gilbert Walmsley has been quoted on an earlier page, as has the briefer mention of Cornelius Ford. In the days of his poverty in Grub Street, Johnson had been friendly with the poet Collins, whose delicate lyric gift largely by-passed Johnson's neoclassic ear but whose fate as a suffering and sensitive man went straight to his capacious heart. Collins had been, like most men of letters in the 1740s, desperately hard up, and Johnson recalled how he had once rescued him from 'a bailiff, that was prowling in the street'. Collins, prompted by Johnson, sent a message to a bookseller, proposing a new edition of Aristotle's *Poetics* with a commentary by himself; Johnson carried the message and returned with an advance which took Collins out of his immediate predicament. In a sudden flash of vivid detail Johnson writes, 'He shewed me the guineas safe in his hand.' One sees the two poets in the shabby room, conscious of the bailiff waiting outside, with the sharp visual precision of a flashlight photograph. In more measured and elegiac vein, Johnson writes of Collins's sad decline:

22. This was however the character rather of his inclination than his genius; the grandeur of wildness, and the novelty of extravagance, were always desired by him, but were not always attained. Yet as diligence is never wholly lost; if his efforts sometimes caused harshness and obscurity, they likewise produced in happier moments sublimity and splendour. This idea which he had formed of excellence, led him to oriental fictions and allegorical imagery; and perhaps, while he was intent upon description, he did not sufficiently cultivate sentiment. His poems are the productions of a mind not deficient in fire, nor unfurnished with knowledge either of books or life, but somewhat obstructed in its progress by deviation in quest of mistaken beauties.

His morals were pure, and his opinions pious: in a long continuance of poverty, and long habits of dissipation, it cannot be expected that any character should be exactly uniform. There is a degree of want by which the freedom of agency is almost destroyed; and long association with fortuitous companions will at last relax the strictness of truth, and abate the fervour of sincerity. That this man, wise and virtuous as he was, passed always unentangled through the snares of life, it would be prejudice and temerity to affirm; but it may be said that at least he preserved the source of action unpolluted, that his principles were never shaken, that his distinctions of right and wrong were never confounded, and that his faults had nothing of malignity or design, but proceeded from some unexpected pressure, or casual temptation.

The latter part of his life cannot be remembered but with pity and sadness. He languished some years under that depression of mind which enchains the faculties without destroying them, and leaves reason the knowledge of right without the power of pursuing it. These clouds which he perceived gathering on his intellects, he endeavoured to disperse by travel, and passed into France: but found himself constrained to yield to his malady, and returned. He was for some time confined in a house of lunatics, and afterwards retired to the care of his sister in Chichester, where death in 1756 came to his relief.

After his return from France, the writer of this character paid him a visit at Islington, where he was waiting for his sister, whom he had directed to meet him: there was then nothing of disorder discernible in his mind by any but himself; but he had withdrawn from study, and travelled with no other book than an English Testament, such as children carry to the school: when his friend took it into his hand, out of curiosity to see what companion a Man of Letters had chosen, *I have but one book*, said Collins, *but that is the best*.

Such was the fate of Collins, with whom I once delighted to converse, and whom I yet remember with tenderness.

He was visited at Chichester, in his last illness, by his learned friends Dr. Warton and his brother; to whom he spoke with disapprobation of his *Oriental Eclogues*, as not sufficiently expressive of Asiatic manners, and called them his Irish Eclogues. He shewed them, at the same time, an ode inscribed to Mr. John Hume, on the superstitions of the Highlands; which they thought superior to his other works, but which no search has yet found.

His disorder was not alienation of mind, but general laxity and feebleness, a deficiency rather of his vital than intellectual powers. What he spoke wanted neither judgement nor spirit; but a few minutes exhausted him, so that he was forced to rest upon the couch, till a short cessation restored his powers, and he was again able to talk with his former vigour.

The approaches of this dreadful malady he began to feel soon after his uncle's death; and, with the usual weakness of men so diseased, eagerly snatched that temporary relief with which the table and the bottle flatter and seduce. But his health continually declined, and he grew more and more burdensome to himself.

With the publication of the *Lives* we approach the end of Johnson's own life. The last chapter is a sad one, inevitably, for Johnson was deeply attached to his old friends and so many of them fell away one after another; this, combined with his own physical deterioration and the shattering blow to him of Hester Thrale's marriage to Gabriele Piozzi and her departure for Italy, caused him deep suffering, which he bore with his customary manly fortitude. One of the worst of his shocks was the death of Robert Levet, that grim, taciturn Yorkshireman who was so long an inmate of Johnson's strange *ménage* in the house off Fleet Street. Levet, though not a qualified medical man, had picked up some skill in physic in the course of a wandering life, and he acted as doctor to many a poor person who could not afford to approach a regular practitioner—and, for that matter, served as medical officer to Johnson and his household. Though Johnson's senior, he was a slender, tough, leathery man who might reasonably have been expected to live to a great age. But it was not to be, and Johnson wrote sadly to Bennet Langton (20 March 1782),

At night, as at Mrs Thrale's I was musing in my chamber, I thought with uncommon earnestness, that however I might alter my mode of life, or whithersoever I might remove, I would endeavour to retain Levet about me, in the morning my servant brought me word that Levet was called to another state, a state for which, I think, he was not unprepared, for he was very useful to the poor. How much soever I valued him, I now wish that I had valued him more.

A few weeks later Johnson wrote his moving elegy, *On the Death of Dr Robert Levet.* Though cloaked as usual in the impersonality of a public utterance, this is a deeply personal statement. Levet was a man of limited powers who had used those powers to the full, very largely to the good of others. Johnson was a man of wide and general powers, haunted by the fear that he was failing to render to his Creator the homage of a total employment of his gifts. He was tormented by the thought of 'That one talent which is death to hide'. Levet, by contrast, had 'well employed' his 'single talent', and in doing so had deserved well of man and of God. Tenderly, sadly, Johnson wrote of his old companion in short, strong, lapidary stanzas, instinct with feeling and experience.

23.   Condemn'd to hope's delusive mine,
      As on we toil from day to day,
By sudden blasts, or slow decline,
      Our social comforts drop away.

Well tried through many a varying year,
      See LEVET to the grave descend;
Officious, innocent, sincere,
      Of ev'ry friendless name the friend.

Yet still he fills affection's eye,
      Obscurely wise, and coarsely kind;
Nor, letter'd arrogance, deny
      Thy praise to merit unrefin'd.

When fainting nature call'd for aid,
      And hov'ring death prepar'd the blow,
His vig'rous remedy display'd
      The power of art without the show.

In misery's darkest caverns known,
      His useful care was ever nigh,
Where hopeless anguish pour'd his groan,
      And lonely want retir'd to die.

No summons mock'd by chill delay,
      No petty gain disdain'd by pride,
The modest wants of ev'ry day
      The toil of ev'ry day supplied.

His virtues walk'd their narrow round,
   Nor made a pause, nor left a void;
And sure th' Eternal Master found
   The single talent well employed.

The busy day, the peaceful night,
   Unfelt, uncounted, glided by;
His frame was firm, his powers were bright,
   Tho' now his eightieth year was nigh.

Then with no throbbing fiery pain,
   No cold gradations of decay,
Death broke at once the vital chain,
   And free'd his soul the nearest way.

That poem represents a peak from which there is no other way than down. But let us end this section on a lighter and more cheerful note. Johnson was keenly interested in his fellow-men, alive to their quirks and oddities, full of relish for the flavour of their individualities. And his conversation, as reported by Boswell, above all, is full of brief, pithy characterizations. He could hit off, in a few words, the outline of a man's life and being. So, coming down from the stately pinnacle of his grief for Levet, here is the fragment of talk about Christopher Smart (Boswell, 24 May 1763) in which Johnson gave his kindly and humorous verdict on the man.

24. Concerning this unfortunate poet, Christopher Smart, who was confined in a mad-house, he had, at another time, the following conversation with Dr. Burney.—BURNEY. 'How does poor Smart do, Sir; is he likely to recover?' JOHNSON. 'It seems as if his mind had ceased to struggle with the disease; for he grows fat upon it.' BURNEY. 'Perhaps, Sir, that may be from want of exercise.' JOHNSON. 'No, Sir; he has partly as much exercise as he used to have, for he digs in the garden. Indeed, before his confinement, he used for exercise to walk to the alehouse; but he was *carried* back again. I did not think he ought to be shut up. His infirmities were not noxious to society. He insisted on people praying with him; and I'd as lief pray with Kit Smart as any one else. Another charge was, that he did not love clean linen; and I have no passion for it.'

Chapter V

Johnson and Women

First, his mother. We have already had a glimpse or two (I, 1, 3) of the relationship between them during Johnson's formative years; we have taken note of his remarking that his parents 'had not much happiness from each other' and that 'poor people's children never respect them'. Sarah was evidently something of a nagger; when she told the ten-year-old Sam that his eating a huge helping of boiled mutton at a relative's house 'would hardly ever be forgotten', we can assume that there was a tinge of reproach in the statement; bodily appetites, even the normal hunger of a large growing boy, were to be associated with guilt.

Johnson saw his mother frequently during the early weeks of 1740, when he stayed for a time in Lichfield. He was not to go there again for twenty-two years, by which time his mother was dead. This long absence has usually been explained by Johnson's poverty, the unremitting necessity to work for the next meal, the difficulty and expense of a journey to Lichfield, etc., etc. In my *Samuel Johnson* (1974) I give my reasons for thinking that he was probably avoiding his mother. He very deeply wished to love her—not only did he feel it to be a duty, but he always longed to love and be loved—without ever actually succeeding, and as he said himself, 'sensation is sensation', if a feeling is not there it cannot be manufactured. This would account for the undercurrent of guilt and self-accusation that made so much the more painful his grief at her death. No one questions that this grief was sincere. The four letters he wrote to her on her deathbed are among the most touching of his personal statements, and the sense of loss in them is unmistakably genuine. But loss of what? The sustaining comfort of a mother's presence? He had known little enough of that. I suspect that the agony came much more from the knowledge (always terrible to Johnson) that the time for making amends and trying again was past. His relationship with his mother had never been entirely satisfactory to either of them, and now it never could be.

1. Honoured Madam,
   The account which Miss gives me of your health pierces my heart. God comfort and preserve you and save you, for the sake of Jesus Christ.
   I would have Miss read to you from time to time the Passion of our Saviour, and sometimes the sentences in the Communion Service, beginning *'Come unto me, all ye that travel and are heavy laden, and I will give you rest'*.
   I have just now read a physical book, which inclines me to think that a strong infusion of the bark would do you good. Do, dear mother, try it.
   Pray, send me your blessing, and forgive all that I have done amiss to you. And whatever you would have done, and what debts you would have paid first, or anything else that you would direct, let Miss put it down; I shall endeavour to obey you.
   I have got twelve guineas to send you, but unhappily am at a loss how to send it to-night. If I cannot send it to-night, it will come by the next post.
   Pray, do not omit any thing mentioned in this letter: God bless you for ever and ever.

I am your dutiful son

Jan. 13, 1758 Sam: Johnson

Endorsement by another hand:
   Pray acknowledge the receipt of this by return of post without fail.

2. Dear honoured Mother
   Your weakness afflicts me beyond what I am willing to communicate to you. I do not think you unfit to face death,

but I know not how to bear the thought of losing you. Endeav-our to do all you ⟨can⟩ for yourself. Eat as much as you can.

I pray often for you; do you pray for me. I have nothing to add to my last letter.

I am, dear, dear mother, Your dutiful son,
Jan. 16, 1759.   Sam: Johnson

3. Dear honoured Mother
I fear you are too ill for long letters; therefore I will only tell you, you have from me all the regard that can possibly subsist in the heart. I pray God to bless you for evermore, for Jesus Christ's sake. Amen.

Let Miss write to me every post, however short.

I am, dear mother, Your dutiful son
Jan. 18, 1759.   Sam: Johnson

4. Dear honoured Mother
Neither your condition nor your character make it fit for me to say much. You have been the best mother, and I believe the best woman in the world. I thank you for your indulgence to me, and beg forgiveness of all that I have done ill, and all that I have omitted to do well. God grant you his Holy Spirit, and receive you to everlasting happiness, for Jesus Christ's sake. Amen. Lord Jesus receive your spirit. Amen.

I am, dear, dear mother, Your dutiful son,
Jan. 20, 1759.   Sam: Johnson

Next—and again of course—his wife Elizabeth, whom he called Tetty, using a then common diminutive form. Opinions have differed about Tetty; she was a widow twenty years older than her husband, and the world is always inclined to be sarcastic about such marriages; but one thing is certain: she understood and appreciated Johnson for what he was. The couple first became acquainted during the melancholy period that followed Johnson's enforced withdrawal from Oxford in 1729. For the young Johnson it was a thin, sour time. He had no prospects, no influential friends, no family support; his father had died in 1731, leaving a failing business and a

few pounds in hand; Johnson was trying to find work as
a schoolmaster, but every job he applied for he either
failed to get or kept only a few months. His friend Edmund
Hector invited him to stay in Birmingham, and this gave
him some relief from melancholy; he met a few people,
picked up some scraps of literary piece-work, and at any
rate managed not to sink into the inertia of despair.
Round about this time he met Harry Porter and his wife
Elizabeth; they were kindly, hospitable, well-to-do; cultivated, too, up to a point. Certainly Elizabeth saw behind
the ugly appearance and alarming physical abnormalities
of the young man who called at the house; after their first
meeting, she turned to her daughter Lucy and said, 'This
is the most sensible man I ever met.' The friendship
prospered, and when Harry Porter unexpectedly died in
his late forties, Elizabeth was more than willing to take
the young Johnson as her second husband. Her family
were scandalized; one son renounced her and never saw
her again, the other took years to swallow his indignation;
only her grown-up daughter, Lucy, stayed at home and
adapted to the new arrangement. She probably had no
choice.

It was a love-match on both sides. Johnson's account of
their wedding, to Boswell, is evidence that the young bridegroom thought it important to assert some kind of authority
over his wife. But it was loving authority; he needed her
respect.

5. I know not for what reason the marriage ceremony was not
performed at Birmingham; but a resolution was taken that it
should be at Derby, for which place the bride and bridegroom
set out on horseback, I suppose in very good humour. But
though Mr. Topham Beauclerk used archly to mention Johnson's having told him with much gravity, 'Sir, it was a love
marriage on both sides', I have had from my illustrious friend
the following curious account of their journey to church upon
the nuptial morn:—'Sir, she had read the old romances, and
had got into her head the fantastical notion that a woman of
spirit should use her lover like a dog. So, Sir, at first she told

me that I rode too fast, and she could not keep up with me : and, when I rode a little slower, she passed me, and complained that I lagged behind. I was not to be made the slave of caprice; and I resolved to begin as I meant to end. I therefore pushed on briskly, till I was fairly out of her sight. The road lay between two hedges, so I was sure she could not miss it; and I contrived that she should soon come up with me. When she did, I observed her to be in tears.'

> Johnson's only surviving letter to Tetty shows him in placating mood, conscious that she has been having a thin time. Having moved to London and set her up in lodgings, he heard of a schoolmastering job that might be going at Appleby, Leicestershire, and went to try his chances. When the job failed to materialize, he stayed on, enjoying the hospitality of John Taylor, spending a few comfortable weeks at his mother's house in Lichfield, and generally enjoying the respite from his laborious London life. Tetty, who must have been lonely and insecure, endured his long absence as best she could, but finally, when she managed to fall somehow and injure a tendon in her leg, she must have written asking him to come home and give her the support of his presence. Johnson's letter is guilty in tone; it sounds almost as if he had not written to her at all during these months; he is recalled to a sense of the duty he owes his wife, and he assures her that his affections have remained constant.

6. Dearest Tetty

After hearing that You are in so much danger, as I apprehend from a hurt on a tendon, I shall be very uneasy till I know that You are recovered, and beg that You will omit nothing that can contribute to it, nor deny Yourself any thing that may make confinement less melancholy. You have already suffered more than I can bear to reflect upon, and I hope more than either of us shall suffer again. One part at least I have often flattered myself we shall avoid for the future, our troubles will surely never separate us more. If M ⟨   ⟩ does not easily succeed in his endeavours, let him not ⟨? scruple⟩ to call in another

Surgeon to consult with him, Y⟨ou may⟩ have two or three visits from Ranby or Shipton, who is ⟨? said⟩ to be the best, for a Guinea, which You need not fear to part with on so pressing an occasion, for I can send you twenty pouns more on Monday, which I have received this night; I beg therefore that You will more regard my happiness, than to expose Yourself to any hazards. I still promise myself many happy years from your tenderness and affection, which I sometimes hope our misfortunes have not yet deprived me of. David wrote to me this day on the affair of Irene, who is at last become a kind of Favourite among the Players, Mr Fletewood promises to give a promise in writing that it shall be the first next season, if it cannot be introduced now, and Chetwood the Prompter is desirous of bargaining for the copy, and offers fifty Guineas for the right of printing after it shall be played. I hope it will at length reward me for my perplexities.

Of the time which I have spent from thee, and of my dear Lucy and other affairs, my heart will be at ease on Monday to give Thee a particular account, especially if a Letter should inform me that thy Leg is better, for I hope You do not think so unkindly of me as to imagine that I can be at rest while I be⟨li⟩eve my dear Tetty in pain.

Be assured, my dear Girl, that I have seen nobody in these rambles upon which I have been forced, that has not contribute to confirm my esteem and affection for thee, though that esteem and affection only contributed to increase my unhappiness when I reflected that the most amiable woman in the world was exposed by my means to miseries which I could not relieve.

I am My charming Love Yours

Jan. 31st 1739/40   Sam: Johnson

Lucy always sends her Duty and my Mother her service.

Tetty was the only woman with whom Johnson had sexual relations. This statement is made under two safeguards: one, that we cannot say with absolute certainty everything that happened or did not happen in the life of someone who lived two hundred years ago; the other, that all the relationships a man has with women are sexual, or at any rate sexually differentiated. Johnson never made the mis-

take of treating women as if they were men. He responded
to them as women, admired their beauty if they had any,
admired their intelligence if they had any, admired them
most of all if they united the two. He held no views about
the innate superiority of men; it was a woman, Mary
Meynell, whom he pronounced to be the most intelligent
person he had ever met; on the other hand, he particularly
liked those women who could acquire a man's skills without losing a woman's. So that he intended high praise when
he remarked, 'My old friend, Mrs. Carter, could make a
pudding as well as translate Epictetus.'

Johnson was susceptible to the beauty and delicacy of
women. He knew what it was to be in love, not only with
his wife but with other ladies whom he worshipped at a
distance. Molly Aston, one of the daughters of Sir Thomas
Aston whom he met in that winter of 1740, particularly
fired his emotions, as witness Mrs Piozzi's *Anecdotes*:

7. When Mr. Thrale once asked him which had been the
happiest period of his past life? he replied, 'it was that year in
which he spent one whole evening with Molly Aston. That
indeed (said he) was not happiness, it was rapture; but the
thoughts of it sweetened the whole year.' I must add, that the
evening alluded to was not passed *tête-à-tête*, but in a select company, of which the present Lord Killmorey was one. 'Molly
(says Dr. Johnson) was a beauty and a scholar, and a wit and
a whig; and she talked all in praise of liberty: and so I made
this epigram upon her—She was the loveliest creature I ever
saw!!!

> Liber ut esse velim, suasisti pulchra Maria,
> Ut maneam liber—pulchra Maria, vale!'

Will it do this way in English, Sir (said I)?

> Persuasions to freedom fall oddly from you;
> If freedom we seek—fair Maria, adieu!

'It will do well enough (replied he); but it is translated by a
lady, and the ladies never loved Molly Aston.' I asked him what
his wife thought of this attachment? 'She was jealous to be
sure (said he), and teized me sometimes when I would let her;

and one day, as a fortune-telling gipsey passed us when we were walking out in company with two or three friends in the coun-try, she made the wench look at my hand, but soon repented her curiosity; for (says the gipsey) Your heart is divided, Sir, between a Betty and a Molly: Betty loves you best, but you take most delight in Molly's company: when I turned about to laugh, I saw my wife was crying. Pretty charmer! she had no reason!'

> Such a man is in no danger of underestimating the power of the tender emotions. On the other hand, Johnson occa-sionally made very down-to-earth remarks about the relations of the sexes, and particularly about marriage, which have caused some people to think of him as the stern moralist who dismisses love-talk as sentimentality.
>
> In such vein he remarked to Boswell on their visit to Lichfield in 1776 that if he had married Edmund Hector's sister Anne, who later married a clergyman named Careless, 'it might have been as happy for me'. Boswell, always eager to sound out Johnson's views, jumped at this with

8. 'Pray, Sir, do you not suppose that there are fifty women in the world, with any one of whom a man may be as happy, as with any one woman in particular?' JOHNSON. 'Ay, Sir, fifty thousand.' BOSWELL. 'Then, Sir, you are not of opinion with some who imagine that certain men and certain women are made for each other; and that they cannot be happy if they miss their counterparts.' JOHNSON. 'To be sure not, Sir. I believe marriages would in general be as happy, and often more so, if they were all made by the Lord Chancellor, upon a due consideration of the characters and circumstances, without the parties having any choice in the matter.'

> On this same visit Johnson, whose mind may have been running on sentimental memories ('Forty years ago, Sir, I was in love with an actress here, Mrs. Emmet, who acted Flora, in "Hob in the Well"'), spoke again of the sexual bond:

9. 'Marriage, Sir, is much more necessary to a man than to a woman: for he is much less able to supply himself with domestic comforts. You will recollect my saying to some ladies the other day, that I had often wondered why young women should marry, as they have so much more freedom, and so much more attention paid to them while unmarried, than when married. I indeed did not mention the *strong* reason for their marrying—the *mechanical* reason.' BOSWELL. 'Why that *is* a strong one. But does not imagination make it much more important than it is in reality? Is it not, to a certain degree, a delusion in us as well as in women?' JOHNSON. 'Why yes, Sir; but it is a delusion that is always beginning again.' BOSWELL. 'I don't know but there is upon the whole more misery than happiness produced by that passion.' JOHNSON. 'I don't think so, Sir.'

Johnson was undoubtedly serious in making these matter-of-fact observations. All the same, there was a deeper stratum of memory and sentiment that he did not always choose to reveal to Boswell. To recall Anne Hector was a sentimental pleasure; to recall Hill Boothby might have been more of a grief, for this seems to have been a genuine opportunity for happiness which fate denied him. Hill Boothby, a spinster one year older than Johnson, whom he probably met during that memorable country sojourn in 1739–40, was sweet, good, pious, witty and spirited. It seems more than likely that after Tetty's death in 1752, when after a decent interval Johnson's thoughts turned to marrying again, Hill Boothby was very much in his mind. But at about this time, a neighbour of hers named William Fitzherbert was widowed, and Hill Boothby honoured an old promise to move in and run his house and look after his family. Even if Johnson had wanted to persuade her to go back on her word, he would never have succeeded in doing so, since her personal standard of integrity was so high. He therefore relinquished all thoughts of her as a wife, but she remained very close to his heart. Three years later, she died, and Johnson wrote six letters to her, during her last illness, that show the warmth and depth of his devotion to her.

10. Dear Madam   Dec. 30, 1755

It is again Midnight, and I am again alone. With what meditation shall I amuse this waste hour of darkness and vacuity. If I turn my thoughts upon myself what do I perceive but a poor helpless being reduced by a blast of wind to weakness and misery. How my present distemper was brought upon me I can give no account, but impute it to some sudden succession of cold to heat, such as in the common road of life cannot be avoided, and against which no precaution can be taken.

Of the fallaciousness of hope, and the uncertainty of schemes every day gives some new proof, but it is seldom heeded till something rather felt than seen awakens attention. This Ilness in which I have suffered something and feared much more, has depressed my confidence and elation, and made me consider all that I have promised myself as less certain to be attained or enjoyed. I have endeavoured to form resolutions of a better life, but I form them weakly under the consciousness of an external motive. Not that I conceive a time of sickness a time improper for recollection and good purposes, which I believe Diseases and Calamities often sent to produce; but because no man can know how little his performance will answer to his promises, and designs are nothing in human eyes till they are realised by execution.

Continue, my Dearest, your prayers for me, that no good reso⟨lu⟩tion may be vain. You think, I believe, better of me than I deserve. I hope to be in time what I wish to be, and what I have hitherto satisfied myself too readily with only wishing.

Your Billet brought me what I much wished to have, a proof that I am still remembred by you at the hour in which I most desire it!

The Doctor is anxious about you. He thinks you too negligent of yourself, if you will promise to be cautious, I will exchange promises, as we have already exchanged injunctions. However, do not write to me more than you can easily bear, do not interrupt your ease to write at all.

Mr Fitzherbert sent to day to offer me some Wine, the people about me say I ought to accept it, I shall therefore be obliged to him if he will send me a Bottle.

There has gone about a report that I died to day which I

mention, lest you should hear it and be alarmed. You see that I think my death may alarm you, which for me is to think very ⟨highly⟩ of earthly friendship. I believe it arose from the death of one of my neighbours. You know Des Cartes's argument, 'I think therefore I am'. It is as good a consequence 'I write therefore I am alive'. I might give another 'I am alive therefore I love Miss Boothby'; but that I hope our friendship may be of far longer duration than life.

I am Dearest Madam with most sincere affection, Your most obliged, and most humble servant Sam: Johnson

11. My Sweet Angel

I have read your book, I am afraid you will think without any great improvement, whether you can read my notes I know not. You ought not to be offended, I am perhaps as sincere as the writer. In all things that terminate here I shall be much guided by your influence, and should take or leave by your direction, but I cannot receive my religion from any human hand. I desire however to be instructed and am far from thinking myself perfect.

I beg you to return the book when you have looked into it. I should not have written what is in the margin, had I not had it from you, or had I not intended to show it you.

It affords me a new conviction that in these books there is little new, except new forms of expression, which may be sometimes taken even by the writer, for new doctrines.

I sincerely hope that God whom you so much desire to serve aright will bless you, and restore you to health, if he sees it best. Surely no human understanding can pray for any thing temporal otherwise than conditionally. Dear Angel do not forget me. my heart is full of tenderness.

It has pleased God to permit me to be much better, which I believe will please you.

Give me leave, who have thought much on Medicine, to propose to you an easy and I think a very probable remedy for indigestion and lubricity of the bowels. Dr Laurence has told me your case. Take an ounce of dried orange peel finely powdered, divide it into scruples, and take one Scruple at a time in any manner; the best way is perhaps to drink it in a glass of hot red port. or to eat it first and drink the wine after it. If you mix cinnamon or nutmeg with the powder it were not worse, but it will be more bulky and so more troublesome. This is a medicine not disgusting, not costly, easily tried, and if not found useful easily left off.

I would not have you offer it to the Doctor as mine. Physicians do not love intruders, yet do not take it without his leave. but do not be easily put off, for it is in my opinion very likely to help you, and not likely to do you harm, do not take too much in haste, a scruple one in three hours or about five scruples a day will be sufficient to begin, or less if you find any aversion. I think using sugar with it might be bad, if Syrup, use old Syrup of Quinces, but even that I do not like. I should think better of conserve of Sloes. Has the Doctor mentioned the bark? in powder you could hardly take it, perhaps you might bear the infusion?

Do not think me troublesome, I am full of care. I love you and honour you, and am very unwilling to lose you.

A Dieu Je vous commende.

I am Madame Your most affectionate humble servant

Sam: Johnson.

My compliments to my dear Miss.

Dec 31

12. Honoured Madam

I beg of you to endeavour to live. I have returned your *Law* which however I earnestly entreat you to give me. I am in great trouble, if you can write three words to me, be pleased to do it. I am afraid to say much, and cannot say nothing when my dearest is in danger.

The Allmercifull GOD have mercy on You.

I am Madam Your

Jan 8. 1756 Sam: Johnson

Hester Piozzi, in her *Anecdotes*, specifically links the death of Hill Boothby with the death of Elizabeth Johnson as two shattering blows in Johnson's life.

13. I have heard Baretti say, that when this lady died, Dr.

Johnson was almost distracted with his grief; and that the friends about him had much ado to calm the violence of his emotion. Dr. Taylor too related once to Mr. Thrale and me, that when he lost his wife, the negro Francis ran away, though in the middle of the night, to Westminster, to fetch Dr. Taylor to his master, who was all but wild with excess of sorrow, and scarce knew him when he arrived : after some minutes however, the doctor proposed their going to prayers, as the only rational method of calming the disorder this misfortune had occasioned in both their spirits. Time, and resignation to the will of God, cured every breach in his heart before I made acquaintance with him, though he always persisted in saying he never rightly recovered the loss of his wife.

To quote from Mrs Piozzi is, inevitably, to remember her as Hester Thrale, vivacious and hospitable mistress of the household where Johnson was an honoured and happy guest for the best part of twenty years, from their first meeting 1765 to the final rupture that followed her marriage to Piozzi in 1784. Hester's relationship with Johnson was deep and ramifying: partly she was a favourite daughter, partly a nurse who helped him through his illnesses—especially those that were mental rather than physical—partly a gracious hostess ('my Mistress'), partly a literary collaborator, always a good and loyal friend until finally, and entirely justifiably, she decided that the demands of her own life must come first. Letters to, and mentions of, Hester Thrale are necessarily scattered all through this volume; those that follow here are a selection which, I hope, reflects in its various facets the relationship Johnson had with her as an older man to a younger woman. The first surviving letter, when the Thrales are delightful new friends who have offered him a holiday by the sea, is full of friendly eagerness.

14. Madam
If you have really so good an opinion of me as you express, it will not be necessary to inform you how unwillingly I miss the opportunity of coming to Brighthelmston in Mr. Thrale's

company, or since I cannot do what I wish first, how eagerly I shall catch the second degree of pleasure by coming to you and Him, as soon as I can dismiss my work from my hands.

I am afraid to make promises even to myself, but I hope that the week after the next, will be the end of my present business. When business is done what remains but pleasure? and where should pleasure be sought but under Mrs Thrale's influence?

Do not blame me for a delay by which I must suffer so much, and by which I suffer alone. If you cannot think I am good, pray think I am mending, and that in time I may deserve to be,

Dear Madam, Your most obedient and most humble servant

London. Aug. 13. 1765   Sam: Johnson

> Some eighteen months later he is sufficiently involved in the relationship to be genuinely uneasy at not having any news of her at a time when he knows she is giving birth to a child. Not to disturb her quiet, but anxious for news, he writes to her mother.

15. Madam

I hope it will not be considered as one of the mere formalities of life, when I declare that to have heard nothing of Mrs Thrale for so long a time has given me pain. My uneasiness is sincere, and therefore deserves to be relieved. I do not write to Mrs Thrale lest it should give her trouble at an inconvenient time. I beg, dear Madam, to know how she does, and shall honestly partake of your grief if she is ill, and of your pleasure if she is well.

I am, Madam, Your most obliged and most humble servant

February the 14th. 1767   Sam: Johnson

> The friendship continues to ripen, and from Lichfield in the summer of 1767 Johnson writes two letters which show how much he misses the company of Hester and her family. He spent a very long time in the country that year, nearly six months in all, and the October letter shows definite impatience to be back.

16. Madam

Though I have been away so much longer than I purposed or expected, I have found nothing that withdraws my affections from the friends whom I left behind, or which makes me less desirous of reposing in that place which your kindness and Mr Thrale's allows me to call my *home*.

Miss Lucy is more kind and civil than I expected, and has raised my esteem by many excellencies very noble and resplendent, though a little discoloured by hoary virginity. Every thing else recals to my remembrance years in which I purposed what, I am afraid, I have not done, and promised myself pleasures which I have not found. But complaint can be of no use, and why then should I depress your hopes by my lamentations? I suppose it is the condition of humanity to design what never will be done, and to hope what never will be obtained. But among the vain hopes let me not number the hope which I have, of being long

Dear Madam Your most obedient and most humble Servant
Lichfield July 20 1767   Sam: Johnson

17. Dear Madam   Lichfield, Oct. 3, 1767.
You are returned, I suppose, from Brighthelmstone, and this letter will be read at Streatham.

—Sine me, liber, ibis in urbem.

I have felt in this place something like the shackles of destiny. There has not been one day of pleasure, and yet I cannot get away. But when I do come, I perhaps shall not be easily persuaded to pass again to the other side of Styx, to venture myself on the irremeable road. I long to see you, and all those of whom the sight is included in seeing you. Nil mihi rescribas; for though I have no right to say Ipsa veni, I hope that ipse veniam. Be pleased to make my compliments.

I am, Madam, Your most humble Servant
Sam: Johnson

In 1768 Johnson went to stay with his young friend Robert Chambers in Oxford. There, his health evidently troubled him, and perhaps she had been ill too, and looked after by her mother, for in a letter which shows that they were close enough to discuss serious issues he shares with her his thoughts on illness.

18. Madam   Oxford, April 28th, 1768.

It is indeed a great alleviation of sickness to be nursed by a mother, and it is a comfort in return to have the prospect of being nursed by a daughter, even at that hour when all human attention must be vain. From that social desire of being valuable to each other, which produces kindness and officiousness, it proceeds, and must proceed, that there is some pleasure in being able to give pain. To roll the weak eye of helpless anguish, and see nothing on any side but cold indifference, will, I hope, happen to none whom I love or value; it may tend to withdraw the mind from life, but has no tendency to kindle those affections which fit us for a purer and a nobler state.

Yet when any man finds himself disposed to complain with how little care he is regarded, let him reflect how little he contributes to the happiness of others, and how little, for the most part, he suffers from their pains. It is perhaps not to be lamented, that those solicitudes are not long nor frequent, which must commonly be vain; nor can we wonder that, in a state in which all have so much to feel of their own evils, very few have leisure for those of another. However, it is so ordered, that few suffer from want of assistance; and that kindness which could not assist, however pleasing, may be spared.

These reflections do not grow out of any discontent at C——'s behaviour: he has been neither negligent nor troublesome; nor do I love him less for having been ill in his house. This is no small degree of praise. I am better, having scarce eaten for seven days. I shall come home on Saturday.

I am, &c.

About this time Johnson begins to speak of Streatham Place as 'home' ('our affairs will not suffer me to come home, till Saturday', 18 May 1769); he has his own room there, and comes and goes as he pleases. In June 1769 she has again been delivered of a child, and he writes a gallant congratulatory note, and begs that she will take care of herself as well as of her children, for that they will grow up to be as good and as useful as she, is an assumption he is willing to make but that no one can prove.

19. Madam

Hesiod, who was very wise in his time, though nothing to such wise people as we, says that the evil of the worst times has some good mingled with it. Hesiod was in the right. These times are not much to my mind, I am not well, but in these times you are safe, and have brought a pretty little Miss. I always wished it might be a Miss, and now that wish is gratified, nothing remains but that I entreat you to take care of yourself, for whatever number of Girls or Boys you may give us, we are far from being certain that any of them will ever do for us, what you can do, it is certain that they cannot now do it, and the ability which they want, they are not likely to gain, but by your precepts and your example; by an example of excellence, and by ⟨the admonitions⟩ of truth.

Mr. Thrale tells me that my furlough is shortened, I am always ready to obey orders, I have not yet found any place from which I shall not willingly depart, to come back to you.

I am, Dearest Lady, Your most obedient and most humble Servant

Oxford. June 29. 1769   Sam: Johnson

The tale of their parting is a sad one. But no part of Johnson's story is without its nobility, and one is heartened to see how quickly generosity and forgiveness catch up with pain and resentment. After Henry Thrale's death in April 1781, the bonds between Johnson and the Thrale family inevitably slackened: Hester, fearful of undue expense now that the breadwinner was gone, sold Streatham Place and moved to a house in town; here, too, Johnson had his own room and some pretence at the old intimacy was kept up, but her thoughts were elsewhere. She wanted to marry the sensitive and understanding Gabriele Piozzi; her daughters were furious, just as Tetty's children had been when she wanted to marry the young Johnson, but the parallel was lost on him and this time he was among the outraged. He was old, and ill; he needed her help and comfort; now she was going to marry a man with a different nationality and a different religion, who would take her far from her family and from him. When he received the letter telling of her decision—and it was a form letter, sent out to all the trustees of her husband's estate, of whom he was one—he replied with that notorious bellow of pain and rage.

20. Madam

If I interpret your letter right, you are ignominiously married, if it is yet undone, let us once talk together. If you have abandoned your children and your religion, God forgive your wickedness; if you have forfeited your Fame, and your country, may your folly do no further mischief.

If the last act is yet to do, I, who have loved you, esteemed you, reverenced you, and served you, I who long thought you the first of human kind, entreat that before your fate is irrevocable, I may once more see you. I was, I once was,

Madam, most truly yours.

July 2. 1784 Sam: Johnson

I will come down if you permit it.

She replied with spirit:

21. Sir— 4 July 1784.

I have this Morning received from You so rough a Letter, in reply to one which was both tenderly & respectfully written, that I am forced to desire the conclusion of a Correspondence which I can bear to continue no longer. The Birth of my second Husband is not meaner than that of my first, his sentiments are not meaner, his Profession is not meaner,—and his Superiority in what he professes—acknowledged by all Mankind.—It is want of Fortune then that is *ignominious*, the Character of the Man I have chosen has no other Claim to such an Epithet. The Religion to which he has been always a zealous Adherent, will I hope teach him to forgive Insults he has not deserved—mine will I hope enable me to bear them at once with Dignity & Patience. To hear that I have forfeited my Fame is indeed the greatest Insult I ever yet received, my Fame is as unsullied as Snow, or I should think it unworthy of him who must henceforward protect it.

I write by the Coach the more speedily and effectually to prevent your coming hither.

140

Perhaps by my Fame (& I hope it is so;) you mean only that Celebrity which is a Consideration of a much lower kind: I care for that only as it may give pleasure to my Husband & his Friends.

Farewell Dear Sir, and accept my best wishes: You have always commanded my Esteem, and long enjoy'd the Fruits of a Friendship never infringed by one harsh Expression on my Part, during twenty Years of familiar Talk. never did I oppose your Will, or controal your Wish: nor can your unmerited Severity itself lessen my Regard—but till you have changed your Opinion of Mr. Piozzi—let us converse no more. God bless you!

> Four days later, Johnson is writing to her in a spirit of forgiveness, wishing her every happiness, and even breathing out one more sigh of tenderness. Their parting was sad; to him, heart-breaking; but it was not bitter.

22. Dear Madam

What you have done, however I may lament it, I have no pretence to resent, as it has not been injurious to me. I therefore breathe out one sigh more of tenderness perhaps useless, but at least sincere.

I wish that God may grant you every blessing, that you may be happy in this world for its short continuance, and eternally happy in a better state, and whatever I can contribute to your happiness, I am very ready to repay for that kindness which soothed twenty years of a life radically wretched.

Do not think slightly of the advice which I now presume to offer. Prevail upon Mr. Piozzi to settle in England. You may live here with more dignity than in Italy, and with more security. Your rank will be higher, and your fortune more under your own eye. I desire not to detail all my reasons; but every argument of prudence and interest is for England, and only some phantoms of imagination seduce you to Italy.

I am afraid, however, that my counsel is vain, yet I have eased my heart by giving it.

When Queen Mary took the resolution of sheltering herself. in England, the Archbishop of St. Andrew's attempting to dissuade her, attended on her journey and when they came to the irremeable stream that separated the two kingdoms, walked by her side into the water, in the middle of which he seized her bridle, and with earnestness proportioned to her danger and his own affection, pressed her to return. The Queen went forward.——If the parallel reaches thus far; may it go no further. The tears stand in my eyes.

I am going into Derbyshire, and hope to be followed by your good wishes, for I am with great affection

Your most humble servant,

London July 8. 1784   Sam: Johnson

> As a coda to this section, here is Johnson's letter to 'a lady' (unidentified) who had asked him a favour he did not feel able to do for her. The refusal is final, but the humanity and courtesy, the understanding and compassion, are qualities that seem to run through all his dealings with people, and especially with women.

23. Madam

I hope you will believe that my delay in answering Your letter could proceed only from my unwillingness to destroy any hope that You had form'd. Hope is itself a species of happiness, & perhaps the chief happiness which this World affords, but like all other pleasures immoderately enjoyed, the excesses of hope must be expiated by pain, & expectations improperly indulged must end in disappointment. If it be asked, what is the improper expectation which it is dangerous to indulge, experience will quickly answer, that it is such expectation, dictated not by reason but by desire; expectation raised not by the common occurrences of life but by the wants of the Expectant; an Expectation that requires the common course of things to be changed, and the general rules of Action to be broken.

When you made Your request to me, You should have considered, Madam, what You were asking. You ask me to solicit a great Man to whom I never spoke, for a young Person whom I had never seen, upon a supposition which I had no means of knowing to be true. There is no reason why amongst all the great, I should chuse to supplicate the Archbishop, nor why among all the possible objects of his bounty, the Archbishop should chuse your Son. I know, Madam, how unwillingly conviction is admitted, when interest opposes it; but surely, Madam, You must allow that there is no reason why that should be done by me which every other man may do with equal reason, and which indeed no man can do properly without some very particular Relation both to the Archbishop & to You. If I could help You in this exigence by any proper means, it would give me pleasure, but this proposal is so very remote from all usual methods, that I cannot comply with it, but at the risque of such answer & suspicions, as I believe you do not wish me to undergo.

I have seen your Son this morning, he seems a pretty Youth, and will perhaps find some better friend than I can procure him, but though he should at last miss the University he may still be wise, useful, & happy.

I am Madam, Your most humble Servant,

Sam : Johnson.

Chapter VI

'A Ship with a Wide Sail'

'The man who is tired of London is tired of life; for there is in London everything that life can afford.' Short, pithy, memorable, this remark has become one of Johnson's most often quoted sayings. Certainly he relished London, especially in his later years when his fame opened all doors and his pension raised him above want. On the strength of this tribute, plus the fact of his long residence in town, Londoners have become accustomed to claiming Johnson as their own, the most metropolitan and city-bound of all great Englishmen, so that as early as 1825 Macaulay could define the limitations of Johnson's vision of life as essentially Cockney limitations.

He was no master of the great science of human nature. He had studied, not the genus man, but the species Londoner. Nobody was ever so thoroughly conversant with all the forms of life and all the shades of moral and intellectual character which were to be seen from Islington to the Thames, and from Hyde Park Corner to Mile-End Green. But his philosophy stopped at the first turnpike-gate. Of the rural life of England he knew nothing . . .

This assessment—it is from Macaulay's review of Croker's edition of Boswell's *Life of Johnson* (*Edinburgh Review*, 1825, *Critical and Historical Essays*, 1843)—is of course wide of the mark, but it was influential in starting a tradition that has not quite died out. Macaulay's judgment obscures not only the fact that Johnson was country-bred (for Lichfield life in the early eighteenth century was hardly urban as we understand that word today) but also

145

his love of travel. Johnson loved journeys. Not only did he love to examine human nature under various geographical and social conditions, not only was he far from being as insensitive to landscape as has been supposed; he enjoyed the actual process of travel. He liked the feeling of wheels under him, and the sight of the countryside flowing past on either hand. As he put it to Boswell, 'If I had no duties, and no reference to futurity, I would spend my life in driving briskly in a postchaise with a pretty woman. But,' he added characteristically, 'she should be one who could understand me and would add something to the conversation.'

No doubt the 'conversation' would have turned frequently on the manners, customs and peculiarities of the people among whom they were travelling. To Johnson, travel was not merely the indulgence of a whim; it was an important source of knowledge and wisdom. It was, he believed, the responsibility of any traveller to keep his eyes open, to inform himself as fully as possible beforehand so that he would have some idea of what he was looking at, and to impart to the world such illumination as his travels brought him. He was irritated with people who fell below this standard. Once, at the Thrales', he was annoyed at the silence of a man who had visited Prague. 'Surely,' he complained, 'the man who has been to Prague might tell us something new and something strange, and not sit silent for want of matter to set his lips in motion.' Another time, in conversation with Boswell (10 April 1778),

1. He talked with an uncommon animation of travelling into distant countries; that the mind was enlarged by it, and that an acquisition of dignity of character was derived from it. He expressed a particular enthusiasm with respect to visiting the wall of China. I caught it for the moment, and said I really believed I should go and see the wall of China had I not children, of whom it was my duty to take care. 'Sir, (said he), by doing so, you would do what would be of importance in raising your children to eminence. There would be a lustre reflected upon them from your spirit and curiosity. They

would be at all times regarded as the children of a man who had gone to view the wall of China.'

Certainly Johnson never wavered from his belief that really long, ambitious journeys were a good thing and benefited the person who undertook them. (What he would have thought of the modern package tour can only be imagined.) The only people he knew, or at any rate knew well, who could afford to travel the earth if they so wished, were Henry and Hester Thrale. In one year, 1777, they did particularly well financially, receiving at one point a lump sum of £14,000 (in modern money, about £280,000); Johnson wrote to Hester, rather wistfully:

2. If I had money enough, what would I do? Perhaps, if you and master did not hold me, I might go to Cairo, and down the Red Sea to Bengal, and take a ramble in India. Would this be better than building and planting? It would surely give more variety to the eye, and more amplitude to the mind. Half fourteen thousand would send me out to see other forms of existence, and bring me back to describe them.

And in the same year he remarked in a letter to John Taylor:

3. Is not mine a kind of life turned upside down? Fixed to a spot when I was young, and roving the world when others are contriving to sit still, I am wholly unsettled. I am a kind of ship with a wide sail, and without an anchor.

For the first half-century of Johnson's life, the anchor was work. After he first arrived in London at the age of twenty-eight, poverty and the pressure of work kept him there almost without interruption for a quarter of a century. But as soon as his circumstances permitted, he established the custom of what he himself called 'my annual ramble into the middle counties'. His usual route was Oxford-Lichfield-Ashbourne-Birmingham. In each case there was a reason. Oxford he loved passionately; almost all his academic contacts were with Oxford men, he worked in the Bodleian Library and enjoyed conviviality in the Common Rooms ('I have drunk three bottles of port without being the worse for it. University College has witnessed this'); he formed lifelong friendships, notably with Thomas Warton and Joseph Adams. Lichfield was of course his birthplace, and he clung tenaciously not only to the scenes but to the people. His step-daughter Lucy Porter lived out her days in the house in Breadmarket Street in which he had been born; on his visits there, Johnson sometimes stayed with her, but more often took rooms at the Three Crowns, next door but one. Ashbourne was the home of his old friend John Taylor, Birmingham of Edmund Hector. The Midlands were very much Johnson's stamping-ground; though he enjoyed travelling anywhere, he needed a regular immersion in Midland sights and sounds. Not that he saw the region through a sentimental mist; as he remarked in a letter to Boswell (27 August 1775),

Time has left that part of the island few antiquities; and commerce has left the people no singularities.

All the more reason why he should grasp at the opportunity to accompany Boswell on a tour of the Hebrides, where he might reasonably expect to see 'antiquities' and a people whose 'singularities' had been left intact. The latter expectation was not, in the end, as amply fulfilled as he had hoped, since the defeat of 1745 and the subsequent measures aimed at bringing the Highlanders more into line with the other inhabitants of the British Isles. Nevertheless, the journey was an important one for Johnson. It brought him into contact with scenes, and aspects of human life, very widely removed from those to which he was accustomed; it put him, at the age of sixty-four, among the inconveniences, the hardships, and sometimes the dangers, of a part of the world far from the centres of trade and the easy routes of communication. Furthermore, it came just in time. Huge and sturdy as he was, he was beginning to lose his strength; he remarks in a letter to Mrs Thrale that his 'nerves' (i.e. muscles) are weak, and he cannot walk far because his knees are unsteady. Just before setting out he had had a severe inflammation in his eye—the only one that was of any use—and this was not altogether better at the time of his departure. With all this, he rode long distances on horseback, clambered over rocks and heather, was tossed in small boats and on one occasion exposed to very real danger of drowning. But of this last adventure he says, characteristically, very little. It happened when he and Boswell were trying to get from Skye to Iona. It was October, and already the seas were dangerous and the daylight short. They were lodged at Armadale, near the Sound of Sleat, in order to be near the water when weather conditions proved favourable and a boat was leaving. A Mr Simpson, owner of a trading vessel of some twelve tons, offered to give them a passage to the Isle of Mull, off whose south-west corner Iona lies. They accepted; and there followed a crossing of fourteen hours in increasingly bad weather, much of it in darkness, and all of it in extremely hazardous water. Johnson nowhere tells this story. When he reaches the appropriate point in his published narrative, he remarks laconically that the wind

blew against us, in a short time, with such violence that we, being no seasoned sailors, were willing to call it a tempest. I was sea-sick and lay down. Mr. Boswell kept the deck. The master knew not well whither to go; and our difficulties might perhaps have filled a very pathetic page, had not Mr. Maclean of Col, who, with every other qualification which insular life requires, is a very active and skilful mariner, piloted us safe into his own harbour.

Thus lightly did Johnson pass over an experience of very real danger. How real, can be gauged from a reading of two accounts: Boswell's (*Journal of a Tour to the Hebrides with Samuel Johnson, LL.D.*, under Sunday 3 October) and a reconstruction by a modern scholar who evidently understands boats and sailing (Francis E. Skipp, 'Johnson and Boswell Afloat' in *The New Rambler: Journal of the Johnson Society of London*, January 1965).

But Johnson's concern was not with adventures of the

body but those of the mind. He travelled in search of illumination. How did these people live? In these latitudes and among these conditions, what shape did human life grow into? He was interested in how the poor crofters scratched a living from the almost non-existent soil; but also, and equally, in the gentry. He who had chosen London with its 'full tide of human existence', whose familiar companions were scholars, wits, poets, statesmen, lawyers, was curious to know how the mind, as well as the body, supported itself among the naked rocks and barren moors. He was impressed; wherever the travellers went, they were hospitably entertained, and the houses even of the most remote Lairds contained not only good company, good food and entertainment, but—what was just as important—good books. 'I have never wanted books in the Isle of Skye', Johnson tells Mrs Thrale; and, considering the rate at which he devoured books, and the lengthy stay he was forced by bad weather to make at some houses, this is remarkable.

His Highland and Island journey afforded Johnson a great deal of solid matter for reflection, and the book he wrote about it (*A Journey to the Western Islands of Scotland*, 1775) is one of his finest achievements. It shows Johnson looking at a society whose ways are not his ways, yet which is ruled by the same government; a government, moreover, which has lately been provoked into severe repressive measures—for the part played by the clans in the rising of 1745 was rewarded by prolonged punitive humiliation, from which they were only just beginning to recover thirty years later. (Indeed, as depopulation and decline argue, the entire way of life may have been damaged beyond repair.) Change was being thrust upon these people; they were being forced out of a patriarchal social organization and a barter economy, and forced to adapt to a mercantile and pluto-democratic manner of existence. The resulting confusion and pain, amounting sometimes to despair, Johnson arrived in time to witness. His testimony is grave and moving. But the book in which he gives it is, perhaps for that very reason, very little use for our present purposes.

It is not autobiographical. Johnson is writing about the Highlands and Islands, not about himself. The narrative structure—a journey in search of the truth—is hardly less formalized than in *Rasselas*.

For a personal account of their adventure one turns to Boswell's brilliant *reportage*. But there is, fortunately, a third account, also very personal and this time written by Johnson himself. It is to be found in the series of long letters he wrote to Mrs Thrale during the journey. He wrote these letters whenever he had leisure, and despatched them by any and every means that came to hand. Thus, after going up the east coast of Scotland from Edinburgh, through St Andrews and Aberdeen to Banff, we find him (4) sitting down to write to Mrs Thrale an account of everything that has happened since he and Boswell left the comfort and security of Edinburgh on 18 August. Extract 5 takes up the story from Dunvegan in Skye.

Johnson spent a hundred days in Scotland; the first four and the last ten in Edinburgh, the rest in his ambitious itinerary. He spent more time in the Hebrides than anywhere else (this is reflected in the title of his book), but there was no characteristic part of Scotland he did not see. Back home in November, he at once began the composition of the book which he knew would be expected of him, and, working rapidly, had the bulk of it completed by the summer of 1774, and the whole finished and proofread by 25 November. Copies were available in the New Year. Below (6) is an extract which, though 'public' and magisterial by comparison with the letters to Hester Thrale, shows Johnson's deeply personal reaction to the wild beauty of the islands, the courtesy of his hosts, and the venerable associations of Iona (he uses the name of the religious foundation, Icolmkill, rather than of the island, Iona), the lump of rock from which Christianity was introduced from Ireland to Scotland and England.

4. Dear Madam   Bamff, Aug. 25. 1773
    It has so happened that though I am perpetually thinking on you, I could seldom find opportunity to write. I have in fourteen

days sent only one Letter. You must consider the fatigues of travel, and the difficulties encountered in a strange Country.

August 18. I passed with Boswel the Firth of Forth, and began our Journey. In the passage We observed an Island which I persuaded my companions to survey. We found it a Rock somewhat troublesome to climb, about a mile long and half a mile broad; in the middle were the ruins of an old fort, which had on one of the stones Maria Re. 1564. It had been only a blockhouse one story high. I measured two apartments of which the walls were entire and found them 27 feet long and 23 broad. The Rock had some grass and many thistles, both cows and sheep were grazing. There was a spring of water. The name is Inchkeith. Look on your Maps.

This visit took about an hour. We pleased ourselves with being in a country all our own, and then went back to the boat, and landed at Kinghorn, a mean town, and travelling through Kirkaldie, a very long town meanly built, and Cowpar, which I could not see because it was night, we came late to St. Andrews, the most ancient of the Scotch universities, and once the See of the Primate of Scotland. The inn was full, but Lodgings were provided for us at the house of the professor of Rhetorick, a Man of elegant manners who showed us in the morning the poor remains of a stately Cathedral, demolished in Knox's reformation, and now only to be imaged by tracing its foundation and contemplating the little ruins that are left. Here was once a religious house. Two of the vaults or cellars of the Subprior are yet entire. In one of them lives an old Woman who claims an hereditary residence in it, boasting that her husband was the sixth tenant of this gloomy mansion in a lineal descent, and claiming by her marriage with this Lord of the cavern, an alliance with the Bruces. Mr. Boswel staid a while to interrogate her, because he understood her language. She told him, that she and her Cat lived together; that she had two sons somewhere, who might perhaps be dead; that when there were quality in the town, notice was taken of her; and that now she was neglected, but did not trouble them. Her habitation contained all that she had, her turf for fire was laid in one place, and her balls of coaldust in another, but her bed seemed to be clean. Boswel asked her if she never heard any noises, but she could tell him of nothing supernatural, though she sometimes wandered in the night among the graves and ruins, only she had some notice by dreams of the death of her relations.

We then viewed the remains of a Castle on the margin of the sea, in which the Archbishops resided, and in which Cardinal Beatoun was killed.

The Professors, who happened to be resident in the vacation, made a publick dinner, and treated us very kindly and respectfully. The⟨y⟩ shewed us their Colleges in one of which there is a library, that for luminousness and elegance may vie at least with the new edifice at Streatham. But Learning seems not to prosper among them, one of their Colleges has been lately alienated, and one of their churches lately deserted. An experiment was made of planting a shrubbery in the church, but it did not thrive.

Why the place should thus fall to decay I know not, for Education, such as is here to be had, is sufficiently cheap. Their term or as they call it their session lasts seven months in the year which the students of the highest rank and greatest expence may pass here for twenty pounds in which are included, Board, Lodging, Books, and the continual instruction of three Professors.

* * *

21 We travelled towards Aberdeen, another University, and in the way dined at Lord Monbodo's, the Scotch Judge who has lately written a strange book about the origin of Language, in which he traces Monkeys up to Men, and says that in some countries the human species have tails like other beasts. He enquired for these longtailed Men of Banks, and was not well pleased, that they had not been found in all his peregrination. He talked nothing of this to me, and I hope, we parted friends, for we agreed pretty well, only we differed in adjusting the claims of merit between a Shopkeeper of London, and a Savage of the American wildernesses. Our opinions were, I think, maintained on both sides without full conviction; Monbodo declared boldly for the Savage, and I perhaps for that reason sided with the Citizen.

We came late to Aberdeen, where I found my dear Mistress's Letter, and learned that all our little people, were happily recovered of the Measles. Every part of your letter was pleasing. I am glad that the presents are made, and that Mr. Perkins is sent to Ireland, and sent with full powers both by my Master and you. I do not well understand the question of the tithes, if you can follow Mr. Robson's advice without open War upon your unkle, it will be best to do it; but it would be wrong to raise new quarrels for a small matter.

There are two cities of the name of Aberdeen. The old town built about a mile inland, once the see of a Bishop, which contains the King's College, and the remains of the Cathedral, and the new town which stands for the sake of trade, upon a firth or arm of the sea, so that ships rest against the Key.

The two cities have their separate Magistrates, and the two Colleges are in effect two Universities which confer degrees independently on each other.

New Aberdeen is a large town, built almost wholly of that Granite which is used for the new pavement in London, which, hard as it is, they square with very little difficulty. Here I first saw the women in plaids. The plaid makes at once a hood and cloak without cutting or sewing, merely by the manner of drawing the opposite sides over the Shoulders. The Maids at the Inns run over the house barefoot, and children, not dressed in rags, go without shoes or stockings. Shoes are indeed not yet in universal use they came late into this country. One of ⟨the⟩ Professors told us, as we were mentioning a fort built by Cromwel, that the Country owed much of its present industry to Cromwel's soldiers. They taught us said he, to raise cabbage, and make shoes. How they lived without shoes may yet be seen, but in the passage through villages, it seems to him that surveys their gardens, that when they had not cabbage they had nothing.

Education is here of the same price as at St. Andrews only the session is but from the first of November to the first of April. The academical buildings, seem rather to advance than decline. They shewed their libraries which were not very splendid, but some manuscripts were so exquisitely penned, that I wished my dear Mistress to have seen them.

I had an unexpected pleasure by finding an old acquaintance, now professor of physick in the King's College. We were on both sides glad of the interview, having not seen nor perhaps thought on one another for many years. But we had no emulation, nor had either of us risen to the other's envy, and our old kindness was easily renewed. I hope We shall never try the effect of so long an absence, and that I shall always be

Madam Your most humble servant

Sam: Johnson

5. Dearest Madam

I am so vexed at the necessity of sending yesterday so short a Letter that I purpose to get a long letter beforehand by writing something every day, which I may the more easily do, as a cold makes me now too deaf to take the usual pleasure in conversation. Lady Macleod is very kind to me, and the place at which we now are, is equal in strength of situation, in the wildness of the adjacent country, and in the plenty and elegance of the domestick entertainment, to a Castle in Gothick romances. The sea with a little Island is before us, cascades play within view. Close to the house is the formidable skeleton of an old Castle probably Danish; and the whole mass of building stands upon a protuberance of rock, inaccessible till of late but by a pair of stairs on the sea side, and secure in ancient times against any Enemy that was likely to invade the kingdom of Skie. Macleod has offered me an Island, if it were not too far off I should hardly refuse it; my Island would be pleasanter than Brighthelmston, if you and Master could come to it, but I cannot think it pleasant to live quite alone. Oblitusque meorum, obliviscendus et illis. That I should be elated by the dominion of an Island to forgetfulness of my friends at Streatham, and I hope never to deserve that they should be willing to forget me.

It has happened that I have been often recognized in my journey where I did not expect it. At Aberdeen I found one of my acquaintance Professor of Physick. Turning aside to dine with a country Gentleman, I was owned at a table by one who had seen me at a Philosophical Lecture. At Macdonald's I was claimed by a Naturalist, who wanders about the Islands to pick up curiosities, and I had once in London attracted the notice of Lady Macleod. I will now go on with my Account.

The Highland Girl made tea, and looked and talked not inelegantly. Her Father was by no means an ignorant or a weak man. There were books in the cottage, among which were some volumes of Prideaux's Connexion. This man's conversation we were glad of while we staid. He had been *out* as they call it, in forty five, and still retained his old opinions. He was going to America, because his rent was raised beyond what he thought himself able to pay.

At night our beds were made, but we had some difficulty in persuading ourselves to lye down in them, though we had put on our own sheets. At last we ventured, and I slept very soundly, in the vale called Glenmorison amidst the rocks and mountains. Next morning our Landlord liked us so well, that he walked some miles with us for our company through a country so wild and barren that the proprietor does not with all his pressure upon his tenants raise more than four hundred a year from near an hundred square miles, or sixty thousand acres. He let us know that he had forty head of black cattle, an hundred Goats, and [and] an hundred sheep upon a farm which he remembred let at five pounds a year, but for which he now paid twenty. He told us some stories of their march into England. At last he left us, and we went forward, winding among mountains sometimes green and sometimes naked, commonly so steep as not easily to be climbed by the greatest vigour and activity. Our way was often crossed by little rivulets, and we were entertained with small streams trickling from the rocks, which after heavy rains must be tremendous torrents.

About noon, we came to a small glen, so they call a valley, which compared with other places appeared rich and fertile. Here our Guides desired us to stop that the horses might graze, for the journey was very laborious, and no more grass would be found. We made no difficulty of compliance, and I sat down to take notes on a green bank, with a small stream running at my feet, in the midst of savage solitude, with Mountains before me, and on either hand covered with heath. I looked round me, and wondered that I was not more affected, but the mind is not at all times equally ready to be put in motion. If my Mistress, and Master, and Queeny had been there we should have produced some reflections among us either poetical or philosophical, for though *Solitude* be *the nurse of woe*, conversation is often the parent of remarks and discoveries.

In about an hour we remounted, and persued our journey.
The lake by which we had travelled from some time ended in a
river, which we passed by a bridge and came to another Glen
with a collection of huts, called Auknashealds, the huts were
generally built of clods of earth held together by the inter-
texture of vegetable fibres, of which earth there are great levels
in Scotland which they call mosses. Moss in Scotland, is Bog in
Ireland, and Moss trooper is Bog trotter. There was however
one hut built of loose stones piled up with great thickness into
a strong though not solid wall. From this house we obtained
some great pails of milk, and having brought bread with us,
were very liberally regaled. The Inhabitants, a very coarse
tribe, ignorant of any language but Earse, gathered so fast
about us, that if we had not had Highlanders with us, they
might have caused more alarm than pleasure. They are called
the clan of Macrae.

We have been told that nothing gratified the Highlanders
so much as snuff and tobacco, and had accordingly stored ourselves with both at fort Augustus. Boswel opened his treasure
and gave them each a piece of tobacco roll. We had more
bread than we could eat for the present, and were more liberal
than provident. Boswel cut it in slices and gave each of them
an opportunity of tasting wheaten bread for the first time. I then
got some halfpence for a shilling and made up the deficiencies
of Boswels distribution, who had given some money among the
children. We then directed that the mistress of the stone house
should be asked what we must pay her, she who perhaps had
never sold any thing but cattle before, knew not, I believe, well
what to ask, and referred herself to us. We obliged her to make
some demand, and our Highlanders settled the account with
her at a shilling. One of the men advised her, with the cunning
that clowns never can be without, to ask more but she said that
a shilling was enough. We gave her half a crown and she offered
part of it again. The Macraes were so well pleased with our
behaviour, that they declared it the best day they had seen
since the time of the old Laird of MacLeod, who I suppose,
like us, stopped in their valley, as he was travelling to Skie.

We were mentioning this view of the Highlander's life at
Macdonald's, and mentioning the Macraes with some degree

of pity, when a Highland Lady informed us, that we might spare our tenderness, for she doubted not, but the Woman who supplied us with milk, was Mistress of thirteen or fourteen milch cows.

I cannot forbear to interrupt my Narrative. Boswel, with some of his troublesome kindness, has informed this family, and reminded me that the eighteenth of September is my birthday. The return of my Birthday, if I remember it, fills with me thoughts which it seems to be the general care of humanity to escape. I can now look back upon threescore and four years, in which little has been done, and little has been enjoyed, a life diversified by misery, spent part in the sluggishness of penury, and part under the violence of pain, in gloomy discontent, or importunate distress. But perhaps I am better than I should have been, if I had been less afflicted. With this I will try to be content.

In proportion as there is less pleasure in retrospective considerations the mind is more disposed to wander forward into futurity, but at sixty four what promises, however liberal of imaginary good, can Futurity venture to make. Yet something will be always promised, and some promises will always be credited. I am hoping, and I am praying that I may live better in the time to come, whether long or short, than I have yet lived, and in the solace of that hope endeavour to repose. Dear Queeney's day is next, I hope, she at sixty four will have less to regret.

I will now complain no more, but tell my Mistress of my travels.

After we left the Macraes, we travelled on through a country like that which we passed in the morning, the highlands are very uniform, for there is little variety in universal barrenness. The rocks however are not all naked, some have grass on their sides, and Birches and Alders on their tops, and in the vallies are often broad and clear streams which have little depth, and commonly run very quick. The channels are made by the violence of wintry floods, the quickness of the stream is in proportion to the declivity of the descent, and the breadth of the channel makes the water shallow in a dry season.

There are Red Deer and Roebucks in the mountains, but we

found only Goats in the road, and had very little entertainment as we travelled either for the eye or ear. There are, I fancy, no singing birds in the Highlands.

Towards Night we came to a very formidable Hill called Rattiken, which we climbed with more difficulty than we had yet experienced, and at last came to Glanelg a place on the Seaside opposite to Skie. We were by this time weary and disgusted, nor was our humour much mended, by an inn, which, though it was built with lime and slate, the highlander's description of a house which he thinks magnificent, had neither wine, bread, eggs, nor any thing that we could eat or drink. When we were taken up stairs, a dirty fellow bounced out of the bed in which one of us was to lie. Boswel blustered, but nothing could be got. At last a Gentleman in the Neighbourhood who heard of our arrival sent us rum and white sugar. Boswel was now provided for in part, and the Landlord prepared some mutton chops, which we could not eat, and killed two Hens, of which Boswel made his servant broil a limb, with what effect I know not. We had a lemon, and a piece of bread, which supplied me with my supper.

When the repast was ended, we began to deliberate upon bed. Mrs Boswel had warned us that we should *catch something*, and had given us Sheets for our security; for Sir Alexander and Lady Macdonald, she said, came back from Skie, so scratching themselves—. I thought sheets a slender defence, against the confederacy with which we were threatned, and by this time our highlanders had found a place where they could get some hay; I ordered hay to be laid thick upon the bed, and slept upon it in my great coat. Boswel laid sheets upon his hay, and reposed in Linen like a Gentleman. The horses were turned out to grass, with a man to watch them. The hill Ratiken, and the inn at Glanelg, are the only things of which we or travellers yet more delicate, could find any pretensions to complain.

Sept. 2.   I rose rustling from the hay, and went to tea, which I forget whether we found or brought. We saw the Isle of Skie before us darkening the horizon with its rocky coast. A boat was procured, and we launched into one of the Straits of the Atlantick Ocean. We had a passage of about twelve miles to the point where Sir Alexander resided, having come from his

Seat in the midland part, to a small house on the shore, as we believe, that he might with less reproach entertain us meanly. If he aspired to meanness his retrograde ambition was completely gratified, but he did not succeed equally in escaping reproach. He had no cook, nor, I suppose, much provision, nor had the Lady the common decencies of her tea table. We picked up our Sugar with our fingers. Boswel was very angry, and reproached him with his improper parsimony. I did not much reflect upon the conduct of a man with whom I was not likely to converse as long at any other time.

You will now expect that I should give you some account of the Isle of Skie, of which though I have been twelve days upon it, I have little to say. It is an Island perhaps fifty miles long, so much indented by inlets of the Sea, that there is no part of it removed from the water more than six miles. No part that I have seen is plain you are always climbing or descending, and every step is upon rock or mire. A walk upon plowed ground in England is a dance upon carpets, compared to the toilsome drudgery, of wandering in Skie. There is neither town nor village in the Island, nor have I seen any house but Macleod's, that is not much below your habitation at Brighthelmston. In the mountains there are Stags and Roebucks, but no hares and few rabbits, nor have I seen any thing that interested me, as Zoologist, except an Otter, bigger than I thought an otter could have been.

You are perhaps imagining that I am withdrawn from the gay and the busy world into regions of peace and pastoral felicity, and am enjoying the reliques of the golden age; that I am surveying Nature's magnificence from a mountain, or remarking her minuter beauties on the flowery bank of a winding rivulet, that I am invigorating myself in the sunshine, or delighting my imagination with being hidden from [from] the invasion of human evils and human passions, in the darkness of a Thicket, that I am busy in gathering shells and pebbles on the Shore, or contemplative on a rock, from which I look upon the water and consider how many waves are rolling between me and Streatham.

The use of travelling is to regulate imagination by reality, and instead of thinking how things may be, to see them as they are. Here are mountains which I should once have climbed, but the (sic) climb steeps is now very laborious, and to descend them dangerous, and I am now content with knowing that by a scrambling up a rock, I shall only see other rocks, and a wider circuit of barren desolation. Of streams we have here a sufficient number, but they murmur not upon pebbles but upon rocks; of flowers, if Chloris herself were here, I could present her only with the bloom of Heath. Of Lawns and Thickets, he must read, that would know them, for here is little sun and no shade. On the sea I look from my window, but am not much tempted to the shore for since I came to this Island, almost every Breath of air has been a storm, and what is worse, a storm with all its severity, but without its magnificence, for the sea is here so broken into channels, that there is not a sufficient volume of water either for lofty surges, or loud roar.

On Sept. 6. We left Macdonald, to visit Raarsa, the Island which I have already mentioned. We were to cross part of Skie on horseback, a mode of travelling very uncomfortable, for the road is so narrow, where any road can be found that only one can go, and so craggy that the attention can never be remitted, it allows therefore neither the gayety of conversation nor the laxity of solitude, nor has it in itself the amusement of much variety, as it affords only all the possible transpositions of Bog, Rock, and Rivulet. Twelve Miles, by computation, make a reasonable journey for a day.

At night we came to a tenants house of the first rank of tenants where we were entertained better than the Landlords. There were books, both English and Latin. Company gathered about us, and we heard some talk of the Second sight and some talk of the events of forty five, a year which will not soon be forgotten among the Islanders. The next day we were confined by a storm, the company, I think, encreased and our entertainment was not only hospitable but elegant. At night, a Minister's sister in very fine Brocade, sung Earse songs. I wished to know the meaning, but the Highlanders are not much used to scholastick questions, and no translation could be obtained.

Next day, Sept. 8. The weather allowed us to depart, a good boat was provided us, and we went to Raarsa, under the conduct of Mr Malcolm Macleod, a Gentleman who conducted

Prince Charles through the mountains in his distresses. The prince, he says, was more active than himself, they were at least one night, without any shelter.

The wind blew enough to give the boat a kind of dancing agitation, and in about three or four hours we arrived at Raarsa, where we were met by the Laird and his friends upon the Shore. Raarsa, for such is his title, is Master of two Islands, upon the smaller of which, called Rona, he has only flocks and herds. Rona gives title to his eldest Son. The money which he raises by rent from all his dominions which contain at least fifty thousand acres, is not believed to exceed two hundred and fifty pounds, but as he keeps a large farm in his own hands, he sells every year great numbers of cattle which he adds to his revenue, and his table is furnished from the Farm and from the sea with little expence, except for those things this country does not produce, and of those he is very liberal. The Wine circulates vigorously, and the tea and Chocolate and Coffee, however they are got [got] are always at hand.

I am Madam Your most obedient servant
Skie. Sept. 21. 1773   Sam: Johnson
We are this morning trying to get out of Skie.

6. . . . Sir Allan, to whom the whole region was well known, told us of a very remarkable cave, to which he would show us the way. We had been disappointed already by one cave, and were not much elevated by the expectation of another.

It was yet better to see it, and we stopped at some rocks on the coast of Mull. The mouth is fortified by vast fragments of stone, over which we made our way, neither very nimbly, nor very securely. The place, however, well repaid our trouble. The bottom, as far as the flood rushes in, was encumbered with large pebbles, but as we advanced was spread over with smooth sand. The breadth is about forty-five feet: the roof rises in an arch, almost regular, to a height which we could not measure; but I think it about thirty feet.

This part of our curiosity was nearly frustrated; for though we went to see a cave, and knew that caves are dark, we forgot to carry tapers, and did not discover our omission till we were wakened by our wants. Sir Allan then sent one of the boatmen into the country, who soon returned with one little candle. We were thus enabled to go forward, but could not venture far. Having passed inward from the sea to a great depth, we found on the right hand a narrow passage, perhaps not more than six feet wide, obstructed by great stones, over which we climbed and came into a second cave, in breadth twenty-five feet. The air in this apartment was very warm, but not oppressive, nor loaded with vapours. Our light showed no tokens of a feculent or corrupted atmosphere. Here was a square stone, called, as we are told, Fingal's Table.

If we had been provided with torches, we should have proceeded in our search, though we had already gone as far as any former adventurer, except some who are reported never to have returned; and, measuring our way back, we found it more than a hundred and sixty yards, the eleventh part of a mile.

Our measures were not critically exact, having been made with a walking pole, such as it is convenient to carry in these rocky countries, of which I guessed the length by standing against it. In this there could be no great errour, nor do I much doubt but the Highlander, whom we employed, reported the number right. More nicety however is better, and no man should travel unprovided with instruments for taking heights and distances.

There is yet another cause of errour not always easily surmounted, though more dangerous to the veracity of itinerary narratives, than imperfect mensuration. An observer deeply impressed by any remarkable spectacle, does not suppose, that the traces will soon vanish from his mind, and having commonly no great convenience for writing, defers the description to a time of more leisure, and better accommodation.

He who has not made the experiment, or who is not accustomed to require rigorous accuracy from himself, will scarcely believe how much a few hours take from certainty of knowledge, and distinctness of imagery; how the succession of objects will be broken, how separate parts will be confused, and how many particular features and discriminations will be compressed and conglobated into one gross and general idea.

To this dilatory notation must be imputed the false relations of travellers, where there is no imaginable motive to deceive.

They trusted to memory, what cannot be trusted safely but to the eye, and told by guess what a few hours before they had known with certainty. Thus it was that Wheeler and Spen described with irreconcilable contrariety things which they surveyed together, and which both undoubtedly designed to show as they saw them.

When we had satisfied our curiosity in the cave, so far as our penury of light permitted us, we clambered again to our boats, and proceeded along the coast of Mull to a headland, called Atun, remarkable for the columnar form of the rocks, which rise in a series of pilasters, with a degree of regularity, which Sir Allan thinks not less worthy of curiosity than the shore of Staffa.

Not long after we came to another range of black rocks, which had the appearance of broken pilasters, set one behind another to a great depth. This place was chosen by Sir Allan for our dinner. We were easily accommodated with seats, for the stones were of all heights, and refreshed ourselves and our boatmen, who could have no other rest till we were at Icolmkill.

The evening was now approaching, and we were yet at a considerable distance from the end of our expedition. We could therefore stop no more to make remarks in the way, but set forward with some degree of eagerness. The day soon failed us, and the moon presented a very solemn and pleasing scene. The sky was clear, so that the eye commanded a wide circle: the sea was neither still nor turbulent: the wind neither silent nor loud. We were never far from one coast or another, on which, if the weather had become violent, we could have found shelter, and therefore contemplated at ease the region through which we glided in the tranquillity of the night, and saw now a rock and now an island grow gradually conspicuous and gradually obscure. I committed the fault which I have just been censuring, in neglecting, as we passed, to note the series of this placid navigation.

We were very near an island, called Nun's Island, perhaps from an ancient convent. Here is said to have been dug the stone that was used in the buildings of Icolmkill. Whether it is now inhabited we could not stay to inquire.

At last we came to Icolmkill, but found no convenience for

landing. Our boat could not be forced very near the dry ground, and our Highlanders carried us over the water.

We were now treading that illustrious island, which was once the luminary of the Caledonian regions, whence savage clans and roving barbarians derived the benefits of knowledge, and the blessings of religion. To abstract the mind from all local emotion would be impossible, if it were endeavoured, and would be foolish, if it were possible. Whatever withdraws us from the power of our senses; whatever makes the past, the distant, or the future predominate over the present, advances us in the dignity of thinking beings. Far from me and from my friends, be such frigid philosophy as may conduct us indifferent and unmoved over any ground which has been dignified by wisdom, bravery, or virtue. That man is little to be envied, whose patriotism would not gain force upon the plain of Marathon, or whose piety would not grow warmer among the ruins of Iona.

If Boswell set up Johnson's most memorable journey, and the Oxford-Lichfield-Ashbourne-Birmingham round provided him with his annual holiday, the Thrales were also good providers of travel. They frequently had him to stay at their Brighton house, where he tasted the joys of sea-bathing, and for that matter Streatham, where they made Johnson so welcome that he spoke of it as 'home', was some six miles out of town; since eighteenth-century London was about the size of modern Oxford, this meant that he was well clear of smoke and noise and in a rural atmosphere for long stretches during almost two decades. The Thrales also took Johnson along on two trips: to North Wales in 1774, and to France in 1775. In each case he kept a diary. The French diary is printed by Boswell in the *Life*; the Welsh diary remained in manuscript until long after both Johnson and Boswell were dead; it was first printed in 1816 by a man named Richard Duppa, who had the advantage of knowing Hester Thrale (by that time Hester Piozzi), who gave him much elucidatory information. Boswell, in the *Life*, reports that Johnson made his journey, but knew nothing of the Diary ('I do not find that he kept any journal or notes of what he saw there'). He did not miss very much; Johnson's diary is laconic; a note, places, names, a few impressions. He began his notes on 5 July with 'We left Streatham'; it took the party twenty-three days to get as far as Chester, and on the return journey fifteen days were spent on the somewhat shorter journey home from Shrewsbury. As usual, Johnson was interested in everything he saw, eager to learn, whether the subject was antiquity, literature or the state of life of the inhabitants.

AUG⟨UST⟩ 4.

7. Ruthlan Castle is still a very noble ruin. All the walls still remain so that a compleat platform, and elevations not very imperfect may be taken. It incloses a square of about thirty yards. The middle space was always open. The wall is I believe about thirty feet high very thick, flanked with six round towers each about eighteen feet, or less, in diameter. Only one tower had a chimney, so that here was commodity of living. It was only a place of strength. The Garrison had perhaps tents in the area.

Stapiltons house is pretty⟨;⟩ there are pleasing shades about it, with a constant spring that supplies a cold bath.

We then went to see a cascade, I trudged unwillingly, and was not sorry to find it dry. The water was however turned on, and produced a very striking cataract. They are paid an hundred pounds a year, for permission to divert the stream to the mines. The River for such it may be termed rises from a single spring, which like that of Winifred is covered with a building.

We called then at another house belonging to Mr. Lloyd which made a handsome appearance. This country seems full of very splendid houses.

Mrs. T⟨hrale⟩ lost her purse. She expressed so much uneasiness that I concluded the sum to be very great, but when I heard of only seven guineas, I was glad to find she had so much sensibility of money.

I could not drink this day either coffee or tea after dinner. I know not when I missed before.

AUG⟨UST⟩ 5.

Last night my sleep was remarkably quiet. little flatus. I know not whether by fatigue in walking, or by forbearance of tea. I gave the Ipecacuanha—Vin. Emet. had failed, so had tartar Emet. The Ipec. did but little.

I dined at Mr. Middleton's of Gwaynynog. The house was a Gentlemans house below the second rate, perhaps below the third⟨,⟩ built of stone roughly cut. The rooms were low, and the passage above stairs gloomy, but the furniture was good. The table was well supplied, except that the fruit was bad. It was truly the dinner of a country Gentleman. Two tables were filled with company not inelegant. After dinner the talk was of preserving the Welsh language. I offered them a scheme. Poor Evan Evans was mentioned as incorrigibly addicted to strong drink. Worthington was commended. Middleton is the only man who in Wales has talked to me of literature. I wish he were truly zealous. I recommended the republication of David ap Rhees's Welsh Grammar.

Two sheets of Hebrides came to me for correction to day, F. G.

AUGUST 6.

Καθ⟨αρσις⟩ δρ⟨αστικὴ⟩. I corrected the two sheets. My sleep last night was disturbed.

Washing at Chester, and here—5s. 1d.

I did not read. Atterbury's version a heap of barbarity. The καθ did not much, but I hope, enough.

I saw to day more of the outhouses at Lleuwenny. It is in the whole a very spacious house.

AUGUST 14.

At Botfarry I heard the second Lesson read, and the sermon preached in Welsh. The text was pronounced both in Welsh and English. The sound of the Welsh in a continued discourse is not unpleasant.

Βρῶσις ὀλίγη. Καθ⟨αρσις⟩ α⟨νευ⟩ φ⟨άρμακων⟩

The Letter of Chrysostom against transubstantiation. Erasmus to the Nuns, full of mystic notions, and allegories.

AUG⟨UST⟩ 15.
Καθ. Imbecillitas genuum non sine aliquantulo doloris inter ambulandum, quem a prandio magis sensi.

AUG⟨UST⟩ 18.
We left Llewenni, and went forwards on our Journey. We came to Abergeler a mean town in which little but Welsh is spoken, and Divine Service is seldom performed in English. Our way then lay by the sea side, at the foot of a Mountain called Penman ross. Here the way was so steep that we walked on the lower edge of the hill to meet the Coach that went upon a road higher on the hill. Our walk was not long nor unpleasant, the longer I walk the less I feel its inconvenience. As I grow warm my breath mends and I think my limbs grow pliable.

We then came to Conway Ferry, and passed in small boats, with some passengers from the Stage coach, Among whom were an Irish Gentlewoman with two maids and three little children of which the youngest was only a few months old. The tide did not serve the large ferry boat, and therefore our Coach could not very soon follow us. We were therefore to stay at the Inn. It is now the day of the race at Conway and the town was so full of company, that no money could purchase lodging. We were not very readily supplied with cold dinner. We would have stayed at Conway, if we could have found entertainment, for we were afraid of passing Penmanmawr over which lay our way to Bangor but by bright daylight, and the delay of our coach made our departure necessarily late. There was however no stay on any other terms than of sitting up all night.

The poor Irish Lady was still more distressed. Her children wanted rest. She would have been content with one bed, but for a time none could be had. Mrs. T⟨hrale⟩ gave her what help she could. At last two gentlemen were persuaded to yield up their room with two beds, for which she gave half a guinea.

Our coach was at last brought and we set out with some anxiety but we came to Penmanmawr by day light, and found a way lately made, very easy and very safe. It was cut smooth and inclosed between parallel walls. The outer of which secures the ⟨traveller?⟩ from the precipice which is deep and dreadful. This wall is here and there broken by mischievous wantonness.

The inner wall preserves the road from the loose stones which the shatter⟨ed⟩ steeps above it would pour down. That side of the mountain seems to have a surface of loose stones which every accident may crumble. The old road was higher and must have been very formidable. The sea beats at the bottom of the way. At Evening the Moon shone eminently bright, and our thoughts of danger being now past, the rest of our journey was very pleasant. At an hour somewhat late we came to Bangor, where we found a very mean Inn, and had some difficulty to obtain lodging. I lay in a room where the other bed had two men. I had a flatulent night.

AUGUST 19.

We obtained a boat to convey us to Anglesea, and saw Lord Bulkley's house and Beaumaris Castle. I was accosted by Mr Lloyd the Schoolmaster of Beaumaris who had seen me at University College and he with Mr. Roberts the Register of Bangor whose boat we borrowed, accompanied us. Lord Bulkeley's house is very mean, but his garden is spacious and shady, with large trees and smaller interspersed. The walks are strait and cross each other with no variety of plan but they have a pleasing coolness and solemn gloom, and extend to a great length.

The Castle is a mighty pile⟨:⟩ the outward wall has fifteen round towers, besides square towers at the angles. There is then a void space between the wall and the castle, which has an area enclosed with a wall which again has towers larger than those of the outer wall; the towers of the inner castle are I think eight. There is likewise a chapel entire, bui⟨l⟩t upon an arch as I suppose, and beautifully arch⟨ed⟩ with a stone roof which is yet unbroken. The entrance into the Chapel is about eight or nine feet high, and was I suppose, higher when there was no rubbish in the area.

This castle corresponds with all the representations of romancing narratives. Here is not wanting the private passage, the dark cavity, the deep dungeon or the lofty tower. We did not discover the well. This is ⟨the⟩ most complete view that I have yet had of an old castle. It had a moat.

The towers.

We returned to Bangor.

AUGUST 20.

We went by water from Bangor to Caernarvon, where we met Paoli and Sir Thomas Wynne. Meeting by chance with one Troughton, an intelligent and loquacious wanderer, Mr. T⟨hrale⟩ invited him to din⟨n⟩er. He attended us to the Castle, an Edifice of stupendous magnitude and strength. It has in it all that we observed at Beaumaris, of much greater dimensions; many of the smaller rooms floored with stone are entire; of the larger rooms, the beams and planks are all lost; this is ⟨the⟩ state of all buildings left to time. We mounted the Eagle tower by 169 steps each of ten inches. We did not find the well, nor did I trace the moat, but moats there were I believe to all castles on the plain, which not only hindred access, but prevented mines. We saw but a very small part of this mighty ruin. And in all these old buildings, the subterraneous works are concealed by the rubbish. To survey this place would take much time. I did not think there had been such buildings. It surpassed my Ideas.

⟨AUGUST⟩ 24.

We went to see Bodvil. Mrs. T⟨hrale⟩ remembred the rooms, and wandred over them, with recollection of her childhood. This species of pleasure is always melancholy. The walk was cut down, and the pond was dry. Nothing was better.

We surveyed the churches, which are mean and neglected to a degree scarcely imaginable. They have no pavement, and the earth is full of holes, the seats are rude benches. The altars have no rails; one of them has a breach in the roof. On the desk I think of each lay a Folio Welsh Bible of the black letter, which the Curate cannot easily read. Mr. T⟨hrale⟩ proposes to beautify the Churches, and, if he prospers, will probably restore the tithes. The two parishes are Llangynnidle and Tydweilliog. The Methodists are here very prevalent. A better church will impress the people with more reverence of public Worship.

Mrs. Thrale visited a house where she had been used to drink milk, which was left with an estate of 200 l a year, by one Lloyd to a married woman who lived with him.

We went to Pwlhely a mean old town at the extremity of the country. Here we bought something to remember the place.

The following year, Johnson had his first and only experience of Continental European travel, when the Thrales took him to France. It was not a particularly ambitious trip, the main purpose being to see Paris, but it put Johnson in France for eight weeks, and he found much to interest him. His diary, long familiar from Boswell's pages, is still worth re-reading in the context of his travels in general. Here are a few extracts.

8. 'Oct. 19. Thursday. At Court, we saw the apartments;—the King's bed-chamber and council-chamber extremely splendid.—Persons of all ranks in the external rooms through which the family passes;—servants and masters.—Brunet with us the second time.

'The introductor came to us;—civil to me.—Presenting.—I had scruples.—Not necessary.—We went and saw the King and Queen at dinner.—We saw the other ladies at dinner.—Madame Elizabeth, with the Princess of Guimené.—At night we went to a comedy. I neither saw nor heard. Drunken women.—Mrs. Th. preferred one to the other.

'Oct. 20. Friday. We saw the Queen mount in the forest.—Brown habit; rode aside: one lady rode aside.—The Queen's horse light grey;—martingale.—She galloped.—We then went to the apartments, and admired them.—Then wandered through the palace.—In the passages, stalls and shops.—Painting in Fresco by a great master, worn out.—We saw the King's horses and dogs.—The dogs almost all English.—Degenerate.

'The horses not much commended.—The stables cool; the kennel filthy.

'At night the ladies went to the opera. I refused but should have been welcome.

'The King fed himself with his left hand as we.

'Saturday, 21. In the night I got round.—We came home to Paris.—I think we did not see the chapel.—Tree broken by the wind.—The French chairs made all of boards painted.

'N. Soldiers at the court of justice.—Soldiers not amenable to the magistrates.—Dijon woman.

'Faggots in the palace.—Everything slovenly, except in the

chief rooms.—Trees in the roads, some tall, none old, many very young and small.

'Women's saddles seem ill made. Queen's bridle woven with silver.—Tags to strike the horse.

'Sunday, Oct. 22. To Versailles, a mean town. Carriages of business passing.—Mean shops against the wall.—Our way lay through Sêve, where the China manufacture.—Wooden bridge at Sêve, in the way to Versailles.—The palace of great extent.—The front long; I saw it not perfectly.—The Menagerie.—Cygnets dark; their black feet; on the ground; tame.—Halcyons, or gulls.—Stag and hind, young.—Aviary, very large: the net, wire.—Black stag of China, small.—Rhinoceros, the horn broken and pared away, which, I suppose, will grow; the basis, I think, four inches 'cross; the skin folds like loose cloth doubled over his body, and cross his hips; a vast animal, though young; as big, perhaps, as four oxen.—The young elephant, with his tusks just appearing.—The brown bear put out his paws;—all very tame.—The lion.—The tigers I did not well view.—The camel, or dromedary with two bunches called the Huguin, taller than any horse.—Two camels with one bunch.—Among the birds was a pelican, who being let out, went to a fountain, and swam about to catch fish. His feet well webbed: he dipped his head, and turned his long bill sidewise. He caught two or three fish, but did not eat them.

'Trianon is a kind of retreat appendant to Versailles. It has an open portico; the pavement, and, I think, the pillars of marble.—There are many rooms, which I do not distinctly remember.—A table of porphyry, about five feet long, and between two or three broad, given to Louis XIV. by the Venetian State.—In the council-room almost all that was not door or window, was, I think, looking-glass.—Little Trianon is a small palace like a gentleman's house.—The upper floor paved with brick.—Little Vienne.—The court is ill paved.—The rooms at the top are small, fit to sooth the imagination with privacy. In the front of Versailles are small basons of water on the terrace, and other basons, I think, below them. There are little courts.—The great gallery is wainscotted with mirrours, not very large, but joined by frames. I suppose the large plates were not yet made.—The play-house was very large.—The chapel I do not remember if we saw.—We saw one chapel, but I am not certain whether there or at Trianon.—The foreign office paved with bricks. The dinner half a Louis each, and, I think, a Louis over.—Money given at Menagerie, three livres; at palace, six livres.

*   *   *

'We then went to Sans-terre, a brewer. He brews with about as much malt as Mr. Thrale, and sells his beer at the same price, though he pays no duty for malt, and little more than half as much for beer. Beer is sold retail at 6d. a bottle. He brews 4,000 barrels a year. There are seventeen brewers in Paris, of whom none is supposed to brew more than he;—reckoning them at 3,000 each, they make 51,000 a year.—They make their malt, for malting is here no trade.

'The moat of the Bastile is dry.

'Oct. 24. Tuesday. We visited the King's library.—I saw the *Speculum humanæ Salvationis*, rudely printed, with ink, sometimes pale, sometimes black; part supposed to be with wooden types, and part with pages cut in boards. The Bible, supposed to be older than that of Mentz, in 62; it has no date; it is supposed to have been printed with wooden types.—I am in doubt; the print is large and fair, in two folios. Another book was shewn me, supposed to have been printed with wooden types;—I think, *Durandi Sanctuarium* in 58. This is inferred from the difference of form sometimes seen in the same letter, which might be struck with different puncheons.—The regular similitude of most letters proves better that they are metal.—I saw nothing but the *Speculum* which I had not seen, I think, before.

'Thence to the Sorbonne.—The library very large, not in lattices like the King's. *Marbone* and *Durandi*, q. collection 14 vol. *Scriptores de rebus Gallicis*, many folios.—*Histoire Genealogique of France*, 9 vol.—*Gallia Christiana*, the first edition, 4to. the last, f. 12 vol.—The Prior and Librarian dined [with us] :—I waited on them home.—Their garden pretty, with covered walks, but small; yet may hold many students. The Doctors of the Sorbonne are all equal;—choose those who succeed to vacancies.—Profit little.

'Oct. 25. Wednesday. I went with the Prior to St. Cloud, to see Dr. Hooke.—We walked round the palace, and had some talk.—I dined with our whole company at the Monastery.—In the library, *Beroald*,—*Cymon*,—*Titus*, from Boccace.—*Oratio Proverbialis* to the Virgin, from Petrarch; Falkland to Sandys;—Dryden's Preface to the third vol. of Miscellanies.

* * *

'Hotel—a guinea a day.—Coach, three guineas a week.—Valet de place, three l. a day.—*Avantcoureur*, a guinea a week.—Ordinary dinner, six l. a head.—Our ordinary seems to be about five guineas a day.—Our extraordinary expences, as diversions, gratuities, clothes, I cannot reckon.—Our travelling is ten guineas a day.

'White stockings, 18l. Wig.—Hat.

'Sunday, Oct. 29. We saw the boarding-school,—The *Enfans trouvés*.—A room with about eighty-six children in cradles, as sweet as a parlour.—They lose a third; take in to perhaps more than seven [years old]; put them to trades; pin to them the papers sent with them.—Want nurses.—Saw their chapel.

'Went to St. Eustatia; saw an innumerable company of girls catechised, in many bodies, perhaps 100 to a catechist.—Boys taught at one time, girls at another.—The Sermon; the preacher wears a cap, which he takes off at the name:—his action uniform, not very violent.

'Oct. 30. Monday. We saw the library of St. Germain.—A very noble collection.—*Codex Divinorum Officiorum*, 1459:—a letter, square like that of the *Offices*, perhaps the same.—The *Codex*, by Fust and Gernsheym.—*Meursius*, 12 v. fol.—*Amadis*, in French, 3 v. fol.—Catholicon *sine colophone*, but of 1460.—Two other editions, one by ——————— *Augustin. de Civitate Dei*, without name, date, or place, but of Fust's square letter as it seems.

'I dined with Col. Drumgold; had a pleasing afternoon.

'Some of the books of St. Germain's stand in presses from the wall, like those at Oxford.

'Oct. 31. Tuesday. I lived at the Benedictines; meagre day; soup meagre, herrings, eels, both with sauce; fryed fish; lentils, tasteless in themselves. In the library; where I found *Maffeus's de Historiâ Indicâ: Promontorium flectere, to double the Cape.* I parted very tenderly from the Prior and Friar Wilkes.

France was interesting. But what Johnson really had his eye on was a visit to Italy, a country he had always longed to see. To Johnson as to Milton, Italy was classic ground. He explained to Boswell how he saw the matter (11 April 1776).

9. A journey to Italy was still in his thoughts. He said, 'A man who has not been in Italy, is always conscious of an inferiority, from his not having seen what it is expected a man should see. The grand object of travelling is to see the shores of the Mediterranean. On these shores were the four great Empires of the world; the Assyrian, the Persian, the Grecian, and the Roman.—All our religion, almost all our law, almost all our arts, almost all that sets us above savages, has come to us from the shores of the Mediterranean.'

In this very year, a visit to Italy with the Thrale family was all planned. When the sad death of their little son, Harry, caused the trip to be cancelled, Johnson was undeniably very disappointed. While sincerely sharing in their grief ('I would have gone to the extremity of the earth to have preserved this boy'), he still hoped that the journey might be only postponed and not cancelled; after all, it would be a good anodyne. But the Thrale family never went to Italy; and when, eight years later, the widowed Hester Thrale married a native of the country that had always meant so much to Johnson, and disappeared from his life, the irony was a dark and bitter one.

There is an interesting essay to be written on the theme of 'Johnson in Italy'. Not that he ever got there in the flesh; but he thought much about Italy, studied its literature from classical Latin to the modern vernacular, and had two fairly close Italian friends, Giuseppe Baretti and Francesco Sastres. As a place of the mind, it meant more to Johnson than any country except his own.

Chapter VII

'Thousand Natural Shocks'

Johnson's health was never good. His early attack of scrofula (tuberculosis of the lymph glands) destroyed the sight of one eye and left the other myopic. He also had troubles of nervous, or neuro-cerebral, origin. He walked clumsily and was almost incapable of sitting still; his limbs twitched and he made frequent convulsive movements.

With all this he was large and strong, and until the onset of dropsy and cardiac asthma in his seventies, his health was not such as to forbid normal activity. He walked long distances in early manhood; until well into middle age he rode a horse tolerably well, and swam in the sea when the Thrales took him to Brighthelmston. In 1771 he noted in a letter to Hester Thrale (7 July), 'The old Rheumatism is come again into my face and mouth, but nothing yet to the lumbago.' Still, he was sixty-two years old, an age at which aches and pains begin to be usual. All in all, if his afflictions had been only physical, we might say that his lot was not much worse than most people's. But his mind was afflicted more grievously than his body.

Johnson's brain was capable of an almost unbelievable degree of concentration. He could read rapidly through a book, assimilate its contents and never forget them. At other times the grip of his mind relaxed almost completely, and he was incapable of any effort. These periods of inertia were usually accompanied by a deep depression.

The first onset of this depression came at a time when he had adequate reasons, outside his own mind, to feel depressed: after coming down from Oxford, and before finding any kind of employment. The family background was sombre, the future uncertain, his spirits dashed by the enforced abandonment of his formal education. His faithful friend Edmund Hector put him up in Birmingham and gave him crucial help; but, though Johnson struggled onto his feet, he was never permanently cured of his depression. In 1756 he wrote to Hector (7 October), 'from that kind of melancholy indisposition which I had when we lived together at Birmingham I have never been free, but have always had it operating against my health and my life with more or less violence.'

To think of Johnson's concern with mental illness is to think of those moving chapters in his fable *Rasselas* (roughly, Chapters 40 to 46) in which he introduces a character, 'the astronomer', who has become deranged through solitude and intense study, and whose mind has fallen prey to a delusion. After long hesitation, he confides to the philosopher Imlac that he is at breaking point under an intolerable responsibility. Now, he will at last bring himself to confess this responsibility to another human being. For the last five years, he has had it in his power to control the weather; to bring floods to one part of the earth, drought to another, to produce plenty or famine.

Rasselas, resisting any temptation to scoff at the unfortunate man, gravely asks whether he is quite sure of this. Of course, answers the astronomer impatiently; as a scientist, a man accustomed to weigh evidence, he refused to admit the truth until it was overwhelmingly forced on him. (Victims of delusion always talk like this.) The astronomer goes on to say that one problem torments him above all others. He is old; in the course of nature his death cannot be far away; what will happen when the sun and the rain have no master? He must find someone to take over his function, which as he rightly says is far more important than that of any mere king or emperor; and at last, in the direct and seasoned Imlac, he has found the right man.

Imlac, still proceeding softly, accepts the responsibility and promises to rule the seasons justly. The astronomer, in a delicious touch, cautions him against trying to bring about any sweeping changes; the system on the whole works well enough as it is, and if he tries to benefit one region he will have to rob another; 'do not . . . indulge thy pride by innovation.' Imlac gravely promises not to, and then returns to his companions to tell them the man's sad story and consider how to help him.

1. The prince heard this narration with very serious regard, but the princess smiled, and Pekuah convulsed herself with laughter. 'Ladies,' said Imlac, 'to mock the heaviest of human afflictions is neither charitable nor wise. Few can attain this man's knowledge, and few practise his virtues; but all may suffer his calamity. Of the uncertainties of our present state, the most dreadful and alarming is the uncertain continuance of reason.'

The princess was recollected, and the favourite was abashed. Rasselas, more deeply affected, enquired of Imlac whether he thought such maladies of the mind frequent, and how they were contracted.

THE DANGEROUS PREVALENCE OF IMAGINATION

'Disorders of intellect', answered Imlac, 'happen much more often than superficial observers will easily believe. Perhaps, if we speak with rigorous exactness, no human mind is in its right state. There is no man whose imagination does not sometimes predominate over his reason, who can regulate his attention wholly by his will, and whose ideas will come and go at his command. No man will be found in whose mind airy notions do not sometimes tyrannise, and force him to hope or fear beyond the limits of sober probability. All power of fancy over reason is a degree of insanity; but while this power is such as we can control and repress it is not visible to others, nor considered as any depravation of the mental faculties: it is not pronounced madness but when it comes ungovernable, and apparently influences speech or action.

'To indulge the power of fiction, and send imagination out upon the wing, is often the sport of those who delight too much in silent speculation. When we are alone we are not always busy; the labour of excogitation is too violent to last long; the ardour of enquiry will sometimes give way to idleness or satiety.

He who has nothing external that can divert him must find pleasure in his own thoughts, and must conceive himself what he is not; for who is pleased with what he is? He then expatiates in boundless futurity, and culls from all imaginable conditions that which for the present moment he should most desire, amuses his desires with impossible enjoyments, and confers upon his pride unattainable dominion. The mind dances from scene to scene, unites all pleasures in all combinations, and riots in delights which nature and fortune, with all their bounty, cannot bestow.

'In time some particular train of ideas fixes the attention; all other intellectual gratifications are rejected; the mind, in weariness or leisure, recurs constantly to the favourite conception, and feasts on the luscious falsehood whenever she is offended with the bitterness of truth. By degrees the reign of fancy is confirmed; she grows first imperious, and in time despotic. Then fictions begin to operate as realities, false opinions fasten upon the mind, and life passes in dreams of rapture or of anguish.

'This, Sir, is one of the dangers of solitude, which the hermit has confessed not always to promote goodness and the astronomer's misery has proved to be not always propitious to wisdom.'

'I will no more', said the favourite, 'imagine myself the queen of Abyssinia. I have often spent the hours which the princess gave to my own disposal in adjusting ceremonies and regulating the court; I have repressed the pride of the powerful, and granted the petitions of the poor; I have built new palaces in more happy situations, planted groves upon the tops of mountains, and have exulted in the beneficence of royalty, till, when the princess entered, I had almost forgotten to bow down before her.'

'And I', said the princess, 'will not allow myself any more to play the shepherdess in my waking dreams. I have often soothed my thoughts with the quiet and innocence of pastoral employments, till I have in my chamber heard the winds whistle and the sheep bleat; sometimes freed the lamb entangled in the thicket, and sometimes with my crook encountered the wolf. I have a dress like that of the village maids, which I put on to help my imagination, and a pipe on which I play softly, and suppose myself followed by my flocks.'

'I will confess', said the prince, 'an indulgence of fantastic delight more dangerous than yours. I have frequently endeavoured to image the possibility of a perfect government, by which all wrong should be restrained, all vice reformed, and all the subjects preserved in tranquillity and innocence. This thought produced innumerable schemes of reformation, and dictated many useful regulations and salutary edicts. This has been the sport, and sometimes the labour, of my solitude; and I start, when I think with how little anguish I once supposed the death of my father and my brothers.'

'Such', says Imlac, 'are the effects of visionary schemes: when we first form them we know them to be absurd, but familiarise them by degrees, and in time lose sight of their folly.'

The delusions of the astronomer, like the disillusion and *accidie* of the hermit in Chapter XXI (see III, 4), are described with an accuracy and depth that reveal Johnson's involvement. He was conscious of the weak spots in his own mind, and critical of its lapses into hopelessness and inertia. He described his own mental state several times, though never, it seems, in English. As far as surviving documents go, we have to rely on a letter in French and a poem in Latin.

The Latin poem, which came first in order of time, is Γνῶθι Σεαυτόν: *Post Lexicon Anglicanum Auctum et Emendatum* (Know Thyself: on finishing the revised edition of the English *Dictionary*). Johnson had worked intensely hard between the summer of 1771 and the autumn of 1772, completely revising his *Dictionary* for its fourth edition, and when the work was at last completed he felt exhausted and depressed. His self-doubt and discouragement found poignant expression in the dignified impersonality of a dead language; almost certainly, he would never have exposed his innermost discouragement and sense of failure in the plainness of English. Even so, sombre as the poem is, and soberly as it anatomizes his sufferings, there is still a flash of Johnsonian humour in the joke that comes in the last line.

In making an approximate translation, I have employed the English alliterative line, not in its pristine Anglo-Saxon form, but in the longer and looser version as developed by the fourteenth century. It seemed to my ear to come closer to the roll and thunder of the hexameter.

2.

Scaliger, when with scant sense of achievement he had scrawled
his lexicon's last page, after prolonged toil, loathing
the mindless menial grind, the small problems piled into mountains,
in hate groaning, he gave his thought to guide grave judges
that the penal system should prescribe for all hard prisoners
found guilty of devilment, the drudgery of making a dictionary—
one punishment, for the most impenitent, all punishments compounding!

How right he was, that rare man, erudite, lofty, rigorous,
worthy of weightier work, better able to serve the world
by enchanting the ear with antique heroines, or the bards' ecstasies;
the shifting sands of governance, the swirl of the shining spheres
his mind could read and unriddle, and the vast earth's revolving.

A large example is dangerous. The dunciad of learned dolts presume
to glare and grumble, presenting their case, princely Scaliger
as if it were yours, master. Let each mind his measure!
I, at least, have realized that to be your rival (in rage
or in knowledge) was never part of my nature. Who can know why?
Is it the lazy flow of my chill blood, or the long idle years that I lost?
or was I just bundled into the world with a bad brain?

As soon as your sterile work was over, and the stiff word-
    stubble
you had pushed through, peerless wisdom the goddess into
    her pure
arcanum accepted you, while all the arts applauded,
and the world's words, their voices so long at variance,
now home from exile joyfully rang about you, gentle master,
    their joiner.

As for me, my task finished, I find myself still fettered to
    myself:
the dull doom of doing nothing, harsher than any drudgery,
stays for me, and the staleness of slow stagnation.
Cares beget cares, and a clamouring crowd of troubles
vex me, and vile dreams, the sour sleep of an empty mind.
What will refresh me? The rattle of all-night roisterers,
or the quiet of solitary spaces? Oh, sleep, sleep, I call,
lying where I fret at the lingering night, but fear day's cold
    finger.
Trembling, I trudge everywhere, peering, prying, into every-
    thing, trying
passionate to know if somewhere, anyhow, a path leads up
    to a more perfect pasture
but glooming over grand schemes I never find my growing-
    point,
and am always forced finally to face myself, to own frankly
that my heart is illiterate, and my mind's strength an illusion
I labour to keep alive. Fool, a mind not fuelled by learning
slides into a morass. Stop the supply of marble
to Phidias our fertile sculptor, and where are his forms and
    faces?
Every endeavour, every avenue, ends in frustration always,
closed in by lack of cash, bound up by a costive mind.
Ah, when that mind reckons up its resources, the sheaves of
    reason
stacked high, matter for self-satisfaction, are conspicuously
    absent:
nor does creation's great king from his high castle
send down daily supplies to ensure its survival.

Regularly the years mount up, regularly the mind's works do
   not mount up:
as for the frills and the friendly honours, fruits of a useful life,
its own harsh judgment forbids it that harmless enjoyment.
Turning to survey its territory, that night-shadowed tundra,
the mind is full of fear—of ghosts, of the fleeting glimmer
of the thin shadows of nothing, the absence of shapes, the
   shimmer.

What then am I to do? Let my declining years go down to
   the dark?
Or get myself together, gather the last of my gall,
and hurl myself at some task huge enough for a hero?

And if that's too much, perhaps my friends might find me
some dull, decent job, undemanding: like making a
   dictionary. . .

Johnson was interested in medicine; he kept fairly well
abreast of the medical science of his day, at least insofar
as it was empirical; he understood his own body, and was
able to write out prescriptions for medicines, so that he
was often taken by apothecaries to be a physician. His
Christian piety was not of the mystical kind which regards
even an illness as sent from God; he vigorously combated
his ailments, believing that it was a man's duty to keep
himself healthy and active if he could; Christian piety
enjoined that one should be useful in the world, and at
least not a burden to others. He made use of the medical
care available in his day, for all his physical sufferings, and
would have done the same for his mental sufferings had
he not been put off by an unfortunate early experience.
During that first depressive collapse in 1729, he wrote a
description of his mental state, in Latin, for the information of Dr Swinfen of Lichfield, the Johnsons' family
doctor and Sam's godfather. Dr Swinfen was impressed
by the clarity and completeness of the young man's self-
analysis; innocently, but in an evil hour, he showed the
manuscript to some of his friends. Johnson, his reticent
nature deeply offended, never forgave Swinfen and never

again confided his psychological troubles to a doctor. If the same thing had happened to Boswell, he would probably have felt rather flattered. But Johnson felt betrayed and shamed.

It was impossible for him, nevertheless, to bear his burdens in complete solitude, and this is why Hester Thrale is so important in the Johnsonian story. Almost from the beginning of their friendship, Johnson confided in her; not only because she was a woman, and in those things in which he is most vulnerable a man will always confide more readily in a woman than in another man, but because he knew her to be discreet and sensible. Though she kept a voluminous journal, scribbling away like a very Boswell, Hester never wrote down the intimate problems which Johnson discussed with her. She came into his life at a moment when he was about to sink beneath his burden of melancholy and self-accusation; they met in 1765, and in 1766 Johnson had a depressive breakdown so severe that the Thrales, in horror and pity at his sufferings, took him into their house and nursed him.

About seven years after he first became a familiar inhabitant of Streatham Place, Johnson wrote to Hester a rather cryptic letter in French. It is impossible here to discuss all the implications of this letter; there is an authoritative scholarly treatment by Miss K. C. Balderston, 'Johnson's Vile Melancholy', in *The Age of Johnson: Essays Presented to C. B. Tinker* (1949), and I discuss it in my *Samuel Johnson*. Here, we will print the text of the letter, with a rough translation, and let it go more or less at that. Clearly, Johnson is appealing to her to take responsibility and make decisions for him. Many years later, when Hester died, there was a sale of her effects in Manchester, and one of the items bore the label, 'Johnson's padlock, committed to my care in the year 1768'. The date is interesting, as showing that Johnson suffered, or feared, a bad breakdown so soon after he first got to know the Thrales. As to the exact significance of the padlock, why he gave it to her and why she kept it, we can only conjecture.

Johnson, we know, was afraid of going mad ('the un-

certain continuance of reason'); since mad people were
in the eighteenth century treated with barbarous cruelty,
it would have been reasonable to ask Hester to lock him
up until the fit had passed; since he commonly divided
the week between Streatham and his own house off Fleet
Street, it is quite likely that he made a similar request to
dour old Levet, who made no written memorandum and
took his secrets silently to the grave. On the other hand, it
is not likely that Johnson addressed Levet in terms of such
plangent appeal as he used to Hester. Johnson's sexual
problems may have included masochistic impulses, and
perhaps Hester had become the node of some of these
fantasies. In any event, she handled the situation with
tact, kindness and wisdom; Johnson recovered his equili-
brium, enough at least to resume normal life; and while
he knew that there were dark and misshapen things in his
mind, he struggled to remain in control, and on the whole
his struggle was successful. In 1771 he wrote in his diary
the laconic entry, *De pedicis et manicis insana cogitatio*, an
insane thought of fetters and handcuffs; this suggests that
he recognized in himself some of the classic symptoms of
what has subsequently come to be known as masochism.
But if Johnson had certain forces within his mind against
which he found it necessary to struggle, so do most of us,
and we do not all struggle as courageously as he.

3. Madame trés honorée

Puisque, pendant que je me trouve chez vous, il faut passer,
tous les jours, plusieures heures dans une solitude profonde,
dites moi, Si vous voulez que je vogue a plein abandon, ou que
je me contienne dans des bornes prescrites. S'il vous plaît, ma
tres chere maîtresse, que je sois lassè a hazard. La chose est
faite. Vous vous souvenez de la sagesse de nôtre ami, *Si je ferai
&c.* Mais, si ce n'est trop d'esperer que je puisse être digne,
comme auparavant, des soins et de la protection d'une ame si
aimable par sa douceur, et si venerable par son elevation, accor-
dez moi, par un petit ecrit, la connoissance de ce que m'est
permis, et que m'est interdit. Et s'il vous semble mieux que je
demeure dans un certain lieu, je vous supplie de m'epargner la

necessitè de me contraindre, en m'ôtant le pouvoir de sortir d'ou vou voulez que je sois. Ce que vous ne coûtera que la peine de tourner le clef dans la porte, deux fois par jour. Il faut agir tout a fait en Maîtresse, afin que vôtre jugement et vôtre vigilance viennent a secours de ma faiblesse.

Pour ce que regarde la table, j'espere tout de vôtre sagesse et je crains tout de vôtre douceur. Tournez, Madame tres honorèe, vos pensèes de ce côte la. Il n'y a pour vous rien de difficile; vous pourrez inventer une regime pratiquable sans bruît, et efficace sans peril.

Est ce trop de demander d'une ame telle qu est la vôtre, que, maîtresse des autres, elle devienne maîtresse de soy-même, et qu'elle triomphe de cette inconstance, qui a fait si souvent, qu'elle a negligèe l'execution de ses propres loix, qu'elle a oublièe tant de promesses, et qu'elle m'a condamnè a tant de solicitations reiterèes que la resouvenance me fait horreur. Il faut ou accorder, ou refuser; il faut se souvenir de ce qu'on accorde. Je souhaite, ma patronne, que vôtre autoritè me soit toûjours sensible, et que vous me tiennez dans l'esclavage que vou scavez si bien rendre heureuse.

Permettez moi l'honeur d'être Madame Vôtre très obeissant serviteur

Very honoured Madam,

Since, during the time that I am under your roof, I am to spend several hours of each day in a profound solitude—tell me, if you will, whether you wish me to wander entirely free, or to keep myself confined within prescribed limits. If it please you, my very dear mistress, that I should be left to my own devices, the thing is done. You will remember the wisdom of our friend, *If I shall do*, etc. But, if it be not too much to hope that I might be worthy, as I formerly was, of the care and protection of a soul so amiable in its gentleness, and so venerable by its loftiness, grant me, by a short written message, the knowledge of what is allowed to me, and what is forbidden. And if it seems better to you that I should remain in one defined place, I beg of you to spare me the necessity of confining myself, by making it impossible for me to leave the place in which you think it best for me to remain. That will cost you no more trouble than the turning of a key in the door, twice every day.

You must act wholly as Mistress, if your judgment and your vigilance are to come to the rescue of my weakness.

As far as the table is concerned, I have everything to hope from your wisdom and everything to fear from your gentleness. Most honoured Madam, turn your thoughts to that subject. There is for you nothing difficult in it; you can devise a regime practicable without fuss, and efficacious without danger.

Is it too much to ask of a spirit like yours, that, holding sway over others, it should hold sway over itself, and triumph over that inconstancy which has so often caused it to neglect the execution of its own decrees, and forgotten so many promises, and condemned me to so many repeated pleadings, of which the remembrance fills me with horror? One must give, or refuse; and one must remember what one has given. I hope, my lady, that your authority over me will always make itself felt, and that you will keep me in that bondage which you know so well how to make into a happiness.

Permit me the honour of being, Madam, your most obedient servant.

Not long after writing that letter Johnson made his tour of the Hebrides with Boswell. He undertook this arduous journey at a time when his physical health was by no means good; he had been unwell for months, his one seeing eye had been put out of action by a persistent inflammation which had made him, for weeks on end, virtually a blind man; when this slowly cleared, he was still shaky; his knees trembled and he could walk only with difficulty. That in spite of all this he launched himself into a journey across wild mountains and rough autumnal seas is an indication of his unwillingness to submit tamely to physical affliction. He fought back; and it was not until the age of seventy-five, after a long stubborn fight, that he accepted death.

From a physical point of view, it could be said that the last eighteen months of Johnson's life were one long delaying action against the advance of death. In June 1783, he suffered a paralytic stroke that robbed him for a time of the power of speech. We have his own detailed account of this in a letter to Hester Thrale. Stoical in its dry account of his physical suffering, the letter is more openly emotional in its appeal for her sympathy and support. But, sunk as she was in her own problems, she made no move towards him.

4. Dear Madam

I am sitting down in no chearful solitude to write a narrative which would once have affected you with tenderness and sorrow, but which you will perhaps pass over now with the careless glance of frigid indifference. For this diminution of regard however, I know not whether I ought to blame You, who may have reasons which I cannot know, and I do not blame myself who have for a great part of human life done You what good I could, and have never done you evil.

I had been disordered in the usual way, and had been relieved by the usual methods, by opium and catharticks, but had rather lessened my dose of opium.

On Monday the 16. I sat for my picture, and walked a considerable way with little inconvenience. In the afternoon and evening I felt myself light and easy, and began to plan schemes of life. Thus I went to bed, and in a short time waked and sat up as has been long my custom, when I felt a confusion and indistinctness in my head which lasted, I suppose about half a minute; I was alarmed and prayed God, that however he might afflict my body he would spare my understanding. This prayer, that I might try the integrity of my faculties I made in Latin verse. The lines were not very good, but I knew them not to be very good, I made them easily, and concluded myself to be unimpaired in my faculties.

Soon after I perceived that I had suffered a paralytick stroke, and that my Speech was taken from me. I had no pain, and so little dejection in this dreadful state that I wondered at my own apathy, and considered that perhaps death itself when it should come, would excite less horrour than seems now to attend it.

In order to rouse the vocal organs I took two drams. Wine has been celebrated for the production of eloquence; I put myself into violent motion, and, I think, repeated it. But all was vain; I then went to bed, and, strange as it may seem, I think, slept. When I saw light, it was time to contrive what I should do. Though God stopped my speech he left me my hand, I enjoyed a mercy which was not granted to my Dear

Friend Laurence, who now perhaps overlooks me as I am writing and rejoices that I have what he wanted. My first note was necessarily to my servant, who came in talking, and could not immediately comprehend why he should read what I put into his hands.

I then wrote a card to Mr Allen, that I might have a discreet friend at hand to act as occasion should require. In penning this note I had some difficulty, my hand, I knew not how nor why, made wrong letters. I then wrote to Dr Taylor to come to me, and bring Dr Heberden, and I sent to Dr Brocklesby, who is my neighbour. My Physicians are very friendly and very disinterested, and give me great hopes, but you may imagine my situation. I have so far recovered my vocal powers, as to repeat the Lord's Prayer with no very imperfect articulation. My memory, I hope, yet remains as it was. But such an attack produces solicitude for the safety of every Faculty.

How this will be received by You I know not, I hope You will sympathise with me, but perhaps

> My Mistress gracious, mild, and good,
> Cries, Is he dumb? 'tis time he shou'd.

But can this be possible, I hope it cannot. I hope that what, when I could speak, I spoke of You, and to You, will be in a sober and serious hour remembred by You, and surely it cannot be remembred but with some degree of kindness. I have loved you with virtuous affection, I have honoured You with sincere Esteem. Let not all our endearment be forgotten, but let me have in this great distress your pity and your prayers. You see I yet turn to You with my complaints as a settled and unalienable friend, do not, do not drive me from You, for I have not deserved either neglect or hatred.

To the Girls, who do not write often, for Susy has written only once, and Miss Thrale owes me a letter, I earnestly recommend as their Guardian and Friend, that They remember their Creator in the days of their Youth.

I suppose you may wish to know how my disease is treated by the physitians. They put a blister upon my back, and two from my ear to my throat, one on a side. The blister on the back has done little, and those on the throat have not risen.

I bullied, and bounced, (it sticks to our last sand) and com-pelled the apothecary to make his salve according to the Edin-burgh dispensatory, that it might adhere better. I have two on now of my own prescription. They likewise give me salt of hartshorn, which I take with no great confidence, but am satis-fied that what can be done is done for me.

O God, give me comfort and confidence in Thee, forgive my sins, and if it be thy good pleasure, relieve my diseases for Jesus Christs sake, Amen.

I am almost ashamed of this querulous letter, but now it is written, let it go.

> I am, Madam Your most humble servant
> Bolt Court Fleet street June 19. 1783   Sam: Johnson.

Finally, some letters to his doctors. Towards the end Johnson was attended by four physicians, Doctors Brocklesby, Heberden, Warren and Butter, and a surgeon, Mr Cruickshank, who gave him such help as they could in living on from day to day.

In the summer of his last year, Johnson as usual spent some time in Staffordshire and Derbyshire, partly in the hope of better health in the country air, but mainly, one suspects, in the well-founded belief that he would have no more chance to see his old friends. To his physicians in London, Dr Brocklesby and Dr Heberden, he wrote accounts of his condition. Brocklesby seems to have advised him to stay where he was and not return to face a winter in London, but (8) Johnson is firm; London is where he feels at home; 'public life', by which he means a life full of sociability in the midst of a large circle of friends to whom he makes himself pretty available, is his 'vocation'.

5. Dear Sir

The kind attention which You have so long shown to my health and happiness, makes it as much a debt of gratitude as a call of interest, to give you an account of what befals me, when accident removes me from your immediate care.

The journey of the first day was performed with very little sense of fatigue, the second day brought me to Lichfield without much lassitude, but I am afraid that I could not have born such violent agitation for many days together. Tell Dr Heberden that in the coach I read Ciceronianus, which I concluded as I entred Lichfield. My affection and understanding went along with Erasmus, except that once or twice he somewhat unskilfully entangles Cicero's civil or moral, with his rhetorical character.

I staid five days at Lichfield, but, being unable to walk, had no great pleasure, and yesterday (19th) I came hither, where I am to try what air and attention can perform.

Of any improvement in my health I cannot yet please myself with the perception. The water has in these summer months made two invasions, but has run off again with no very formidable tumefaction, either by the efficacy of the Squils, which I have used very diligently, or because it is the course of the distemper, when it is at a certain height, to discharge itself.

The Asthma has no abatement. Opiates stop the fit, so as that I can sit and sometimes lie easy, but they do not now procure me the power of motion; and I am afraid that my general strength of body does not encrease. The weather indeed is not benign; but how low is he sunk whose strength depends upon the weather? I still pass the night almost without sleep.

I am now looking into Floyer, who lived with his asthma to almost his ninetieth year. His book by want of order is obscure, and his asthma, I think, not of the same kind with mine. Something however I may perhaps learn.

My appetite still continues keen enough, and what I consider as a symptom of radical health, I have a voracious delight in raw summer fruit, of which I was less eager a few years ago.

One of the most troublesome attendants on my Malady is costiveness, which is perhaps caused by the opiates, though I have not for some months taken any thing more potent than diacodium, and of that not more than twice an ounce at a time, and seldom an ounce in twenty four hours; but I can seldom go ⟨ ⟩ the garden without a cathartick. The aloes mixed with the ⟨? Squills⟩ even when I exceed the quantity prescribed, has not any effect.

You will be pleased to communicate this account to d⟨ear⟩ Dr Heberden, and if any thing is to be done, let me have your joint opinion.

Now—*abite curæ*—let me enquire after the club. I hope You meet, and do not forget, Dear Sir, Your obliged humble Servant, Ashbourne, Derbyshire. July 21. 1784   Sam : Johnson

6. Dear Sir

If nothing is better than when I wrote last, nothing is worse. But I think every thing grows gradually better. By a pertinacious use of the Squils, or by some other cause while I used them, the Flux of water has encreased. My thighs are no longer hard, nor are my legs in any remarkable degree tumid. The Asthma, I think, continues to remit, and my breath passes with more freedom to day than yesterday. I have since the *nox jucunda*, set down *nox felix somno* and *nox placida cum somno*. Such Nights it is long since I have known.

Mr Windham has been here to see me, he came I think, forty miles out of his way, and staid about a day and [and] a half, perhaps I make the time shorter than it was. Such conversation I shall not have again till I come back to the regions of literature and even there Windham is—inter stellas Luna minores.

Your squil pils, are perfect bullets, I commonly divide one into four. They begin now to purge me, which I suppose you intended, and that they produce their effect is to me another token that Nature is recovering its original powers, and the functions returning to their proper state. God continue his mercies, and grant me to use them rightly. I am, dear Sir, Your most obliged and most humble Servant,
Ashbourne. Sept. 2. 1784   Sam : Johnson

7. Though I doubt not but Dr. Brocklesby would communicate to you any incident in the variation of my health which appeared either curious or important, yet I think it time to give you some account of myself.

Not long after the first great efflux of the water, I attained as much vigour of limbs and freedom of breath, that without rest or intermission, I went with Dr. Brocklesby to the top of the painters' Academy. This was the greatest degree of health that I have obtained, and this, if it could continue, were perhaps sufficient; but my breath soon failed, and my body grew weak.

At Oxford (in June) I was much distressed by shortness of breath, so much that I never attempted to scale the library: the water gained upon me, but by the use of squills was in a great measure driven away.

In July I went to Lichfield, and performed the journey with very little fatigue in the common vehicle, but found no help from my native air. I then removed to Ashbourn, in Derby-shire, where for some time I was oppressed very heavily by the asthma; and the dropsy had advanced so far, that I could not without great difficulty button me at my knees. Something was now to be done; I took opium as little as I could, for quiet and squills, as much as I could, for help; but in my medical journal, August 10, I find these words, nec opio, nec squillis quidquam sensi effectum. Animus jacet. But I plied the vinegar of squills to an hundred drops a day, and the powder to 4 grains. From the vinegar I am not sure that I ever perceived any consequence.

'Here follow statements of the effect produced by these and other medicines.'

I rose in the morning with my asthma perceptibly mitigated, and walked to Church that day with less struggle than on any day before.

The water about this time ran again away, so that no hydro-pical tumour has been lately visible. The relaxation of my breath has not continued as it was at first. But neither do I breathe with the same *angustiæ* and distress as before the remis-sion. The summary of my state is this:

I am deprived by weakness and the asthma of the power of walking beyond a very short space.

I draw my breath with difficulty upon the least effort, but not with suffocation or pain.

The dropsy still threatens, but gives way to medicine.

The Summer has passed without giving me any strength.

My appetite is, I think, less keen than it was, but not so abated as that its decline can be observed by any one but myself.

Be pleased to think on me sometimes.

I am, Sir, Your most obliged and most humble servant,
Lichfield, Oct. 13, 1784.   Sam: Johnson.

8. Dear Sir

You write to me with a zeal that animates, and a tenderness that melts me. I am not afraid either of a journey to London or a residence in it. I came down with little fatigue, and I am now not weaker. In the smoky atmosphere I was delivered from the dropsy, which I consider as the original and radical disease. The town is my element, there are my friends, there are my books to which I have not yet bidden farewell, and there are my amusements. Sir Joshua told me long ago that my vocation was to publick life, and I hope still to keep my station, till God shall bid me *Go in peace.*

I have not much to add of medical observation. I believe some vigorous pill must be contrived to counteract the costiveness which opiate⟨s⟩ now certainly produce, and to which it is too troublesome to oppose a regular purge. If You can order such a pill send me the prescription next post.

I now take the squils without the addition of aloes from which I never found other effect, than that it made the pill more bulky and more nauseous, but if it be of any use I will add it again. I am Sir Your most obliged and most humble Servant
Lichfield. Oct. 25. 1784   Sam: Johnson

9. Dear Sir

Nothing now goes well, except that my Asthma is not oppressive to the degree that I have sometimes suffered. The water encreases almost visibly and the squills which I get here are utterly inefficacious. My Spirits are extremely low. Yet I have recovered from a worse state. I have supported myself with opiates till they have made me comatous. I have disobeyed Dr Heberden, and taken Squills in too great a quantity for my Stomach. My Stomach at least is less vigorous, and the Squills I have taken in great quantities.

I am endeavouring to make haste to town. Do not write any more hither. I am Dear Sir Your most humble Servant
Lichfield Nov. 6. 1784   Sam: Johnson

So he returned to London, and it was there that death came to him, peacefully enough, on 13th December.

Chapter VIII

Johnson and His God

Johnson was a lifelong Church of England Christian: at any rate, almost lifelong. His early upbringing was pious and orthodox; for a time, during adolescence, he drifted a certain distance away from religious belief; what caused him to return, never again to waver, is a story that makes one of the best-known passages of Boswell's *Life*:

1. He communicated to me the following particulars upon the subject of his religious progress. 'I fell into an inattention to religion, or an indifference about it, in my ninth year. The church at Lichfield, in which we had a seat, wanted reparation, so I was to go and find a seat in other churches; and having bad eyes, and being awkward about this, I used to go and read in the fields on Sunday. This habit continued till my fourteenth year; and still I find a great reluctance to go to church. I then became a sort of lax *talker* against religion, for I did not much *think* against it; and this lasted till I went to Oxford, where it would not be *suffered*. When at Oxford, I took up Law's "Serious Call to a Holy Life," expecting to find it a dull book, (as such books generally are), and perhaps to laugh at it. But I found Law quite an overmatch for me; and this was the first occasion of my thinking in earnest of religion, after I became capable of rational enquiry.' From this time forward religion was the predominant object of his thoughts; though, with the just sentiments of a conscientious christian, he lamented that his practice of its duties fell far short of what it ought to be.

From that time forth, Johnson adhered to his Christian beliefs and did his erratic best to bring his life into complete alignment with them. This struggle involved him in a great deal of torment and self-reproach; his phenomenally tender conscience never allowed him to feel satisfied with his own performance, and, characteristically, he applied higher standards to himself than he would have done to anyone else. Conscious as he was of great powers, he felt that his Creator's demands on him would be correspondingly heavy. The God whom Johnson worshipped was a jealous God, and it must be sadly confessed that he, a good man if ever a good man trod this earth, spent more time trembling in fear of eternal punishment than in rejoicing at the existence of Heaven.

Religious illumination was very much at the head of Johnson's list of essentials. He disapproved of voyages of exploration and colonial exploitation generally, but he approved of missionary activity. To him, the Island of Iona was

that illustrious island, which was once the luminary of the Caledonian regions, whence savage clans and roving barbarians derived the benefits of knowledge, and the blessings of religion.

That puts it with typical Johnsonian precision: knowledge is a benefit, but religion is a blessing, and to deny it to any people, if by any conceivable effort we can give it to them, is a grave sin. Hence his magnificently lofty rebuke to a body of Scottish divines, conveyed in his letter to William Drummond, bookseller, of Edinburgh (13 August 1766). These reverend gentlemen were exercised over whether or not the New Testament should be translated into Gaelic. It would be an expensive undertaking, and if the Highlanders were forced to learn English in order to read the Scriptures, that would help in breaking down their social and political isolation. Johnson's judgment is uncompromising.

2. Sir

I did not expect to hear that it could be, in an assembly convened for the propagation of Christian knowledge, a question whether any nation uninstructed in religion should receive instruction; or whether that instruction should be imparted to them by a translation of the holy books into their own language. If obedience to the will of God be necessary to happiness, and knowledge of his will be necessary to obedience, I know not how he that with-holds this knowledge, or delays it, can be said to love his neighbour as himself. He, that voluntarily continues ignorance, is guilty of all the crimes which ignorance produces; as to him, that should extinguish the tapers of a lighthouse, might justly be imputed the calamities of shipwrecks. Christianity is the highest perfection of humanity; and as no man is good but as he wishes the good of others, no man can be good in the highest degree, who wishes not to others the largest measures of the greatest good. To omit for a year, or for a day, the most efficacious method of advancing Christianity, in compliance with any purposes that terminate on this side of the grave, is a crime of which I know not that the world has yet had an example, except in the practice of the planters of America, a race of mortals whom, I suppose, no other man wishes to resemble.

The Papists have, indeed, denied to the laity the use of the bible; but this prohibition, in few places now very rigorously enforced, is defended by arguments, which have for their foundation the care of souls. To obscure, upon motives merely political, the light of revelation, is a practice reserved for the reformed; and, surely, the blackest midnight of popery is meridian sunshine to such a reformation.

The Christian, by definition, is concerned for other people's souls as well as his own. Johnson's Christianity always shows in its fairest light when he is helping or comforting others: witness the touching episode of his deathbed visit to Catherine Chambers, his mother's maid and companion. Boswell extracted Johnson's account of this and printed it at the appropriate point of the *Life*, but it actually occurs in the *Prayers and Meditations*. Here now is a selection from that mixed but majestic work, of which a description is given in the Introduction: a selection substantial enough, I hope, to convey its range and not to leave out many of the gems.

3. PRAYER ON NEWYEAR'S DAY. [8.]

Jan. 1, 1744/5

Almighty and everlasting God, in whose hands are life and death, by whose will all things were created, and by whose providence they are sustained, I return thee thanks that Thou hast given me life, and that thou hast continued it to this time, that thou hast hitherto forborn to snatch me away in the midst of Sin and Folly, and hast permitted me still to enjoy the means of Grace, and vouchsafed to call me yet again to Repentance. Grant, O merciful Lord, that thy Call may not be vain, that my Life may not be continued to encrease my Guilt, and that thy gracious Forbearance may not harden my heart in wickedness. Let me remember, O my God, that as Days and Years pass over me, I approach nearer to the Grave, where there is no repentance, and grant, that by the assistance of thy Holy Spirit, I may so pass through this Life, that I may obtain Life everlasting, for the Sake of our Lord Jesus Christ. Amen.

PRAYERS COMPOSED BY ME ON THE DEATH OF MY WIFE, AND REPOSITED AMONG HER MEMORIALS, MAY 8, 1752.[1]
Deus exaudi.—Heu!

[13.]
April 25, 1752.

O Lord, our heavenly Father, almighty and most merciful God, in whose hands are life and death, who givest and takest away, castest down and raisest up, look with mercy on the affliction of thy unworthy servant, turn away thine anger from me, and speak peace to my troubled soul. Grant me the assistance and comfort of thy Holy Spirit, that I may remember with thankfulness the blessings so long enjoyed by me in the society of my departed wife; make me so to think on her precepts and example, that I may imitate whatever was in her life acceptable in thy sight, and avoid all by which she offended Thee. Forgive me, O merciful Lord, all my sins, and enable me to begin and perfect that reformation which I promised her, and to persevere in that resolution, which she implored Thee to continue, in the purposes which I recorded in thy sight, when she lay dead before me, in obedience to thy laws, and faith in

[1] She had died on March 17, O.S. (March 28, N.S.) of this year.

thy word. And now, O Lord, release me from my sorrow, fill me with just hopes, true faith, and holy consolations, and enable me to do my duty in that state of life to which thou hast been pleased to call me, without disturbance from fruitless grief, or tumultuous imaginations; that in all my thoughts, words, and actions, I may glorify thy Holy Name, and finally obtain, what I hope Thou hast granted to thy departed servant, everlasting joy and felicity, through our Lord Jesus Christ. Amen.

[14.]
April 26, 1752, being after 12 at Night of the 25th.

O Lord! Governour of heaven and earth, in whose hands are embodied and departed Spirits, if thou hast ordained the Souls of the Dead to minister to the Living, and appointed my departed Wife to have care of me, grant that I may enjoy the good effects of her attention and ministration, whether exercised by appearance, impulses, dreams or in any other manner agreeable to thy Government. Forgive my presumption, enlighten my ignorance, and however meaner agents are employed, grant me the blessed influences of thy holy Spirit, through Jesus Christ our Lord. Amen.

HILL BOOTHBY'S DEATH.[1]
[29.]
January, 1756.

O Lord God, almighty disposer of all things, in whose hands are life and death, who givest comforts and takest them away, I return Thee thanks for the good example of Hill Boothby, whom Thou hast now taken away, and implore thy grace, that I may improve the opportunity of instruction which Thou hast afforded me, by the knowledge of her life, and by the sense of her death; that I may consider the uncertainty of my present state, and apply myself earnestly to the duties which Thou hast set before me, that living in thy fear, I may die in thy favour, through Jesus Christ our Lord. Amen.

I commend, &c. W. and H. B.

Transcribed June 26, 1768.

---

[1] She died on January 16. 'I have heard Baretti say,' writes Mrs. Piozzi, 'that when this lady died Johnson was almost distracted with his grief.' Piozzi's *Anecdotes*, p. 161. William was a common name in the Boothby family. Perhaps 'W. and H. B.' stands for William and Hill Boothby. [G.B.H.]

WHEN MY EYE WAS RESTORED TO ITS USE. [30.]

February 15, 1756.

Almighty God, who hast restored light to my eye, and enabled me to persue again the studies which Thou hast set before me; teach me, by the diminution of my sight, to remember that whatever I possess is thy gift, and by its recovery, to hope for thy mercy: and, O Lord, take not thy Holy Spirit from me; but grant that I may use thy bounties according to thy will, through Jesus Christ our Lord. Amen.

[41.]

EASTER DAY, *April 15, 1759.*

Almighty and most merciful Father, look down with pity upon my sins. I am a sinner, good Lord; but let not my sins burthen me for ever. Give me thy grace to break the chain of evil custom. Enable me to shake off idleness and sloth; to will and to do what thou hast commanded; grant me chaste in thoughts, words and actions; to love and frequent thy worship, to study and understand thy word; to be diligent in my calling, that I may support myself and relieve others.

Forgive me, O Lord, whatever my mother has suffered by my fault, whatever I have done amiss, and whatever duty I have neglected. Let me not sink into useless dejection; but so sanctify my affliction, O Lord, that I may be converted and healed; and that, by the help of thy holy spirit, I may obtain everlasting life through Jesus Christ our Lord.

And, O Lord, so far as it may be lawful, I commend unto thy fatherly goodness my father, brother, wife, and mother, beseeching thee to make them happy for Jesus Christ's sake. Amen.

[42.]

Sept. 18, 1760, resolved D.j.[1]

To combat notions of obligation.[2]

To apply to study.

[1] Deo juvante.

[2] He had, I conjecture, been tempted to bind himself by a vow in order to force himself to do what he thought he ought to do. Against vows he more than once strongly protested. 'Do not accustom yourself,' he wrote to Boswell, 'to enchain your volatility by vows; they will sometime leave a thorn in your mind, which you will perhaps never be able to extract or eject.' *Life*, ii. 21. 'A vow is a horrible thing, it is a snare for sin.' *Ib*. iii. 357. [G.B.H.]

To reclaim imagination.
To consult the resolves on Tetty's coffin.
To rise early.
To study Religion.
To go to Church.
To drink less strong liquors.
To keep Journal.
To oppose laziness, by doing what is to [be] done to morrow.
Rise as early as I can.
Send for books for Hist. of war.¹
Put books in order.²
Scheme life.

[46.]
April 20, 1764, GOOD FRYDAY.

I have made no reformation, I have lived totally useless, more sensual in thought and more addicted to wine and meat, grant me, O God, to amend my life for the sake of Jesus Christ. Amen.

I hope
To put my rooms in order.* ³
I fasted all day.

* Disorder I have found one great cause of idleness.

¹ Boswell assumes that he meant to write a history of the war that the first Pitt was carrying on in a succession of triumphs. It is possible that it was a history of war in general that he had in view. *Ib.* i. 354. [G.B.H.]

² 'On Wednesday, April 3, [1776], in the morning I found him very busy putting his books in order, and as they were generally very old ones clouds of dust were flying around him. He had on a pair of large gloves such as hedgers use. His present appearance put me in mind of my uncle Dr. Boswell's description of him, "A robust genius, born to grapple with whole libraries."' *Life*, iii. 7. [G.B.H.]

³ 'We cannot but reflect on that inertness and laxity of mind which the neglect of order and regularity in living, and the observance of stated hours, in short the waste of time, is apt to lead men to: this was the source of Johnson's misery throughout his life; all he did was by fits and starts, and he had no genuine impulse to action, either corporal or mental.' *Hawkins*, p. 205. [G.B.H.]

[47.]
April 21, 1764,–3–m.

My indolence, since my last reception of the Sacrament, has sunk into grosser sluggishness, and my dissipation spread into wilder negligence. My thoughts have been clouded with sensuality, and, except that from the beginning of this year I have in some measure forborn excess of Strong Drink my appetites have predominated over my reason. A kind of strange oblivion has overspread me, so that I know not what has become of the last year, and perceive that incidents and intelligence pass over me without leaving any impression.

This is not the life to which Heaven is promised. I purpose to approach the altar again to morrow. Grant, O Lord, that I may receive the Sacrament with such resolutions of a better life as may by thy grace be effectual, for the sake of Jesus Christ. Amen.

[48.]

April 21. I read the whole Gospel of St. John. Then sat up till the 22d.

My Purpose is from this time
To reject or expel sensual images, and idle thoughts.
To provide some useful amusement for leisure time.
To avoid Idleness.
To rise early.
To study a proper portion of every day.
To Worship God diligently.
To read the Scriptures.
To let no week pass without reading some part.
To write down my observations.
I will renew my resolutions made at Tetty's death.

I perceive an insensibility and heaviness upon me. I am less than commonly oppressed with the sense of sin, and less affected with the shame of Idleness. Yet I will not despair. I will pray to God for resolution, and will endeavour to strengthen my faith in Christ by commemorating his death.

I prayed for Tett.

[49.]
Ap. 22, EASTER DAY.

Having before I went to bed composed the foregoing meditation and the following prayer, I tried to compose myself but slept unquietly. I rose, took tea, and prayed for resolution and perseverance. Thought on Tetty, dear poor Tetty, with my eyes full.

I went to church, came in at the first of the Psalms, and endeavoured to attend the service which I went through without perturbation. After sermon I recommended Tetty in a prayer by herself, and my Father, Mother, Brother, and Bathurst, in another. I did it only once, so far as it might be lawful for me.

I then prayed for resolution and perseverance to amend my Life. I received soon, the communicants were many. At the altar it occurred to me that I ought to form some resolutions. I resolved, in the presence of God, but without a vow, to repel sinful thoughts to study eight hours daily, and, I think, to go to church every Sunday, and read the Scriptures. I gave a shilling, and seeing a poor girl at the Sacrament in a bedgown, gave her privately a crown, though I saw Hart's hymns [1] in her hand. I prayed earnestly for amendment, and repeated my prayer at home. Dined with Miss W.[2] went to Prayers at church; went to Davies's, spent the evening not pleasantly. Avoided wine and tempered a very few glasses with Sherbet.[3] Came home, and prayed.

I saw at the Sacrament a man meanly dressed whom I have always seen there at Easter.[4]

[1] *Hymns composed on Various Subjects.* By J. Hart. London 1759. In the Preface Hart describes his 'Experience'—his sins and 'the Clouds of Horror with which he was overwhelmed till Whitsunday 1757; when' he says, 'I happened to go to the Moravian Chapel in Fetter Lane, where I had been several times before . . . I was hardly got home, when I felt myself melting away into a strange Softness of Affection . . . Thenceforth I enjoyed sweet Peace in my Soul.' In the hymn entitled *The Author's own Confession* (p. 40), he says:—

> 'I strove to make my Flesh decay
> With foul Disease and wasting Pain.
> I strove to fling my Life away,
> And damn my Soul—but strove in vain.'

This Hymn-book was so popular that in 1811 it reached its twentieth edition. [G.B.H.]

[2] Miss Williams. He often dined in a tavern, though he always took tea with her. *Life*, i. 421. [G.B.H.]

[3] Johnson defines *Sherbet* as 'the juice of lemons or oranges mixed with water and sugar.' [G.B.H.]   [4] See below, 54.

[51.]

Sept. 18, 1764, about 6 evening.

This is my fifty-sixth birth-day, the day on which I have concluded fifty five years.

I have outlived many friends. I have felt many sorrows. I have made few improvements. Since my resolution formed last Easter I have made no advancement in knowledge or in goodness; nor do I recollect that I have endeavoured it. I am deected but not hopeless.

O God for Jesus Christ's Christ's sake have mercy upon me.

[52.]

7 in the evening.

I went to church prayed *to be loosed from the chain of my sins.*[1]

I have now spent fifty five years in resolving, having from the earliest time almost that I can remember been forming schemes of a better life.[2] I have done nothing, the need of doing therefore is pressing, since the time of doing is short. O God grant me to resolve aright, and to keep my resolutions for Jesus Christ's sake. Amen.

  Haec limina vitae.   STAT.

  I resolve

to study the Scriptures. I hope in the original Languages. Six hundred and forty verses every Sunday will nearly comprise the Scriptures in a year.

  To read good books. To study Theology.

  to treasure in my mind passages for recollection.

  to rise early. Not later than six if I can I hope sooner, but as soon as I can.

  to keep a journal both of employment and of expences. to keep accounts.

  to take of my health by such means as I have designed.

  to set down at night some plan for the morrow.

  Last year I prayed on my birth-day by accommodating the Morning collect for Grace, putting *year* for *day.* This I did this day.

---

[1] 'Though we be tied and bound with the chain of our sins, yet let the pitifulness of thy great mercy loose us.' *Book of Common Prayer.*

[2] Johnson was but fifty-five years old, so that he began resolving, it seems, from his birth.

[54.]

EASTER DAY, *Apr. 7, 1765, about 3 in the morning.*
I purpose again to partake of the blessed Sacrament, yet when
I consider how vainly I have hitherto resolved at this annual
commemoration of my Saviour's death, to regulate my life by
his laws, I am almost afraid to renew my resolutions. Since the
last Easter I have reformed no evil habits, my time has been
unprofitably spent, and seems as a dream that has left nothing
behind. My memory grows confused, and I know not how the
days pass over me.
Good Lord deliver me.

I will call upon God to morrow for repentance and amendment. O heavenly Father, let not my call be vain, but grant
me to desire what may please thee, and fulfill those desires for
Jesus Christs sake. Amen.

My resolutions, which God perfect, are,
1. to avoid loose thoughts.
2. to rise at eight every morning.

I hope to extend these purposes to other duties, but it is
necessary to combat evil habits singly. I purpose to rise at
eight because though I shall not yet rise early it will be much
earlier than I now rise, for I often lye till two, and will gain me
much time, and tend to a conquest over idleness and give time
for other duties. I hope to rise yet earlier.

Almighty and most merciful Father, who hatest nothing that
thou hast made, nor desirest the Death of a Sinner, look down
with mercy upon me, and grant that I may turn from my
wickedness and live. Forgive the days and years which I have
passed in folly, idleness, and sin. Fill me with such sorrow for
the time mispent, that I may amend my life according to thy
holy word; Strengthen me against habitual idleness, and enable
me to direct my thoughts to the performance of every duty;
that while I live I may serve thee in the state to which thou
shalt call me, and at last by a holy and happy death be delivered
from the struggles and sorrows of this life, and obtain eternal
happiness by thy mercy, for the sake of Jesus Christ our Lord.
Amen.
O God, have mercy upon me.

At church I purpose
before I leave the pew to pray the occasional prayer, and
read my resolutions.
To pray for Tetty and the rest [1]
the like after Communion.
at intervals to use the collects of Fourth after Trinity, and
First and Fourth after Epiphany and to meditate.

After church, 3 p.m.

This was done, as I purposed, but with some distraction. I
came in at the Psalms, and could not well hear. I renewed my
resolutions at the altar. God perfect them. When I came home
I prayed, and have hope, grant O Lord for the sake of Jesus
Christ that my hope may not be in vain.

I invited home with me the man whose pious behaviour I
had for several years observed on this day, and found him a
kind of Methodist, full of texts, but ill-instructed. I talked to
him with temper, and offered him twice wine, which he refused.
I suffered him to go without the dinner which I had purposed
to give him. I thought this day that there was something
irregular and particular in his look and gesture, but having
intended to invite him to acquaintance, and having a fit opportunity by finding him near my own seat after I had missed him,
I did what I at first designed, and am sorry to have been so
much disappointed. Let me not be prejudiced hereafter against
the appearance of piety in mean persons, who, with indeter-
minate notions, and perverse or inelegant conversation perhaps
are doing all that they can.

At night I used the occasional prayer with proper collects.

[55.]

July 2. I paid Mr. Simpson ten guineas, which he had formerly
lent me in my necessity and for which Tetty expressed her
gratitude.

July 8. I lent Mr. Simpson ten guineas more.

July 16. I received seventy-five pounds. Lent Mr. Davis
twenty-five.

---

[1] The previous Easter he had joined with her his father, mother, brother,
and Bathurst.

[62.]

GOOD FRIDAY, *March 28, 1766*. On the night before I used proper Collects, and prayed when I arose in the morning. I had all the week an awe upon me, not thinking on Passion week till I looked in the almanack. I have wholly forborne M [?meat] and wines, except one glass on Sunday night.

In the morning I rose, and drank very small tea without milk, and had nothing more that day.

This was the day on which Tetty died. I did not mingle much men [?mention] of her with the devotions of this day, because it is dedicated to more holy subjects. I mentioned her at church, and prayed once solemnly at home. I was twice at church, and went through the prayers without perturbation, but heard the sermons imperfectly. I came in both times at the second lesson, not hearing the bell.

When I came home I read the Psalms for the day, and one sermon in Clark.[1] Scruples distract me, but at church I had hopes to conquer them.

I bore abstinence this day not well, being at night insupportably heavy, but as fasting does not produce sleepyness, I had perhaps rested ill the night before. I prayed in my study for the day, and prayed again in my chamber. I went to bed very early—before eleven.

After church I selected collects for the Sacraments.

Finding myself upon recollection very ignorant of religion, I formed a purpose of studying it.

I went down and sat to tea, but was too heavy to converse.

[63.]

Saturday, 29. I rose at the time now usual, not fully refreshed. Went to tea. A sudden thought of restraint hindered me. I drank but one dish. Took a purge for my health. Still uneasy. Prayed, and went to dinner. Dined sparingly *on fish* [added in different

---

[1] Dr. Samuel Clarke, of whose sermons, though he was 'a condemned heretic as to the doctrine of the Trinity,' Johnson thought highly. 'He had made it a rule not to admit his name in his Dictionary'; nevertheless he recommended them on his death-bed, 'because he is fullest on the propitiatory sacrifice.' *Life*, iii. 248; iv. 416. Clarke's *Scripture Doctrine of the Trinity* had been condemned by the Lower House of Convocation. Smollett's *Hist. of Eng.* ii. 303. [G.B.H.]

ink] about four. Went to Simpson. Was driven home by my physic. Drank tea, and am much refreshed. I believe that if I had drank tea again yesterday, I had escaped the heaviness of the evening. Fasting that produces inability is no duty, but I was unwilling to do less than formerly.

I had lived more abstemiously than is usual the whole week, and taken physic twice, which together made the fast more uneasy.

Thus much I have written medically, to show that he who can fast long must have lived plentifully.

[64.]
Saturday, March 29, 1766. I was yesterday very heavy. I do not feel myself to-day so much impressed with awe of the approaching mystery. I had this day a doubt, like Baxter,[1] of my state, and found that my faith, though weak, was yet faith. O God! strengthen it.

[70.]
August 17, 1767.
I am now about to receive with my old friend Kitty Chambers the sacrament, preparatory to her death. Grant, O God, that it may fit me. I purpose temperance for my resolution. O God, enable me to keep my purpose to thy glory.

5.32 p.m. I have communicated with Kitty, and kissed her. I was for some time distracted but at last more composed. I commended my friends and Kitty. Lucy and I were much affected. Kitty is, I think, going to heaven.

O God, grant that I may practise such temperance in Meat, Drink, and Sleep, and all bodily enjoyments, as may fit me for the duties to which thou shalt call me, and by thy blessing procure me freedom of thought and quietness of mind, that I may so serve Thee in this short and frail life, that I may be received by Thee at my death to everlasting happiness. Take not O Lord thy Holy Spirit from me, deliver me not up to vain fears, but have mercy on me, for the sake of Jesus Christ our Lord. Amen.

O God who desirest not the Death, &c.

---

[1] Baxter describes the doubts of his own salvation which exercised him many years. *Reliquiae Baxterianae*, ed. 1696, p. 6.

O Lord grant us encrease—
O God,—pardon and Peace.
O God who knowest our necessities.[1]
Our Father.

[71.]
Oct. 18, 1767, Sunday.

Yesterday, *Oct. 17*, at abou tten in the morning I took my leave for ever of my dear old friend Catherine Chambers, who came to live with my mother about 1724, and has been but little parted from us since. She buried my Father, my Brother, and my Mother. She is now fifty-eight years old.

I desired all to withdraw, then told her that we were to part for ever, that as Christians we should part with prayer, and that I would, if she was willing say a short prayer beside her. She expressed great desire to hear me, held up her poor hands, as she lay in bed, with great fervour, while I prayed kneeling by her, nearly in the following words:

Almighty and most merciful Father, whose loving-kindness is over all thy works, behold, visit, and relieve this thy Servant, who is grieved with sickness. Grant that the sense of her weakness may add strength to her faith, and seriousness to her Repentance. And grant that by the help of thy Holy Spirit after the pains and labours of this short life, we may all obtain everlasting happiness through Jesus Christ our Lord, for whose sake hear our prayers. Amen. Our Father.

I then kissed her. She told me that to part was the greatest pain that she had ever felt, and that she hoped we should meet again in a better place. I expressed with swelled eyes and great emotion of tenderness the same hopes. We kissed, and parted. I humbly hope, to meet again, and to part no more.

BED-TIME.

[72.]
Lent 2, [1768.]

Almighty God, who seest that I have no power of myself to help myself; keep me both outwardly in my body, and inwardly in my soul, that I may be defended from all adversities that

[1] He has apparently in mind the Absolution and the Collects for the fourteenth and twenty-first Sundays after Trinity and the last Collect but one in the Communion Service in the Book of Common Prayer. [G.B.H.]

may happen to the body, and from all evil thoughts which may assault and hurt the soul, through Jesus Christ our Lord. Amen.

This prayer may be said before or after the entrance into bed, as a preparative for sleep.

When I transcribed this Prayer, it was my purpose to have made this book[1] a Collection.

SCRUPLES. [73.]

O Lord, who wouldst that all men should be saved, and who knowest that without thy grace we can do nothing acceptable to thee, have mercy upon me. Enable me to break the chain of my sins, to reject sensuality in thought, and to overcome and suppress vain scruples; and to use such diligence in lawful employment as may enable me to support myself and do good to others. O Lord, forgive me the time lost in idleness; pardon the sins which I have committed, and grant that I may redeem the time misspent, and be reconciled to thee by true repentance, that I may live and die in peace, and be received to everlasting happiness. Take not from me, O Lord, thy Holy Spirit, but let me have support and comfort for Jesus Christ's sake. Amen.

STUDY OF TONGUES. [74.]

Almighty God, giver of all knowledge, enable me so to pursue the study of tongues, that I may promote thy glory and my own salvation.

Bless my endeavours, as shall seem best unto Thee; and if it shall please Thee to grant me the attainment of my purpose, preserve me from sinful pride; take not thy Holy Spirit from me, but give me a pure heart and humble mind, through Jesus Christ. Amen.

Of this Prayer there is no date, nor can I tell when it was written; but I think it was in Gough-square, after the Dictionary was ended. I did not study what I then intended.

Transcribed June 26, 1768.

[75.]

July 26, 1768. I shaved my nail by accident in whetting the

---

[1] A parchment book containing such of these Prayers as are marked *transcribed*. Note by G. Strahan.

knife, about an eighth of an inch from the bottom, and about a fourth from the top. This I measure that I may know the growth of nails; the whole is about five eighths of an inch.

[81.]
November 5, 1769.

Almighty God, merciful Father, whose providence is over all thy works, look down with pity upon the diseases of my body, and the perturbations of my mind. Give thy Blessing, O Lord, to the means which I shall use for my relief, and restore ease to my body, and quiet to my thoughts. Let not my remaining life be made useless by infirmities, neither let health, if thou shalt grant it, be employed by me in disobedience to thy laws; but give me such a sense of my pains, as may humble me before thee; and such remembrance of thy mercy as may produce honest industry, and holy confidence. And, O Lord, whether Thou ordainest my days to be past in ease or anguish, take not from me thy Holy Spirit; but grant that I may attain everlasting life, for the sake of Jesus Christ our Lord. Amen.

This I found Jan. 11, —72; and believe it written when I began to live on milk. I grew worse with forbearance of solid food.

[83.]
1770, March 28, Wednesday.

This is the day on which in —52, I was deprived of poor dear Tetty. Having left off the practice of thinking on her with some particular combinations, I have recalled her to my mind of late less frequently, but when I recollect the time in which we lived together, my grief for her departure is not abated, and I have less pleasure in any good that befals me, because she does not partake it. On many occasions I think what she would have said or done. When I saw the sea at Brighthelmston, I wished for her to have seen it with me. But with respect to her no rational wish is now left, but that we may meet at last where the mercy of God shall make us happy, and perhaps make us instrumental to the happiness of each other. It is now eighteen years.

[84.]
1770, April 11. Cupped.

[85.]
1770, April 14.

This week is Passion week.

I have for some weeks past been much afflicted with the Lumbago, or Rheumatism in the Loins, which often passes to the muscles of the belly, where it causes equal, if not greater pain. In the day the sunshine mitigates it, and in cold or cloudy weather such as has for some time past remarkably prevailed the heat of a strong fire suspends it. In the night it is so troublesome, as not very easily to be borne. I lye wrapped in Flannel with a very great fire near my bed, but whether it be that a recumbent posture encreases the pain, or that expansion by moderate warmth excites what a great heat dissipates, I can seldom remain in bed two hours at a time without the necessity of rising to heat the parts affected at the fire.

One night, between the pain and the spasms in my stomach I was insupportably distressed. On the next night, I think, I laid a blister to my back, and took opium; my night was tolerable, and from that time the spasms in my stomach which disturbed me for many years, and for two past harassed me almost to distraction, have nearly ceased; I suppose the breast is relaxed by the opium.

Having passed Thursday in Passion Week at Mr. Thrales, I came home on Fryday morning, that I might pass the day unobserved. I had nothing but water once in the morning and once at bed-time. I refused tea after some deliberation in the afternoon. They did not press it. I came home late, and was unwilling to carry my Rheumatism to the cold church in the morning, unless that were rather an excuse made to myself. In the afternoon I went to Church but came late, I think at the Creed. I read Clarkes Sermon on the Death of Christ, and the Second Epistle to Timothy in Greek, but rather hastily. I then went to Thrale's, and had a very tedious and painful night. But the Spasms in my Throat are gone and if either the pain or the opiate which the pain enforced has stopped them the relief is very cheaply purchased. The pain harasses me much, yet many have the disease perhaps in a much higher degree with want of food, fire, and covering, which I find thus grievous with all the succours that riches and kindness can buy and give.

On Saturday I was not hungry and did not eat much breakfast. There was a dinner and company at which I was persuaded, or tempted to stay. At night I came home sat up, and
composed the prayer, and having ordered the maid to make the
fire in my chamber at eight went to rest, and had a tolerable
night.

[97.]
April 26.

I was some way hinderd from continuing this contemplation
in the usual manner, and therefore try at the distance of a week
to review the last Sunday.

I went to Church early having first, I think, used my prayer.
When I was there I had very little perturbation of mind. During
the usual time of Meditation, I considered the Christian Duties
under the three principles of Soberness; Righteousness; and
Godliness; and purposed to forward Godliness by the *annual
perusal of the Bible*; Righteousness *by settling something for Charity*,
and Soberness *by early hours*. I commended as usual with preface
of permission, and, I think, mentioned Bathurst. I came
home, and found Paoli and Boswel waiting for me. What
devotions I used after my return home I do not distinctly
remember. I went to prayers in the evening; and, I think,
entred late.

I have this week endeavoured every day but one to rise early,
and have tried to be diligent, but have not performed what I
required from myself.

On Good Fryday, I paid Peyton without requiring work.

Since Easter —71 I have added a collect to my Evening
devotion.

I have been less indulgent to corporal inactivity. But I have
done little with my mind.

It is a comfort to me, that at last, in my sixty-third year,
I have attained to know, even thus hastily, confusedly, and
imperfectly, what my Bible contains.

May the good God encrease and sanctify my knowledge.

I have never yet read the apocrypha. When I was a boy I
have read or heard Bel and the dragon, Susannah, some of
Tobit, perhaps all. Some at least of Judith, and some of Eccle-
siasticus; and I suppose, the Benedicite. I have some time

looked into the Maccabees, and read a chapter containing the question, *Which is the strongest?* [1] I think in Esdras.

In the afternoon of Easter day, I read Pococke's commentary.[2]

I have this last week scarcely tried to read, nor have I read any thing this day.

I have had my mind weak and disturbed for some weeks past.

Having missed Church in the morning I went this evening, and afterwards sat with Southwel.[3]

Having not used the prayer, except on the day of communion; I will offer it this night, and hope to find mercy. On this day little has been done and this is now the last hour. In life little has been done, and life is very far advanced. Lord, have mercy upon me.

[99.]

GOOD FRIDAY, *April* 9, 1773.

On this day I went twice to Church and Boswel was with me.[4] I had forborn to attend Divine Service for some time in the winter, having a cough which would have interrupted both my own attention and that of others, and when the cough grew less troublesome I did not regain the habit of going to church, though I did not wholly omit it. I found the service not burthensome nor tedious, though I could not hear the lessons. I hope in time to take pleasure in public Worship.

On this whole day I took nothing of nourishment but one cup

---

[1] 'The first [of three young men that were of the guard that kept the king's body] wrote, Wine is the strongest.

The second wrote, The king is the strongest.

The third wrote, Women are strongest: but above all things Truth beareth away the victory.' I Esdras iii. 10.

[2] Edward Pococke's *Commentary on Micah, Malachi, Hosea and Joel*, 1677-91.

[3] Presumably the Edward Southwell whom Baretti conducted to Venice in the capacity of tutor, in 1760. Johnson was acquainted with Southwell and his family.

[4] 'On the 9th of April, being Good Friday, I breakfasted with him on tea and cross-buns. . . . He carried me with him to the church of St. Clement Danes, where he had his seat; and his behaviour was, as I had imaged to myself, solemnly devout. I never shall forget the tremulous earnestness with which he pronounced the awful petition in the Litany: "In the hour of death, and in the day of judgement, good Lord deliver us."' *Life*, ii. 214.

of tea without milk, but the fast was very inconvenient. Towards night I grew fretful, and impatient, unable to fix my mind, or govern my thoughts, and felt a very uneasy sensation both in my stomach and head, compounded as it seemed of laxity and pain.

From this uneasiness, of which when I was not asleep I was sensible all night, I was relieved in the morning by drinking tea, and eating the soft part of a penny loaf.

This I have set down for future observation.

[102.]
June 18, 1773, Friday.

This day after dinner died Mrs Salusbury,[1] she had for some days almost lost the power of speaking. Yesterday as I touched her hand and kissed it, she pressed my hand between her two hands, which she probably intended as the parting caress. At night her speech returned a little; and she said among other things to her daughter, I have had much time, and I hope I have used it. This morning being called about nine to feel her pulse I said at parting God bless you, for Jesus Christs sake. She smiled, as pleased. She had her senses perhaps to the dying moment.

[103.]
July 22, —73.

This day I found this book [2] with the resolutions, some of which I had forgotten, but remembered my design of reading the Pentateuch and Gospels, though I have not perused it.

Of the time past since these resolutions were made I can give no very laudable account. Between Easter and Whitsuntide, having always considered that time as propitious to study, I attempted to learn the low Dutch Language, my application was very slight, and my memory very fallacious, though whether more than in my earlier years, I am not very certain. My progress was interrupted by a fever, which, by the imprudent use of a small print, left an inflammation in my useful eye, which was not removed but by two copious bleedings, and the daily use of cathartics for a long time. The effect yet remains.

[1] Mrs. Salusbury, Hester Thrale's mother, who was dying of cancer.
[2] A book in which this and the preceding Meditations on Good Friday and Easter Sunday are written. Note by G. Strahan.

My memory has been for a long time very much confused. Names, and Persons, and Events, slide away strangely from me. But I grow easier.

The other day looking over old papers, I perceived a resolution to rise early always occurring. I think I was ashamed, or grieved, to find how long and how often I had resolved, what yet except for about one half year I have never done. My Nights are now such as give me no quiet rest, whether I have not lived resolving till the possibility of performance is past, I know not. God help me, I will yet try.

[127.]
Monday, Apr. 20 (1778).

After a good night, as I am forced to reckon, I rose seasonably, and prayed, using the collect for yesterday.

In reviewing my time from Easter —77, I find a very melancholy and shameful blank. So little has been done that days and months are without any trace. My health has indeed been very much interrupted. My nights have been commonly not only restless but painful and fatiguing. My respiration was once so difficult, that an asthma was suspected. I could not walk but with great difficulty, from Stowhill to Greenhill.[1] Some relaxation of my breast has been procured, I think, by opium, which, though it never gives me sleep, frees my breast from spasms.

I have written a little of the Lives of the poets, I think with all my usual vigour.[2] I have made sermons, perhaps as readily as formerly.[3] My memory is less faithful in retaining names, and, I am afraid, in retaining occurrences. Of this vacillation and vagrancy of mind I impute a great part to a fortuitous and unsettled life, and therefore purpose to spend my time with more method.

---

[1] Two gentle eminences on the outskirts of Lichfield.

[2] He had a proof-sheet of his *Life of Waller* on Good Friday, though he would not look at it on that day. He seems to have finished first the *Lives of Denham, Butler and Waller. Cowley* he had sent to the printer by the end of the following July. *Milton* was not yet begun by that time, though 'in *Dryden* he was very far advanced.' [G.B.H.]

[3] *Life*, v. 67.

This year, the 28th of March passed away without memorial. Poor Tetty, whatever were our faults and failings, we loved each other. I did not forget thee yesterday. Couldest thou have lived!—— I am now, with the help of God, to begin a new life.

[129.]

1779, GOOD FRIDAY, *Apr. 2.*

After a night restless and oppressive, I rose this morning somewhat earlier than is usual, and having taken tea which was very necessary to compose the disorder in my breast, having eaten nothing I went to church with Boswel.[1] We came late, I was able to attend the litany with little perturbation. When we came home I began the first to the Thess. having prayed by the collect for the right use of the Scriptures. I gave Boswel Les Pensées de Pascal that he might not interrupt me. I did not, I believe, read very diligently, and before I had read far, we went to Church again, I was again attentive. At home I read again, then drank tea with a bun and an half, thinking myself less able to fast, than at former times; and then concluded the Epistle. Being much oppressed with drowsiness, I slept about an hour by the fire.

11 p.m.

I am now to review the last year, and find little but dismal vacuity, neither business nor pleasure; much intended and little done. My health is much broken; my nights afford me little rest. I have tried opium, but its help is counter-balanced with great disturbance; it prevents the spasms, but it hinders sleep. O God, have mercy on me.

Last week I published the lives of the poets, written I hope in such a manner as may tend to the promotion of Piety.

In this last year I have made little acquisition, I have scarcely read any thing. I maintain Mrs. Desmoulins and her daughter,

---

[1] Boswell records of this visit, that 'finding that we insensibly fell into a train of ridicule upon the foibles of one of our friends, a very worthy man, I, by way of a check, quoted some good admonition from *The Government of the Tongue,* that very pious book.' *Life,* iii, 379. *Worthy* is almost always applied to Langton. His foibles were a common subject of their talk. *Ib.* iii. 48. [G.B.H.]

other good of myself I know not where to find, except a little Charity.

But I am now in my seventieth year; what can be done ought not to be delayed.

[130.]

EASTER EVE, *April 2*, [*1779*], *11 p.m.*

This is the time of my annual review, and annual resolution. The review is comfortless. Little done. Part of the life of Dryden and the Life of Milton have been written; but my mind has neither been improved nor enlarged. I have read little, almost nothing. And I am not conscious that I have gained any good, or quitted any evil habits.

Of resolutions I have made so many with so little effect, that I am almost weary, but, by the Help of God, am not yet hopeless. Good resolutions must be made and kept. I am almost seventy years old, and have no time to lose. The distressful restlessness of my nights, makes it difficult to settle the course of my days. Something however let me do.

[140.]

Apr. 13, GOOD FRIDAY, *1781.*

I forgot my Prayer and resolutions, till two days ago I found this paper.

Sometime in March I finished the lives of the Poets, which I wrote in my usual way, dilatorily and hastily, unwilling to work, and working with vigour and haste.

On Wednesday 11, was buried my dear Friend Thrale who died on Wednesday, 4; and with him were buried many of my hopes and pleasures. On Sunday 1st his Physician warned him against full meals, on Monday I pressed him to observance of his rules, but without effect, and Tuesday I was absent, but his Wife pressed forbearance upon him, again unsuccessfully. At night I was called to him, and found him senseless in strong convulsions. I staid in the room, except that I visited Mrs. Thrale twice. About five, (I think), on Wednesday morning he expired; I felt almost the last flutter of his pulse, and looked for the last time upon the face that for fifteen years had never been turned upon me but with respect or benignity. Farewel. May God that delighteth in mercy, have had mercy on thee.

I had constantly prayed for him some time before his death.

The decease of him from whose friendship I had obtained many opportunities of amusement, and to whom I turned my thoughts as to a refuge from misfortunes, has left me heavy. But my business is with myself.

Sept. 18. My first knowledge of Thrale was in 1765. I enjoyed his favour for almost a fourth part of my life.

[141.]

EASTER EVE, *Apr. 14, 1781.*

On Good Friday I took in the Afternoon some coffee and buttered cake, and to-day I had a little bread at breakfast, and potatoes and apples in the afternoon, the tea with a little toast, but I find myself feeble and unsustained, and suspect that I cannot bear to fast so long as formerly.

This day I read some of Clark's Sermons. I hope that since my last Communion I have advanced, by pious reflections in my submission to God, and my benevolence to Man, but I have corrected no external habits, nor have kept any of the resolutions made in the beginning of the year, yet I hope still to be reformed, and not to lose my whole life in idle purposes. Many years are already gone, irrevocably past, in useless Misery, that what remains may be spent better grant O God.

By this awful Festival is particularly recommended Newness of Life; and a new Life I will now endeavour to begin by more diligent application to useful employment, and more frequent attendance on public Worship.

I again with hope of help from the God of mercy, resolve

To avoid Idleness.

To read the Bible.

To study religion.

Almighty God, merciful Father, by whose Protection I have been preserved, and by whose clemency I have been spared, grant that the life which thou hast so long continued may be no longer wasted in idleness or corrupted by wickedness. Let my future purposes be good, and let not my good purposes be vain. Free me O Lord from vain terrours, and strengthen me in diligent obedience to thy laws. Take not from me thy Holy Spirit, but enable me so to commemorate the death of my Saviour Jesus Christ, that I may be made partaker of his merits, and may finally, for his sake obtain everlasting happiness. Amen.

EASTER SUNDAY, *1781.*

I rose after eight, and breakfasted, then went early to church, and before service read the prayer for the Church Militant. I commended my Θ¹ friends as I have formerly done. I was one of the last that communicated. When I came home I was hindred by Visitants, but found time to pray before dinner. God send thy Blessing upon me.

Thursday, March 28, 1782.

This is the day on which in 1752 dear Tetty died. I have now uttered a prayer of repentance and c̄. ;² perhaps Tetty knows that I prayed for her. Perhaps Tetty is now praying for me. God help me. Thou, God, art merciful, hear my prayers, and enable me to trust in Thee.

We were married almost seventeen years, and have now been parted thirty.

I then read 11 p. from Ex. 36. to Lev. 7. I prayed with Fr[ancis] and used the prayer for Good Friday.

29. GOOD FRIDAY. After a night of great disturbance and solicitude, such as I do not remember, I rose, drank tea, but without eating, and went to Church. I was very composed, and coming home, read Hammond on one of the Psalms for the day.³ I then read Leviticus. Scot ⁴ came in which hindred me from Church in the afternoon. A kind letter from Gastrel ⁵ I read on, then went to Evening prayers, and afterwards drank tea with bunns; then read till I finished Leviticus 24 pages et sup.

To write to Gastrel to morrow.

To look again into Hammond.

30. Sat. Visitors Paradise and I think Horseley. Read 11 pages of the Bible. I was faint, dined on herrings and potatoes.

---

¹ Θ is Johnson's shorthand for 'dead' (Greek θάνατος).

² Contrition.

³ Hammond's *Commentary on the Psalms* (1659).

⁴ Scott had chambers hard by in the Temple, where Johnson and Boswell dined with him on April 10, 1778. *Life,* iii. 261. [G.B.H.]

⁵ Mrs Gastrell of Lichfield. For Johnson's answer to her letter, see *Letters,* ii. 248.

At Prayers, I think, in the Evening. I wrote to Gastrel, and received a kind letter from Hector. At night Lowe. Pr[ayed] with Francis.

31. EASTER DAY. Read 15 pages of the Bible.

[154.]
[*On Leaving Streatham.*]
October 6, 1782.

Almighty God, Father of all mercy, help me by thy Grace that I may with humble and sincere thankfulness remember the comforts and conveniences which I have enjoyed at this place, and that I may resign them with holy submission, equally trusting in thy protection when Thou givest and when Thou takest away. Have mercy upon me, O Lord, have mercy upon me.

To thy fatherly protection, O Lord, I commend this family. Bless, guide, and defend them, that they may so pass through this world as finally to enjoy in thy presence everlasting happiness, for Jesus Christs sake. Amen.

O Lord, so far as, &c.—Thrale.

Oct. 7. I was called early. I packed up my bundles, and used the foregoing prayer, with my morning devotions somewhat, I think, enlarged. Being earlier than the family I read St. Pauls farewel in the Acts, and then read fortuitously in the Gospels, which was my parting use of the library.

[155.]
Sunday, went to church at Streatham. *Templo valedixi cum osculo.*[1]

PRAYER FOR MRS. WILLIAMS DURING HER ILLNESS
PRECEDING HER DEATH IN 1783.

[163.]
[*August, 1783.*]

Almighty God, who in thy late visitation hast shewn mercy to me, and now sendest to my companion disease and decay, grant me grace so to employ the life which thou hast prolonged, and the faculties which thou hast preserved, and so to receive the admonition which the sickness of my friend, by thy appoint-

---

[1] 'I bade the church farewell with a kiss.'

ment, gives me, that I may be constant in all holy duties, and be received at last to eternal happiness.

Permit, O Lord, thy unworthy creature to offer up this prayer for Anna Williams now languishing upon her bed, and about to recommend herself to thy infinite mercy. O God, who desirest not the death of a sinner, look down with mercy upon her: forgive her sins and strengthen her faith. Be merciful, O Father of Mercy, to her and to me: guide us by thy holy spirit through the remaining part of life; support us in the hour of death, and pardon us in the day of judgement, for Jesus Christ's sake. Amen.

[164.]
September 6.

I had just heard of Williams's Death.

Almighty and most merciful Father, who art the Lord of life and death, who givest and who takest away, teach me to adore thy providence, whatever Thou shalt allot me; make me to remember, with due thankfulness, the comforts which I have received from my friendship with Anna Williams. Look upon her, O Lord, with mercy, and prepare me, by thy grace, to die with hope, and to pass by death to eternal happiness, through Jesus Christ our Lord. Amen.

[167.]
EASTER DAY, *Apr. 11, 1784.*

Almighty God, my Creator and my Judge, who givest life and takest it away, enable me to return sincere and humble thanks for my late deliverance from imminent death.[1] So govern my future life by the Holy Spirit, that every day which thou shalt permit to pass over me, may be spent in thy service, and leave me less tainted with wickedness, and more submissive to thy will.

[175.]

[The following Prayer was composed and used by Doctor Johnson previous to his receiving the Sacrament of the

---

[1] Ten days later he wrote to Mrs. Thrale:—'After a confinement of one hundred and twenty-nine days, more than the third part of a year, and no inconsiderable part of human life, I this day returned thanks to God in St. Clement's Church for my recovery.' *Letters*, c. 955.

Lord's Supper, on Sunday December 5, 1784. Note by G. Strahan.]

Almighty and most merciful Father, I am now, as to human eyes it seems, about to commemorate, for the last time, the death of thy Son Jesus Christ our Saviour and Redeemer. Grant, O Lord, that my whole hope and confidence may be in his merits, and thy mercy; enforce and accept my imperfect repentance; make this commemoration available to the confirmation of my faith, the establishment of my hope, and the enlargement of my charity; and make the death of thy Son Jesus Christ effectual to my redemption. Have mercy upon me, and pardon the multitude of my offences. Bless my friends; have mercy upon all men. Support me, by the grace of thy Holy Spirit, in the days of weakness, and at the hour of death; and receive me, at my death, to everlasting happiness, for the sake of Jesus Christ. Amen.

In spite of his heroic piety, the threat of damnation continued to prey on Johnson's mind into old age. Since death meant judgment, he clung to continued life as holding out the possibility of continued progress towards redemption. Sometimes he came close to maintaining that life in torment was better than no life at all, as in the amusing story, related by Boswell from Anna Seward, about the educated pig.

4. 'I told him (says Miss Seward) in one of my latest visits to him, of a wonderful learned pig, which I had seen at Nottingham; and which did all that we have observed exhibited by dogs and horses. The subject amused him. 'Then, (said he,) the pigs are a race unjustly calumniated. *Pig* has, it seems, not been wanting to *man*, but *man* to *pig*. We do not allow *time* for his education, we kill him at a year old.' Mr. Henry White, who was present, observed that if this instance had happened in or before Pope's time, he would not have been justified in instancing the swine as the lowest degree of groveling instinct. Dr. Johnson seemed pleased with the observation, while the person who made it proceeded to remark, that great torture must have been employed, ere the indocility of the animal could have been subdued.—"Certainly, (said the Doctor;) but, (turning to me,) how old is your pig?" I told him, three years old. "Then, (said he,) the pig has no cause to complain; he would have been killed the first year if he had not been *educated*, and protracted existence is a good recompence for very considerable degrees of torture."'

In more sober vein, Boswell records two conversations that took place when they visited Oxford together in June 1784, the last summer of Johnson's life. One concerned the Roman Catholic faith, with its much more guaranteed road to salvation than Protestantism could indicate.

5. On the Roman Catholic religion he said, 'If you join the Papists externally, they will not interrogate you strictly as to your belief in their tenets. No reasoning Papist believes every article of their faith. There is one side on which a good man might be persuaded to embrace it. A good man of a timorous disposition, in great doubt of his acceptance with GOD, and pretty credulous, may be glad to be of a church where there are so many helps to get to heaven. I would be a Papist if I could. I have fear enough; but an obstinate rationality prevents me. I shall never be a Papist, unless on the near approach of death, of which I have a very great terrour. I wonder that women are not all Papists.' BOSWELL. 'They are not more afraid of death than men are.' JOHNSON. 'Because they are less wicked.' DR. ADAMS. 'They are more pious.' JOHNSON. 'No, hang 'em, they are not more pious. A wicked fellow is the most pious when he takes to it. He'll beat you all at piety.'

'A good man of a timorous disposition, in great doubt of his acceptance with God', comes close to a description of Johnson himself, though his 'timorous disposition' showed itself only in relation to Heaven, never to earth. Even more sombre was the conversation between Johnson and Adams of Pembroke, on this same visit, about hell and eternal punishment.

6. Mr. Henderson, with whom I had sauntered in the vener-

able walks of Merton-College, and found him a very learned and pious man, supped with us. Dr. Johnson surprised him not a little, by acknowledging with a look of horrour, that he was much oppressed by the fear of death. The amiable Dr. Adams suggested that GOD was infinitely good. JOHNSON. 'That he is infinitely good, as far as the perfection of his nature will allow, I certainly believe; but it is necessary for good upon the whole, that individuals should be punished. As to an *individual*, therefore, he is not infinitely good; and as I cannot be *sure* that I have fulfilled the conditions on which salvation is granted, I am afraid I may be one of those who shall be damned.' (looking dismally.) DR. ADAMS. 'What do you mean by damned!' JOHNSON. (passionately and loudly) 'Sent to Hell, Sir, and punished everlastingly.' DR. ADAMS. 'I don't believe that doctrine.' JOHNSON. 'Hold, Sir, do you believe that some will be punished at all?' DR. ADAMS. 'Being excluded from Heaven will be a punishment; yet there may be no great positive suffering.' JOHNSON. 'Well, Sir; but, if you admit any degree of punishment, there is an end of your argument for infinite goodness simply considered; for, infinite goodness would inflict no punishment whatever. There is no infinite goodness physically considered; morally there is.' BOSWELL. 'But may not a man attain to such a degree of hope as not to be uneasy from the fear of death?' JOHNSON. 'A man may have such a degree of hope as to keep him quiet. You see I am not quiet, from the vehemence with which I talk; but I do not despair.' MRS. ADAMS. 'You seem, Sir, to forget the merits of our Redeemer.' JOHNSON. 'Madam, I do not forget the merits of my Redeemer; but my Redeemer has said that he will set some on his right hand and some on his left.'—He was in gloomy agitation, and said, 'I'll have no more on't.'

One is the more glad to be able to report that Johnson did not die with these fears about him. A few weeks before he died, his mind became calm, he felt a sense of forgiveness and of reconciliation with God; as far as could be seen from the outside, he seemed to be passing from this world with no terrors about the world to come.

Chapter IX

Last Will and Testament

Johnson's will has been familiar ever since it was printed by Boswell, but it is still worth including in a collection of his personal documents. Its chief feature, of course, is Johnson's dying generosity towards his Jamaican servant Frank Barber. Frank had been born into chattel slavery; he was the property of Colonel Bathurst, father of the amiable physician Richard Bathurst of whom Johnson was very fond. When Colonel Bathurst returned from overseas service, he brought Frank with him, and Johnson in 1753, the year after his wife's death, took the lad under his care; Richard Bathurst was quite probably the intermediary.

Johnson always treated Frank as a son, sending him to school, providing a home for him, and, in the fulness of time, for his English wife Betsy and their children, and taking responsibility for his religious instruction; habitually, they prayed together and Johnson explained to Frank passages in the Scriptures. Nominally, Frank was Johnson's servant, but he was not remarkable either for industry or efficiency; Johnson never seems to have found fault with him, and indeed went to great lengths to spare Frank's feelings. He would not, for instance, send him out to buy oysters (at that time, a cheap food) for their cat Hodge; Johnson always did this errand himself, in case Frank should feel lowered by having to attend on an animal. Neither would he ever instruct Frank to tell callers that he was not at home, as busy people often did; he reasoned that if Frank became accustomed to telling small untruths on his, Johnson's, behalf, he might slide that more easily into being untruthful in other matters. And Johnson was determined to give the lad all possible aid towards full spiritual development.

The story of their relationship is, in fact, a blend of the touching and the farcical, especially in those incidents when Frank ran away and got into situations from which Johnson had to rescue him. He once joined the navy (why anyone should voluntarily join the eighteenth-century navy is a mystery, but Frank did), and then Johnson had to write letters and pull strings to get him released. But affection between them always persisted, and Johnson's protective care for the negro lad continued from the grave. He advised Frank to settle in Lichfield, as being a quieter and safer environment than London; Frank did so, but still managed to run through his money and reduce himself to dire poverty. Profiting by the education that Johnson had paid for, he opened a little school in Burntwood, a village near by; so that in a sense he lived out his life under Johnson's wing.

At Johnson's London house in Gough Square, that familiar shrine to the London literary pilgrim, they tell a story that seems to me good enough to go in here. One evening a few minutes before the end of visiting time, a man arrived on the doorstep wanting to see the house. The curatrix mildly protested; they were about to close; perhaps he could come back in the morning. He could not; moreover, he had come all the way from Australia and must shortly return. The curatrix relented and he went up the stairs while she waited by the door. After seeing the rooms and exhibits the man came down the stairs again, thanked the lady, and was just leaving. 'I can lock up now', she said. 'You're the last.' 'Oh, no', said the Australian. 'There's someone else up there . . . a black man.'

Normally I do not believe ghost stories, but when I have one of those moods in which I think that some of them are probably true, that is the one I believe most easily.

'IN THE NAME OF GOD. AMEN. I, SAMUEL JOHNSON, being in full possession of my faculties, but fearing this night may put an end to my life, do ordain this my last Will and Testament. I bequeath to GOD, a soul polluted with many sins, but I hope purified by JESUS CHRIST.—I leave seven hundred and fifty pounds in the hands of Bennet Langton, Esq.: three hundred pounds in the hands of Mr. Barclay and Mr. Perkins, brewers; one hundred and fifty pounds in the hands of Dr. Percy, Bishop of Dromore; one thousand pounds, three *per cent.* annuities, in the public funds; and one hundred pounds now lying by me in ready money: all these before-mentioned sums and property I leave, I say, to Sir Joshua Reynolds, Sir John Hawkins, and Dr. William Scott, of Doctors Commons, in trust, for the following uses:—That is to say, to pay to the representatives of the late William Innys, bookseller, in St. Paul's Church-yard, the sum of two hundred pounds; to Mrs. White, my female servant, one hundred pounds stock in the three *per cent.* annuities aforesaid. The rest of the aforesaid sums of money and property, together with my books, plate, and household furniture, I leave to the before-mentioned Sir Joshua Reynolds, Sir John Hawkins, and Dr. William Scott, also in trust, to be applied, after paying my debts, to the use of Francis Barber, my manservant, a negro, in such a manner as they shall judge most fit and available to his benefit. And I appoint the aforesaid Sir Joshua Reynolds, Sir John Hawkins, and Dr. William Scott, sole executors of this my last will and testament, hereby revoking all former wills and testaments whatever. In witness whereof I hereunto subscribe my name, and affix my seal, this eighth day of December, 1784.

'SAM. JOHNSON, (L.S.)

'Signed, sealed, published, declared, and delivered, by the said testator, as his last will and testament, in the presence of us, the word *two* being first inserted in the opposite page.

'GEORGE STRAHAN.

'JOHN DESMOULINS.'

'By way of Codicil to my last Will and Testament, I, SAMUEL JOHNSON, give, devise, and bequeath, my messuage or tenement situate at Lichfield, in the county of Stafford, with the appurtenances, in the tenure or occupation of Mrs. Bond, of Lichfield aforesaid, or of Mr. Hinchman, her under-tenant, to my executors, in trust, to sell and dispose of the same; and the money arising from such sale I give and bequeath as follows, viz. to Thomas and Benjamin, the sons of Fisher Johnson, late of Leicester, and —— Whiting, daughter of Thomas Johnson, late of Coventry, and the grand-daughter of the said Thomas Johnson, one full and equal fourth part each; but in case there shall be more grand-daughters than one of the said Thomas Johnson, living at the time of my decease, I give and bequeath the part or share of that one to and equally between such grand-daughters. I give and bequeath to the Reverend Mr. Rogers, of Berkley, near Froome, in the county of Somerset, the sum of one hundred pounds, requesting him to apply the same towards the maintenance of Elizabeth Herne, a lunatic. I also give and bequeath to my god-children, the son and daughter of Mauritius Lowe, painter, each of them, one hundred pounds of my stock in the three *per cent.* consolidated annuities, to be applied and disposed of by and at the discretion of my Executors, in the education or settlement in the world of them my said legatees. Also I give and bequeath to Sir John Hawkins, one of my Executors, the Annales Ecclesiastici of Baronius, and Holinshed's and Stowe's Chronicles, and also an octavo Common Prayer-Book. To Bennet Langton, Esq. I give and bequeath my Polyglot Bible. To Sir Joshua Reynolds, my great French Dictionary, by Martiniere, and my own copy of my folio English Dictionary, of the last revision. To Dr. William Scott, one of my Executors, the Dictionnaire de Commerce, and Lectius's edition of the Greek Poets. To Mr. Windham, Poetæ Græci Heroici per Henricum Stephanum. To the Reverend Mr. Strahan, vicar of Islington, in Middlesex, Mill's Greek Testament, Beza's Greek Testament by Stephens, all my Latin Bibles, and my Greek Bible by Wechelius. To Dr. Heberden, Dr. Brocklesby, Dr. Butter, and Mr. Cruikshank the surgeon who attended me, Mr. Holder my apothecary, Gerard Hamilton, Esq. Mrs. Gardiner, of Snow-hill, Mrs. Frances Reynolds, Mr. Hoole, and the Reverend Mr. Hoole, his son, each a book at their election, to keep as a token of remembrance. I also give and bequeath to Mr. John Desmoulins, two hundred pounds consolidated three *per cent.* annuities; and to Mr. Sastres, the Italian master, the sum of five pounds, to be laid out in books of piety for his own use. And whereas the said Bennet Langton hath agreed, in consideration of the sum of seven hundred and fifty pounds, mentioned in my Will to be in his hands, to grant and secure an annuity of seventy pounds, payable during the life of me and my servant Francis Barber, and the life of the survivor of us, to Mr. George Stubbs in trust for us; my mind and will is, that in case of my decease before the said agreement shall be perfected, the said sum of seven hundred and fifty pounds, and the bond for securing the said sum, shall go to the said Francis Barber; and I hereby give and bequeath to him the same, in lieu of the bequest in his favour, contained in my said Will. And I hereby empower my Executors to deduct and retain all expences that shall or may be incurred in the execution of my said Will, or of this Codicil thereto, out of such estate and effects as I shall die possessed of. All the rest, residue, and remainder, of my estate and effects, I give and bequeath to my said Executors, in trust for the said Francis Barber, his Executors and Administrators. Witness my hand and seal this ninth day of December, 1784.

'SAM. JOHNSON, (L.S.)

'Signed, sealed, published, declared, and delivered by the said Samuel Johnson, as, and for a Codicil to his last Will and Testament, in the presence of us, who, in his presence, and at his request, and also in the presence of each other, have hereto subscribed our names as witnesses.

'JOHN COPLEY.
'WILLIAM GIBSON.
'HENRY COLE.'

Chronological Table of Samuel Johnson's Life

1709 Born, 7/18 September, in Breadmarket Street, Lichfield.
1712 Taken to London to be touched by Queen Anne for scrofula ('the King's Evil').
      His brother, Nathaniel Johnson, born.
1714 Learns to read at Dame Oliver's school, Dam Street, Lichfield.
1716 Enters Lichfield Grammar School.
1725 Visit to his older cousin, Cornelius Ford, at Pedmore, near Stourbridge. Makes the acquaintance of the Stourbridge circle of his relations.
      Refused re-entry to Lichfield Grammar School after prolonged absence; enters Stourbridge Grammar School.
1728 Enters Pembroke College, Oxford (October). Translates Pope's *Messiah* into Latin (published 1731).
1729 Unable to keep up payment of fees at Pembroke; returns to Lichfield (December). Depression solaced by friendship with Gilbert Walmsley, Registrar of the Ecclesiastical Court.
1731 Death of Michael Johnson.
1732 Brief, bitter experience as 'usher' at Market Bosworth School; mutually hostile relationship with his patron, Sir Wolstan Dixie.
1733 Sojourn in Birmingham. Acquaintance with circle including Edmund Hector (his schoolfellow), Harry and Elizabeth Porter, Elizabeth Desmoulins, Warren the publisher.
      Translates Father Lobo's *Voyage to Abyssinia*.
1734 Back to Lichfield, February.

Issues Proposals for an edition of the poems of Politian (August).

First approach to Edward Cave, publisher of the *Gentleman's Magazine*, by letter (November).

1735 Marriage to Elizabeth Porter, née Jervis, at St. Werburgh's Church, Derby, 9 July.

Opens school at Edial, Staffordshire (December, or early 1736). David and Peter Garrick among the pupils.

1736 Begins composition of his tragedy, *Irene*.

1737 Edial School closed, February.

Death of Nathaniel Johnson, March.

Leaves for London, March. Begins work for Edward Cave.

Returns to Lichfield in the summer, finishes *Irene*, back to London with his wife to set up permanent home.

1738 Staff writer for *Gentleman's Magazine*; publishes *London*, his first major poem, also *Life of Sarpi* and (probably by J.) *State of Affairs in Lilliput* (preface to *Debates in the Senate of Lilliput*, disguised Parliamentary reporting).

1739 Writes two Swiftian anti-government pamphlets, *Marmor Norfolciense* and *A Compleat Vindication of the Licensers of the Stage*.

Friendship with Richard Savage; May, Savage leaves for Wales.

Autumn, extended visit to the Midlands. One last attempt to get a headmastership, at Appleby, Leicestershire, unsuccessful; lingers on, enjoying country society—Appleby, Tissington, Ashbourne, Lichfield—into the next year. Last visit to Lichfield for 22 years; last sight of his mother.

1740 Helping William Guthrie with *Debates in the Senate of Lilliput*. Lives of Blake, Drake, Barretier, in *Gentleman's Magazine*.

1741 Sole writer of *Debates*. Writes Proposals for Dr James's *Medicinal Dictionary*.

1742 Continues with *Debates*.

Publishes *Proposals for Printing Bibliotheca Harleiana*.

1743 Death of Savage.

Johnson works on *Debates, Medicinal Dictionary*, cataloguing of Harleian Library.

1744 Publishes *Life of Savage*, his first major prose work.

Harleian Miscellany (selections by William Oldys; introduction by Johnson, 'Essay on Small Tracts and Fugitive Pieces').

1745 *Début* as Shakespearean critic with *Miscellaneous Observations on the Tragedy of Macbeth*.

1746 Signs contract for *Dictionary*.

Makes acquaintance of Robert Levet, physician extraordinary and lifelong friend.

1747 Prologue for opening of Drury Lane Theatre.

Publishes *Plan of an English Dictionary*.

1748 Preface to new magazine, *The Preceptor*, to which he also contributes 'The Vision of Theodore the Hermit'.

Writes (according to Boswell) *The Vanity of Human Wishes*.

1749 Working on *Dictionary*.

Publishes *Vanity of Human Wishes*.

Irene produced at Drury Lane, and published.

Forms the Ivy Lane Club with Bathurst, Hawkesworth, Hawkins (qq.v.) and others.

1750 Working on *Dictionary*.

Begins *The Rambler* (continued to 1752).

Writes Prologue for *Comus*, Proposals for Anna Williams's *Miscellanies*, Preface to Lauder's *Essay on Milton*.

1751 Working on *Dictionary* and *Rambler*.

Dictates to Lauder a letter acknowledging his fraud in 'detecting' 'plagiarisms' in Milton's poetry.

Life of Cheynel.

Death of Gilbert Walmsley (Johnson had long since lost touch with him by this time).

1752 Working on *Dictionary*; concludes *Rambler*.

Death of Elizabeth Johnson.

Anna Williams, blind daughter of a Welsh physician, makes her home with him.

Takes Frank Barber (q.v.) under his care.

Meets Sir Joshua Reynolds.

1753 Working on *Dictionary*.

Contributes to periodical, *The Adventurer*.

Charlotte Lennox (q.v.) introduces him to Giuseppe Baretti (q.v.).

1754 Working on *Dictionary*.

Life of Cave in *Gentleman's Magazine*.

Five-week visit to Oxford, summer.

Beginning of friendship with Thomas Warton (q.v.).

Makes acquaintance with Arthur Murphy (q.v.).

1755 Becomes Oxford M.A.

Dictionary published.

Letter to Lord Chesterfield.

1756 Publishes abridged edition of *Dictionary*.

Contributing editor of *The Literary Magazine*. Publishes edition of Browne's *Christian Morals* with Life; writes Preface to Rolt's *Dictionary of Trade and Commerce*, Preface and Dedication to Payne's *Game of Draughts*, etc.

Issues Proposals for an edition of Shakespeare.

Meets Thomas Percy (q.v.).

Portrait painted by Reynolds.

1757 Editing Shakespeare.

Writes review of Soame Jenyns' *A Free Enquiry into the Nature and Origin of Evil*, in the *Literary Magazine* (his fiercest controversial work).

1758 Editing, or wishing to edit, Shakespeare.

Arrested for debt of £40, February.

Begins *Idler*.

1759 Editing, or wishing to edit, Shakespeare.

Continues *Idler*.

Writes and publishes *Rasselas*.

Death of Sarah Johnson, his mother.

Moves from Gough Square to Staple Inn.

1760 Editing, or wishing to edit, Shakespeare.

Writes Dedication of Baretti's *Dictionary of the English and Italian Languages*; *The Bravery of the English Common Soldiers*; Introduction to *Proceedings of the Committee for Clothing French Prisoners*.

1761 Editing, or wishing to edit, Shakespeare.

Probably meets Adam Smith.

1762 Editing, or wishing to edit, Shakespeare.
      Five-week visit to Lichfield (winter of 1761/2).
      Awarded pension of £300 p.a., July.
      Trip to Devon with Reynolds. First sight of the sea.
      Reynolds (according to Malone) suggests, at Johnson's
        fireside, formation of 'the Club'.

1763 Editing, or wishing to edit, Shakespeare.
      Winter of 1762/3: 'the Club' founded. Meetings at the
        Turk's Head, Gerrard Street. Original members:
        Johnson, Reynolds, Burke, Nugent, Beauclerk, Lang-
        ton, Goldsmith, Chamier, Hawkins.
      First meets Boswell, 16 May.

1764 Finishing edition of Shakespeare.
      A peripatetic year. Visit to Langton (q.v.) in Lincoln-
        shire, part of January and February; to Percy at
        Easton Maudit, Northants., part of July and August;
        Oxford, October.

1765 Meets Henry and Hester Thrale.
      Edition of Shakespeare published.
      LL.D., Dublin.
      Takes house in Fleet Street.

1766 Helps Robert Chambers (q.v.) with Vinerian Lectures,
        an important series of Oxford lectures on law.
      Severe depressive breakdown. Taken in by the Thrales.

1767 Interview with George III, February.
      Summer and autumn in Lichfield, nearly six months in
        all.
      Death of Catherine Chambers, 17 October. ('She buried
        my father, my brother and my mother.')

1768 Writes election publicity for Thrale.
      Visit to Chambers at Oxford, some two months.
      Boswell introduces himself to Mrs Thrale, June.

1769 Character witness at Baretti's trial for murder.
      Oxford, from end of May to at least end of June. Short
        visit to Lichfield, August.

1770 *The False Alarm*, January.
      Contributes concluding lines to Goldsmith's *The
        Deserted Village*.
      Serious illness, spring.

Lichfield and Ashbourne, July.

1771   *Thoughts on Falkland's Islands*, March.

Lichfield and Ashbourne, about 20 June to beginning of August.

Summer, begins work on revised (4th) edition of *Dictionary*.

1772   Finishes revised edition of *Dictionary*, October; writes confessional poem, *Post Lexicon Anglicanum Auctum et Emendatum*.

Boswell (*Journal*, 31 March) tells him of his intention to write his, Johnson's, biography.

Lichfield and Ashbourne, autumn.

1773   4th edition of *Dictionary* published, March.

Bad health; fever; eye infection.

Nevertheless, tour of Hebrides with Boswell, 6 August–26 November.

On return, begins work at once on *Journey to the Western Islands of Scotland*.

1774   Journey to North Wales with the Thrales, July–September.

Hasty return home on hearing of dissolution of Parliament, to enable Henry Thrale to contest his seat in the General Election.

Johnson helps with election publicity.

The Patriot, November.

1775   *A Journey to the Western Islands of Scotland*, January.

Taxation No Tyranny, March.

Summer at Oxford, Lichfield and Ashbourne.

Visit to France with Thrales, autumn.

1776   Lichfield, with Boswell. Hurries home to console Thrales on the death of their nine-year-old son, Harry, March.

Dinner with Wilkes, May. (See the hilarious account in Boswell's *Life*.)

Projected visit to Italy with the Thrales called off owing to Harry's death.

Moved to 8, Bolt Court, off Fleet Street, his last house.

1777   First meeting with Fanny Burney (q.v.).

Concerned with trial of Dr Dodd.

Begins *Lives of the Poets*.

Several months at Lichfield and Ashbourne; Boswell visits him there, September.

1778 Johnson's edition of Shakespeare re-issued with revisions by George Steevens.

Visit to Langton at Warley Camp, Essex, September.

1779 First group of *Lives* published.

Consults with Lord Marchmont for *Life of Pope*, May.

Lichfield and Ashbourne, May and June.

Henry Thrale suffers paralytic stroke, June; Hester Thrale miscarries and is ill; henceforth, Johnson's welcome at Streatham is never quite as warm; the family have less time to spare from their own troubles.

1780 Working on *Lives of the Poets*. Hester Thrale meets Gabriele Piozzi, or at any rate gets to know him well for the first time.

1781 Remaining *Lives* published.

Death of Henry Thrale, April.

Oxford, Birmingham, Lichfield, Ashbourne, autumn.

1782 Death of Robert Levet, January.

Sale of Thrale's brewery to John Perkins, Sylvanus Bevan and David and Robert Barclay.

Mrs Thrale lets Streatham and takes a house in London for the winter.

1783 Paralytic stroke, June.

Visit to Langton at Rochester, July, and to William Bowles at Heale, Salisbury, August.

1784 Marriage of Hester Thrale to Piozzi, July.

Oxford, 3–16 June.

Sees Boswell for the last time, 30 June.

Lichfield, Ashbourne, Birmingham, Oxford.

Back home, makes his will, naming Frank Barber as principal heir. 13 December, dies.

Who's Who

ADAMS, William, 1706–89, Fellow of Pembroke College, Oxford. After the departure of Jorden, he would have been Johnson's tutor had the latter not been forced by poverty to leave the University. Later Master of the College.

ASTON, Mary ('Molly'), 1706–c.1765, daughter of Sir William Aston. Johnson met her in 1740, and deeply admired her.

BARBER, Francis, ?1745–1801, Johnson's negro servant. Born in Jamaica, brought to England by Colonel Bathurst, sent to school by Johnson. With the exception of a brief period at sea he remained in Johnson's service until the latter's death. He was present at his deathbed.

BARETTI, Giuseppe, 1719–89, Italian writer who settled in England in 1751. Johnson and other members of the Club appeared as witnesses when he was tried for murder in 1769.

BATHURST, Richard, d. 1762, physician and friend of Johnson. Francis Barber, Johnson's servant, was originally his father's slave.

BEAUCLERK, the Hon. Topham, 1739–80, believed to be descended from Charles II and Nell Gwynne. Johnson first met him with Bennet Langton in Oxford, and he became one of the original members of the Club. Wild, witty and eccentric.

BOOTHBY, Hill, 1708–56, Johnson probably met her in 1739–1740, and remained devoted to her until her death. 'I never did exchange letters regularly but with dear Miss Boothby.'

BURKE, Edmund, 1729–97, Whig politician and writer. A member of the Club.

BURNEY, Frances (Mme d'Arblay), 1752–1840, novelist and diarist, daughter of the musician Charles Burney.

CARTER, Elizabeth, 1717–1806, poet and translator. 'My old friend, Mrs Carter, could make a pudding, as well as translate Epictetus.'

CAVE, Edward, 1691–1754, printer and first publisher of Johnson's work. After his death Johnson wrote his biography.

CHAMBERS, Sir Robert, 1737–1803, Indian judge. Johnson helped him in the composition of his Vinerian lectures on law at Oxford.

CHESTERFIELD, Philip Dormer Stanhope, Earl of, 1694–1773, politician.

COLLINS, William, 1721–59, poet. Johnson was always sympathetic to the melancholy which afflicted Collins, and in 1763 published a Character of him which he later expanded in *The Lives of the Poets*.

ELPHINSTON, James, 1721–1809, educationalist. Arranged for the publication of *The Rambler* in Scotland in an edition of 'uncommon elegance'.

GARRICK, David, 1717–79, actor. Born in Lichfield, educated at Lichfield Grammar School, later at Johnson's school at Edial. Garrick was responsible for the production of *Irene*.

HAWKESWORTH, Dr John, ?1715–73, writer. With Johnson was one of the contributors to the short-lived periodical *The Adventurer*. Was so adept at imitating Johnson that their contributions were said to be indistinguishable.

HAWKINS, Sir John, 1719–89, author of the official *Life of*

Johnson. Of him Johnson is quoted by Fanny Burney as having said, 'Sir John was a most *unclubable* man.'

HECTOR, Edmund, 1708–94, school and life-long friend of Johnson. He was either the son or nephew of George Hector, the 'man-midwife', who assisted at Johnson's birth.

JAMES, Robert, 1705–76, a schoolfellow of Johnson's who later became a physician. Johnson helped him to write Proposals for his *Medicinal Dictionary* and the *Dictionary* itself.

JOHNSON, Elizabeth ('Tetty'), 1698–1752, née Jervis, widow of Harry Porter, wife of Samuel Johnson.

JOHNSON, Michael, 1656–1731, Johnson's father, bookseller at Lichfield. Son of a small tenant farmer, he became Sheriff of Lichfield in 1709, and also served as junior and senior bailiff of the town. From him Johnson said he inherited 'a vile melancholy'.

JOHNSON, Sarah, 1669–1759, née Ford; Johnson's mother. 'Descended of an ancient race of substantial yeomanry in Warwickshire.'

LANGTON, Bennet, 1737–1801, son of a country squire, introduced to Johnson by Robert Levet. A contemporary of Topham Beauclerk at Oxford; 'a very tall, meagre, long-visaged man.'

LENNOX, Charlotte, 1720–1804, novelist, translator and woman of letters.

LEVET, Robert, 1705–82, 'an obscure practiser in physic amongst the lower people'. Lived for many years in Johnson's house.

LEVET, Theophilus, 1693–1746, Town Clerk of Lichfield.

MACPHERSON, James, 1736–96; published what he alleged to be

translations of ancient Gaelic poems written by 'Ossian'. Although they had a great vogue at the time, Johnson consistently attacked him.

PERCY, Dr Thomas, 1729–1811, Bishop of Dromore, editor of *Reliques of Ancient English Poetry*, a member of the Club.

PORTER, Lucy, 1715–86, step-daughter of Johnson. Although he was very fond of her, she lived in Lichfield during the whole of her life and never visited him in London.

REYNOLDS, Sir Joshua, 1723–92, painter, member of the Club, and first President of the Royal Academy. Painted many portraits of Johnson and his circle.

RICHARDSON, Samuel, 1689–1761, novelist, author of *Clarissa*.

SAVAGE, Richard (d. 1743), poet, prodigal, conversationalist; claimed to be the illegitimate son of the Countess of Macclesfield and Lord Rivers, a claim believed by Johnson, who drew a poignant picture of his friend's sufferings in the *Life of Savage* (1744).

STRAHAN, Rev. George, 1744–1824, son of the following. He edited Johnson's *Prayers and Meditations* after his death.

STRAHAN, William, 1715–85, publisher and King's Printer; publisher of the *Dictionary*.

SWINFEN, Dr Samuel, c. 1679–1736, a young doctor lodging with Johnson's parents at the time of his birth. He became one of his godfathers, and diagnosed his scrofula.

TAYLOR, Rev. John, 1711–88, educated at Lichfield Grammar School and Christ Church. Rector of Ashbourne in Derbyshire where Johnson frequently visited him although intellectually they had little in common.

WALMSLEY, Gilbert, 1680–1751, Registrar of the Ecclesiastical

Court, Lichfield. Befriended the young Johnson who spent, some of the happiest times of his early life in the cultivated household in the Bishop's Palace in Lichfield.

WARTON, Dr Joseph, 1722–80, elder brother of Thomas Warton, literary critic and Headmaster of Winchester. A member of the Club.

WARTON, Rev. Thomas, 1728–90, Fellow of Trinity College, Oxford. Professor of Poetry there 1757–67, Poet Laureate in 1785. Member of the Club. Literary historian who gave Johnson help, friendship and advice.

WILLIAMS, Anne, 1706–83, cultivated daughter of a Welsh physician. She visited London for an unsuccessful operation on cataract in her eyes, became blind, was befriended by Mrs Johnson, and after Tetty's death spent the rest of her life under Johnson's roof.